Creating the Constitution

Thornton Anderson

Creating the

Constitution

The
Convention of 1787
and the
First Congress

The Pennsylvania State University Press
University Park, Pennsylvania

Library of Congress Cataloging-in-Publication Data

Anderson, Thornton, 1915–
    Creating the Constitution : the Convention of 1787 and the first Congress
/ Thornton Anderson.
        p.   cm.
    Includes bibliographical references and index.
    ISBN 0-271-00913-6 (cloth : alk. paper)—ISBN
0-271-00920-9 (pbk.)
    1. United States—Constitutional history. 2. Federal government
—United States—History. 3. United States—Politics and
government—1783–1809. 4. Constitutional conventions—United
States—History. 5. United States. Constitutional Convention
(1787) 6. United States. Congress (1st : 1789–1791) I. Title.
KF4541.A88   1993
342.73′0292—dc20
[347.302292]   92-31502
                                               CIP

Published by The Pennsylvania State University Press,
Suite C, Barbara Building, University Park, PA 16802-1003

It is the policy of The Pennsylvania State University Press to use acid-free paper for
the first printing of all clothbound books. Publications on uncoated stock satisfy the
minimum requirements of American National Standard for Information Sciences—
Permanence of Paper for Printed Library Materials, ANSI Z39.48–1984.

For my parents
    Keturah Hogan Anderson
    Thornton Hatfield Anderson
    who taught me independence

Contents

Convention Chronology

Target meeting date: 5-14
Quorum achieved (seven states): 5-25
Virginia Plan presented: 5-29
Report of the Committee of the Whole: 6-13
New Jersey Plan presented: 6-15
New Jersey Plan rejected: 6-19
Committee on representation elected: 7-2
Committee on representation reported: 7-5
[Jillson's first realignment (vote 156): 7-16]
Connecticut Compromise voted: 7-16
Committee of Detail elected: 7-24
Convention adjourned to await report: 7-26
Committee of Detail reported: 8-6
Committee on commerce and the slave trade appointed: 8-22
[Jillson's second realignment (vote 351): 8-23]
Committee on commerce and the slave trade reported: 8-24
Commerce and slave trade compromise voted: 8-25 to 8-29
Brearley Committee on postponed matters elected: 8-31
[Jillson's third realignment (vote 441): 9-3]
Brearley Committee made its main report: 9-4
Presidential election method voted: 9-5
Style Committee elected: 9-8
Style Committee reported: 9-12
Final approval of the Constitution: 9-17

The Delegates

BY STATE, FROM NORTH TO SOUTH, WITH THE QUORUM EACH STATE REQUIRED

			Attendance
	NEW HAMPSHIRE (2)		
	c	Nicholas Gilman	7-23 to end
	c	John Langdon	7-23 to end
	MASSACHUSETTS (3)		
n d	c	Elbridge Gerry*	5-29 to end
	c	Nathaniel Gorham	5-28 to end
	c	Rufus King	5-21 to end
n		Caleb Strong	5-28 to 8-17
	CONNECTICUT (1)		
n	c	Oliver Ellsworth	5-28 to 8-23
	c	William Samuel Johnson	6-2 to end
d	c	Roger Sherman	5-30 to end
	NEW YORK (2)		
	c	Alexander Hamilton*	5-18 to end
n	c	John Lansing, Jr.	6-2 to 7-10
n		Robert Yates	5-18 to 7-10
	NEW JERSEY (3)		
		David Brearley	5-25 to end
	c	Jonathan Dayton	6-21 to end
n	c	William Churchill Houston	5-25 to 6-5
	c	William Livingston*	6-5 to end
		William Paterson	5-25 to 7-23
	PENNSYLVANIA (4)		
d	c	George Clymer	5-28 to end
	c	Thomas Fitzsimons	5-25 to end
d	c	Benjamin Franklin	5-28 to end
	c	Jared Ingersoll	5-28 to end
	c	Thomas Mifflin	5-28 to end
	c	Gouverneur Morris*	5-25 to end
d	c	Robert Morris	5-25 to end
d	c	James Wilson	5-25 to end
	DELAWARE (3)		
		Richard Bassett	5-21 to end
	c	Gunning Bedford, Jr.	5-28 to end

			Attendance
		Jacob Broom	5-21 to end
	c	John Dickinson	5-29 to 9-14
d	c	George Read	5-19 to end
	MARYLAND (1)		
	c	Daniel Carroll	7-9 to end
	c	Daniel of St. Thomas Jenifer	6-2 to end
	c	James McHenry*	5-28 to end
n	c	Luther Martin*	6-9 to 9-3
n	c	John Francis Mercer	8-6 to 8-17
	VIRGINIA (3)		
		John Blair	5-15 to end
n		James McClurg	5-15 to 7-26
	c	James Madison	5-14 to end
n		George Mason	5-17 to end
n	c	Edmund Randolph	5-15 to end
	c	George Washington	5-14 to end
n d	c	George Wythe	5-15 to 6-4
	NORTH CAROLINA (3)		
	c	William Blount*	6-20 to end
n		William Richardson Davie	5-23 to 8-12
n		Alexander Martin	5-25 to 8-17
	c	Richard Dobbs Spaight	5-19 to end
	c	Hugh Williamson	5-25 to end
	SOUTH CAROLINA (2)		
	c	Pierce Butler	5-25 to end
	c	Charles Pinckney	5-17 to end
		Charles Cotesworth Pinckney	5-25 to end
	c	John Rutledge	5-17 to end
	GEORGIA (2)		
	c	Abraham Baldwin	6-11 to end
	c	William Few*	5-19 to end
n	c	William Houstoun	6-1 to 7-26
n	c	William Pierce	5-31 to 6-30

c   present or former member of Congress
d   signer of the Declaration of Independence
n   nonsigner of the Constitution (Gerry, Mason, and Randolph were present)
*   Eight delegates had gaps in attendance: Blount 7-3 to 8-6; Few 6-30 to 8-6; Gerry 7-27 to 8-9; Hamilton 6-30 to 9-6, with occasional attendance; Livingston 7-3 to 7-19; L. Martin 7-27 to 8-12, except 8-6; McHenry 6-1 to 8-6; and G. Morris 5-31 to 6-30. The Convention did not meet 7-27 to 8-5, and ended 9-17-1787.

Preface

When, in *The Social Contract*, Rousseau confronted the possibility that the people, while willing the good, might not always be able to see the good, he reached back to ancient Greek and Roman traditions and suggested the Legislator, the extraordinary individual with sufficient wisdom to establish a system of laws and institutions that would enable a society to manage its affairs in peace and justice.

Our Founding Fathers were not much influenced by Rousseau, but they were faced with the same difficulty, not as a matter of theory but of practical experience: the people did not always see clearly, so republican governments sometimes did unjust things. Moreover, the existing institutional structure seemed to be failing in ways that brought republicanism itself into doubt. Could men, ordinary men, really govern themselves?

So the Convention of 1787 was thrust into the role of Rousseau's Legislator, like Solon creating the best government that the people would accept.

At the outset I confess an ambivalent attitude toward its work. It did, and failed to do, good things and bad things. The bicentennial has seen the publication of much good research and interpretation, but quite insufficient critique. The Convention was not a gathering of demigods, but it was a meeting of some powerful minds, experienced politicians who felt themselves at least partially emancipated from the influence of public opinion. They made the second American revolution, thereby obviating some perceived difficulties residual from the original Revolution. They also, however, created a structure capable of dangerous and uncontrollable concentration of power.

The Convention did not aim at democracy, or even at majority rule. It rejected the notion of popular sovereignty—as anything more than political rhetoric. In fact, it rejected all forms of internal sovereignty in favor of mutual collaboration of states and nation in a single system of divided responsibilities.

Nor did the Convention think rights—human, civil, or religious—to be very important. From that attitude proceeded two seminal errors.

The failure to provide a bill of rights led to unnecessary conflict in the ratification and fixed an atmosphere of suspicion and majority domination on the new system. This destroyed whatever chance there may have been to establish in the new regime the sort of mutual restraint the Convention itself had achieved and tried to institutionalize. Operating in that atmosphere, the First Congress could remedy the defect only in part, since the original opportunity to provide protection by Convention consensus had been lost.

The opportunity was also lost to provide a terminal date for slavery, as well as for the slave trade. A simple sentence, "All persons born in the United States after _____ shall be free citizens at _____ years of age," might have led, in that era before the cotton gin, when slaveholders (like George Mason on August 22) were speaking against slavery, to a compromise.

The achievements of the Convention, however, clearly outweigh these and other failures.

The delegates found a solution to the riddle of a durable rule of law. They grasped, more firmly than any predecessors, the idea of a constitution as written positive law, enforceable through the courts against the legislative power itself, and even against the people.

They found, in an era of kings, an unprecedented basis for the largest republic since Roman times. It should rest, they proposed, neither on the states nor on the people. The circumstances required that approval of the new system be derived from the states *and* the people; it must therefore be based on both. And fortunately so, for this provided an escape from each of two potential tyrannies: popular sovereignty and excessive centralization.

Their achievement has been widely admired, but it has not been widely understood because of two unexpected developments. First, the Constitution was implemented by the Washington administration in such distorted ways that even Madison was driven into opposition. The ideas of mutual restraint and respect that the Convention had tried to establish were replaced by party conflict and the pursuit of majority power. This led, second, to the regime (which had been planned, not as a ballot-box democracy, but as a system for the distillation of political wisdom) becoming instead a matter of manipulation of the people's votes.

We are thus left in danger of both the potential tyrannies.

The Convention did not intend, or expect, any such result. I hope to make clear the difference between what it did and what the nationalists wanted it to do by looking closely at its proceedings. We shall see that some basic parts of the Constitution were derived neither from the nationalists nor from the state-sovereignty men. They came, instead, from the principles of a third group of delegates whom I call the state federalists, and they were established over the determined opposition of the nationalists.

Since the nationalists achieved control of the new system in the first federal elections, it is further necessary to distinguish the Convention's Constitution from the distortions of its implementation. The massive Federalist majority in both House and Senate encouraged the extremists to find and exercise powers the Convention had refused to grant. Its idea of collaborative federal and state pursuit of consensus was replaced, step by step, by party and sectional polarization. A Constitution designed to reflect the dual nature of American society as both one nation and several nations has been operated as a high-stakes zero-sum game. The result has been a civil war, the alienation of that large fraction of the citizenry who do not vote, and an inability to face and solve even the most urgent problems of public policy.

I thank the students in my seminar on the Convention who have sharpened my understanding over the years and my colleagues at the University of Maryland who have commented on earlier drafts. I am especially indebted to Professors Leslie Anderson, Herman Belz, Erwina Godfrey, Calvin Jillson, and Donald S. Lutz.

I also thank Maryland's Computer Science Center for statistical support and the Department of Government and Politics for secretarial assistance.

Thornton Anderson
College Park, Maryland

1

Introduction

Like the theses of Nietzsche and Tolstoi that the perversion of Christianity began with the Apostle Paul, the thesis here expounded suggests that the misinterpretation—even the deliberate distortion—of the American Constitution began with its earliest and strongest defenders.

We of the 1990s have the advantage of two centuries of thinking and writing in our attempts to understand the Convention of 1787. Yet we can not say with confidence that it is now understood. On a topic so thoroughly explored, on which little new evidence has come to light,[1] an author may feel apologetic in adding yet another study to the list, and the reader is entitled to wonder what another book can contribute.

After a lengthy and penetrating analysis of six recent books on the

---

1. A fine survey of recent articles and books is Peter S. Onuf, "Reflections on the Founding: Constitutional Historiography in Bicentennial Perspective," *William and Mary Quarterly* 46 (April 1989): 341–75. The evidence accumulated since Max Farrand's *Records of the Federal Convention of 1787* (New Haven, 1911) is conveniently edited by James H. Hutson as a *Supplement* to Farrand (New Haven, 1987). The *Records* will be cited hereafter in parentheses in the text, by volume and page.

American founding, Richard K. Matthews concluded with the observation that "not one was critical of the founding itself" or "could be considered a critical analysis."[2] Perhaps the complacency and self-righteousness of the Reagan years have blighted bicentennial scholarship, but such an observation would not have been made in the 1960s regarding Hannah Arendt's *On Revolution*. Appreciating the uniqueness of the American Revolution and its attendant circumstances and achievements, Arendt was nonetheless able to see that the Revolution, "while it had given freedom to the people, had failed to provide a space where this freedom could be exercised. Only the representatives of the people, not the people themselves, had an opportunity to engage in those activities of 'expressing, discussing and deciding' which in a positive sense are the activities of freedom." And she pointed precisely to the men of the Philadelphia Convention, who had failed to find a way to embrace without smothering the winged hopes of the ordinary people caught up in those great events: "Paradoxical as it may sound, it was in fact under the impact of the Revolution that the revolutionary spirit in this country began to wither away, and it was the Constitution itself, this greatest achievement of the American people, which eventually cheated them of their proudest possession."[3]

2. "Liberalism, Civic Humanism, and the American Revolution: Understanding Genesis," *Journal of Politics* 49 (November 1987): 1127–53. Important recent additions to this literature include Terence Ball and J.G.A. Pocock, eds., *Conceptual Change and the Constitution* (Lawrence, Kans., 1988); Richard Beeman et al., eds., *Beyond Confederation: Origins of the Constitution and American National Identity* (Chapel Hill, 1987); Herman Belz et al., eds., *To Form a More Perfect Union: The Critical Ideas of the Constitution* (Charlottesville, 1992); Leonard W. Levy and Dennis J. Mahoney, eds., *The Framing and Ratification of the Constitution* (New York, 1987); Michael Lienesch, *New Order of the Ages: Time, the Constitution, and the Making of Modern American Political Thought* (Princeton, 1988); David E. Narrett and Joyce S. Goldberg, eds., *Essays in Liberty and Federalism: The Shaping of the United States Constitution* (College Station, Tex., 1988); Thomas L. Pangle, *The Spirit of Modern Republicanism: The Moral Vision of the American Founders and the Philosophy of Locke* (Chicago, 1988); and Niel L. York, ed., *Toward a More Perfect Union: Six Essays on the Constitution* (Provo, Utah, 1988).

3. *On Revolution* (New York, 1965); quotations, pp. 238, 242. Drawing on Lewis Mumford, and through him on Ralph Waldo Emerson, Arendt found in the New England towns a type of self-regulating grass-roots government, parallel to the *sociétés populaires* (crushed by Robespierre), the early soviets (crushed by the Bolsheviks), and the German *Räte*, which similarly found no role in the Weimar constitution; pp. 238, 265–66, 290. For a valuable examination of Arendt's reading of the Declaration see Bonnie Honig, "Declarations of Independence: Arendt and Derrida on the Problem of Founding a Republic," *American Political Science Review* 85 (March 1991): 97–113. On Arendt's public sphere see Dana R. Villa, "Postmodernism and the Public Sphere," *American Political Science Review* 86 (September 1992): 712–21, and Seyla Benhabib, "Models of Public Space: Hannah Arendt, the Liberal Tradition, and Jürgen Habermas," in Craig Calhoun, ed., *Habermas and the Public Sphere* (Cambridge, Mass., 1992).

Arendt credited Jefferson, late in life, as the only one of the Founders to sense that the constitutional system had repressed the democratic spirit that, especially in the New England towns, had provided the dynamic of the Revolution. Yet he too had failed seriously, at the moment of opportunity, by omitting the word "public" in his felicitous phrase "the pursuit of happiness," thereby including the drive for private happiness where public happiness should stand. And the people, denied a public space for political action, turned instead to the private space of economic enterprise—selfishness thus triumphing over community.[4] The old distinction between the rulers and the ruled, reestablished permanently by the Constitution, left the ordinary citizen with a political role to play only in the saturnalia of election day.

This critique, oriented from ideas of participatory democracy, may suffer from anachronistic difficulties, yet Arendt was on target in stressing the enormous and still-unresolved problem of how to preserve, in the establishment of an enduring regime, the political freedom attained in the making of a revolution. The Americans, it seems, surrendered their freedom of political action for the security of civil liberties.

Even so, they came closer than other revolutionaries, before and since, to making a successful transition from liberation to establishment, aided, no doubt, not only by the absence of mass poverty but also by their own extensive experience in government in the colonies and in the states.

I shall attempt to show that a better understanding of the Convention and of the Constitution can be achieved by: (1) a broader grasp of the English developments out of which the Revolution arose, particularly the strengths and weaknesses of Court Whiggery and its impact both in and after the Convention; (2) closer attention to the complex ideologic, as well as eco-

4. Arendt, *On Revolution*, pp. 235–38, 252–59. In Europe two works stressing public happiness had recently appeared. The Italian Ludivico Muratori published *Della pubblica felicità* (Lucca, 1749; French translation, two vols., Lyons, 1772), and the Marquis de Chastellux, later a correspondent and friend of Jefferson, published *De la Félicité Publique* (Amsterdam, 1772; English translation, two vols., London, 1774). See "The Pursuit of Happiness" (1974) in *Absolute Liberty: A Selection from the Articles and Papers of Caroline Robbins*, ed. Barbara Taft (Hamden, Conn., 1982), pp. 292–310. For a cogent analysis of Jefferson's wards see Jean Yarbrough, "Republicanism Reconsidered: Some Thoughts on the Foundation and Preservation of the American Republic," *Review of Politics* 41 (January 1979): 61–95 at 84–95.

Michael Lienesch has argued that the "Constitutionalists" deliberately discouraged civic activity and encouraged private enterprise to build a constitutional tradition of obedient citizenship. See "The Constitutional Tradition: History, Political Action, and Progress in American Political Thought, 1787–1793," *Journal of Politics* 42 (February 1980): 2–30, especially pp. 17–20.

nomic, divisions within the Convention, which will reveal a third group,
standing between the nationalists and the localists, with a different agenda;
(3) a realization that the relative strength of the different groups was not
constant from June to September, but that it both controlled, and was
controlled by, the decisions made at different stages of the Convention's
progress; and (4) a further realization that the implementation of the
Constitution by the First Congress was both a continuation and a distortion
of the work of the Convention.

To anticipate briefly, I shall argue that the nationalists tried to ride a
ground swell of renewed appreciation for English government in the age of
Walpole. They succeeded only in part in the Convention, being defeated by
some special American circumstances and the continuing strength of the
opposition Whig ideology that had sparked the Revolution. After the Constitution went into operation, however, under the leadership of Washington
and Hamilton the nationalists bent it toward central and executive power in
ways not intended by the Convention, ways that, if they had been foreseen,
would have prevented ratification.

The initial reaction to its handiwork, when the Constitution emerged
from its cloak of secrecy on September 18, was a great blaze of controversy.
For nine months its adoption remained in doubt while able writers defended
and attacked it.

Since that time students of the Convention have varied widely in their
assessments, from the adulation of George Bancroft to the iconoclasms of J.
Allen Smith and Charles A. Beard. This literature is too well known to need
detailed review. In the 1950s elaborate attempts were made by Robert E.
Brown and Forrest McDonald to slay and bury the Beardian dragon once
and for all, with only partial success.[5] In the 1960s interest shifted from the
economic backgrounds and motives of the Framers to the ideological milieu
in which they worked.

5. See John P. Diggins, "Power and Authority in American History: The Case of Charles A.
Beard and His Critics," *American Historical Review* 86 (October 1981): 701–30; Robert A.
McGuire and Robert L. Ohsfeldt, "Economic Interests and the American Constitution: A
Quantitative Rehabilitation of Charles A. Beard," *Journal of Economic History* 44 (June 1984):
509–19; Pope McCorkle, "The Historian as Intellectual: Charles Beard and the Constitution
Reconsidered," *American Journal of Legal History* 28 (October 1984): 314–63; and the
literature that they cite.

William E. Nelson denies that the Convention is best understood in terms of compromises
of group interests, but rather should be interpreted in terms of instrumental reasoning in
pursuit of the common good; see his "Reason and Compromise in the Establishment of the
Federal Constitution, 1787–1801," *William and Mary Quarterly* 44 (July 1987): 458–84.

An Approach through Ideas

Beginning with Zera S. Fink's *Classical Republicans* and Caroline Robbins's seminal *Eighteenth-Century Commonwealthman*,[6] the strong influence of the English Country, or opposition, Whigs (as distinguished from the Court Whigs) was rediscovered. Bernard Bailyn, J.G.A. Pocock, H. Trevor Colbourn, and others traced the development of the Country ideology in England from the 1620s through the Augustan Age and into the Americans' dispute with Britain. They were more interested in the Revolution, but their researches were relevant to the Convention because it was in that great dispute that the minds of the older Framers were conditioned. Continuing this emphasis on ideas, Gordon S. Wood's monumental *Creation of the American Republic, 1776–1787* gave a penetrating and perceptive analysis of Country Whig influences on the new revolutionary governments, including the drafting and ratification of the Constitution.[7]

It may be the case, however, that the use of the Country ideology as an explanation of eighteenth-century American political ideas has been overdone. Effectively as it may account for the ideological roots of the Revolution and of the early state governments, it cannot explain the work of the Constitutional Convention nor the public's acceptance of it. The Constitution is left as something of an anomaly, a new departure, even a Thermidorian reaction from exaggerated expectations, without old ideological roots.

Less attention has been given to the ideas and influence of the Court Whigs.[8] It should not be forgotten, however, that prior to the Stamp Act the prevailing view in America, as in England, was that the British government was "the best in the world." It was precisely the government managed by the Court Whigs that elicited such admiration and that retained the loyalty

6. Respectively subtitled *An Essay in the Recovery of a Pattern of Thought in Seventeenth-Century England* (Evanston, 1945) and *Studies in the Transmission, Development, and Circumstances of English Liberal Thought from the Restoration of Charles II until the War with the Thirteen Colonies* (Cambridge, Mass., 1959).

7. Chapel Hill, 1969. See pp. 10–45 on Country Whig influences in America throughout the eighteenth century; see also Donald S. Lutz, "Bernard Bailyn, Gordon S. Wood, and Whig Political Theory," *Political Science Reviewer* 7 (Fall 1977): 111–44.

8. The admirable study by Donald S. Lutz, for example, *Popular Consent and Popular Control: Whig Political Theory in the Early State Constitutions* (Baton Rouge, 1980), does not distinguish Court Whig influences from those of the opposition Whigs; instead, the Antifederalists are seen as the heirs of the Whigs and the Federalists as a new native pattern of thought. See especially his chapter 8 and the Conclusion. E. James Ferguson, *The Power of the Purse* (Chapel Hill, 1961), is aware of the English parallel, but he presents the nationalists' program as if it were original with Robert Morris. See his chapters 6, 7, and 13.

of the American tories at great personal cost during the Revolution.[9] And
the patriots also, in their arguments and in their resistance, always claimed
to be defending the liberties of the English constitution against distortions
begun in 1765.[10] The inflexible British claim to a power to tax the colonies,
coupled with the departure of many of the loyalists, however, resulted in
the ascendancy in America of opposition Whig thought and the temporary
eclipse of the shining virtues of British government.

A Convention to Regain Unity?

During the war the Americans began to experience the problems of republican government. The military effort having required the personal and
financial participation of many who had previously left politics to their
"betters," some among these "new men" began to challenge successfully
the old leadership. Their concerns began to appear on public agendas.[11]

Responding to these concerns, the new state legislatures sometimes
enacted economic policies (paper money, debtor relief, etc.) that seemed—
to the wealthy—to be fundamentally unjust and to bring into question the
long-term viability of the new system of large-scale republican governments.
To the less wealthy, on the other hand, the failure to enact such policies (as
in Massachusetts) was not only unjust, and not only placed property above
persons, but also raised a suspicion that republican government, in the
wrong hands, could be as unresponsive as the British monarchy. These
differences of economic perspective were thus given strongly moral interpretations, the one side fearing ever-bolder attacks on property, the other
sensing a conspiracy to destroy popular government. Such fears reinforced
what has been called the "paranoid style" in American politics.[12]

9. See Jeffrey M. Nelson, "Ideology in Search of a Context: Eighteenth-Century British
Political Thought and the Loyalists of the American Revolution," *Historical Journal* 20 (September 1977): 741–49.

10. Their petitions and pamphlets are eloquent evidence of this, and John Adams's *Thoughts
on Government* (1776) is based on English ideas of balanced government. Adams later shifted
from the balancing of estates to the balancing of interests (rich versus poor), an idea that
prevented him from really embracing popular sovereignty. See his *Works*, ed. Charles F.
Adams (Boston, 1850–56), 4:379–82, 579–88; 6:224–99, and passim; for a cogent analysis, see
John R. Howe, Jr., *The Changing Political Thought of John Adams* (Princeton, 1966), pp. 9–99
and chapter 6.

11. See Jackson T. Main, "Government by the People: The American Revolution and the
Democratization of the Legislatures," *William and Mary Quarterly* 23 (July 1966): 391–407.

12. Richard Hofstadter in an Oxford address of 1963, published in his *Paranoid Style in*

And these worries were not without foundation. Legal-tender and install-ment laws were enacted, and the growing population of the piedmont continually threatened the political power of the tidewater. On the other side, the 1780 enactment of half pay for life for the officers of the army (but not for the soldiers) and the establishment of the hereditary Society of the Cincinnati both reflected and aggravated existing class conflicts.

The Philadelphia Convention must be seen, in this atmosphere, as a momentous step in the ongoing efforts of the old colonial ruling class to retain its position and to contain the thrust of the "new men" aroused to political action by the events of the protracted war.

Yet the handiwork of the Convention was both conservative and radical. The men at Philadelphia chose to preserve the fundamentals, as they saw them, by the use of innovations in structures and powers. The Articles of Confederation, drafted in wartime, seemed to require more consensus among the states than was available in peacetime. The nationalists, swinging to the other extreme, sought to convert the external sovereignty of the new nation into a new central sovereignty—a unitary system. They found, however, after weeks of sometimes bitter conflict, that this program would not go down. The states were not ready to become counties. Their spokes-men believed that a degree of consensus was still present and was preferable to uniformity.

The illusion that the Convention was a gathering of like-minded men cannot survive close study of the records. The delegates did agree on many things, but they also disagreed so fundamentally that even in their agree-ments they frequently stood on different ground. The old distinction of large- and small-state men is useful, particularly with regard to representa-tion but also on other state-related issues. More revealing, however, is a trichotomy of nationalists, localist state-sovereignty men, and state federal-ists. This last phrase is used in this study to designate a group, not large in numbers nor so well known as the leading nationalists, who conceived American society in a different way that enabled them to find an original, quite unprecedented, form of government. There is no accepted or satisfac-

---

American Politics (New York, 1965), pp. 3–40. Bernard Bailyn has well described the similar style in earlier eighteenth-century English politics and its influence in America: see his *Origins of American Politics* (New York, 1968), pp. 24–58, and his *Ideological Origins of the American Revolution* (Cambridge, Mass., 1967), chapter 2, and especially the "Note on Conspiracy," pp. 144–59. Gordon S. Wood has gone deeply into the subject in "Conspiracy and the Paranoid Style: Causality and Deceit in the Eighteenth Century," *William and Mary Quarterly* 39 (July 1982): 401–41. See also James H. Hutson, "The Paranoid Style in American Politics," in David D. Hall, John M. Murrin, and Thad W. Tate, eds., *Saints and Revolutionaries* (New York, 1984).

tory name for this third group. They stood between the others and supported mutual cooperation and restraint of states and nation, without rivalry or antagonism, and without internal sovereignty. They were able, over the opposition of the nationalists, to write their major concepts into the Constitution. The customary view of the Constitution as a triumph of the nationalists also cannot survive close study without major qualifications. It is necessary to distinguish between what was said and what was done. A handful of leaders, mostly nationalists,[13] made most of the speeches, and their remarks are frequently and sometimes correctly taken for the tenor of the Convention; yet they often disagreed among themselves and were also often defeated by a largely (but not entirely) silent majority.

A major reason for the prevailing opinion that the Constitution was a nationalist document—aside from the fact that they, calling themselves Federalists, fought for its ratification—has been their success in interpreting and implementing it at the beginning *as if* it were the document they wanted. But this was far from being the case. In the struggles in the Convention between them and the other two groups, the nationalists suffered some fundamental defeats; yet, younger and more ambitious than the state federalists, they quickly attained positions of power in the new government and proceeded to tilt it toward the idea of national sovereignty and a more active role, at the expense of the states, than the Convention had been willing to accept.

A Secret Convention

It needs to be remembered that the new government was set up and operated for more than fifty years before Madison's notes of the Convention debates were published. The whole structure of interpretations and expectations was thus created and established without utilizing the explanatory power of the debates. For the first twenty years only Luther Martin's *Genuine Information* was available, and it was impugned because he opposed ratification. The same stigma attached to the brief extracts from Robert Yates's notes published in 1808.[14] So it was not until 1819 (when John

13. This may reflect a preference in Madison's note taking for speakers of the nationalist orientation. His bias is most evident in his reporting of Luther Martin, but it is more general. James H. Hutson accepts the integrity of Madison's notes but estimates that he recorded only a tenth, or less, of what was said. "The Creation of the Constitution: The Integrity of the Documentary Record," *Texas Law Review* 65 (November 1986): 1–38, p. 34.

14. Both the *Genuine Information* (Baltimore, 1788) and Yates's notes as published by E.C.É. Genêt (New York, 1808) are reprinted in Farrand, 3:172–232 and 410–16.

Quincy Adams, then Secretary of State, edited and published the official *Journal* of the Convention as recorded by its secretary, William Jackson) that any extensive and reliable information about the Convention became publicly available; and even this presented a record of the actions of the Convention but no debates.

It is clear that the nationalist leaders did not intend that public knowledge of the proceedings at Philadelphia should influence the shaping of the new government. During these years former delegates to the Convention held office in all three branches, but they displayed considerable reluctance to hear recollections of the Convention used in later debates.[15] Indeed, Madison himself, although in a better position than anyone else to draw upon the wisdom of the Convention, said on the floor of the House of Representatives in 1796:

> After all, whatever veneration might be entertained for the body of men who formed our Constitution, the sense of that body could never be regarded as the oracular guide in expounding the Constitution. As the instrument came from them it was nothing more than the draft of a plan, nothing but a dead letter, until life and validity were breathed into it by the voice of the people, speaking through the several State Conventions. (3:374)

Why did he take this position?

The rule of the Convention "That nothing spoken in the House be printed, or otherwise published, or communicated without leave" (1:15) is frequently pointed to in explanation. But it was understood at the time, by some of the delegates at least, as intended to apply "during the sitting of the Convention" (Mason, 3:33) or "till their Deliberations are moulded firm for the public Eye" (A. Martin, 3:64) or as "not otherwise enjoined than as prudence may dictate to each individual" (Gilman, 3:66). No contrary conception of permanent secrecy was expressed while the Convention sat; but later Hamilton held that "the deliberations of the convention, which were carried on in private, were to *remain unmolested*" (1791; 3:368). The other delegates who took notes during the sessions appear to have shared his view: one and all, they went to their graves without publishing them.

A secrecy rule was not at all unusual in eighteenth-century deliberative

<hr/>

15. Compare Elbridge Gerry in the House of Representatives, February 7, 1791 (3:362). Washington created a stir in 1796 by using the *Journal*, which was still secret, against the House in connection with Jay's treaty (3:371–74).

bodies. It was believed conducive to candid debate, and it served to insulate the deliberations against outside pressures. Those purposes ceasing at the end of a session, however, the rule was frequently then rescinded—the First Continental Congress, for example, immediately published its journal. Of course, the publication of debates carries implications not entailed in the publication of journals. However, the four-page newspapers of the time routinely published debates in state legislatures. The Convention's departure from that practice suggests that some motive other than candor was in operation. The fact that the departure continued for so many years further suggests a quite long-range purpose.[16]

Madison may have felt himself to be under another restraint also. Having been given for his record copies of numerous speeches when they were delivered, he could not violate the confidence thus reposed in him by making them public later without permission. The early division of the group into Federalists and Republicans may have made such permissions difficult to obtain, and would have given any proposed publication of his notes a political character.

But why did he not publish before that division occurred? Why were the matters of secrecy and the future of the notes not raised and clarified at the end of the Convention? If the delegates believed that their final product was justified by the debates that had led up to it, they might very well have seen in the records of their work the best of all answers to those who might question their proposals during ratification. It is obvious, and was, no doubt, obvious to them, that their enemies would have found therein ammunition against them as individuals. This may, of course, be the ultimate explanation of the continued secrecy; but is it reasonable to suppose that, on the whole, they thought their speeches and votes so discreditable that they could not bear the light of day?

Rufus King of Massachusetts may have thought so. On the last day of the Convention he proposed that the journals "be either destroyed, or deposited in the custody of the President," because, "if suffered to be made public, a bad use would be made of them" (2:648). Wilson replied that "he had at one time liked the first [alternative] best; but as false suggestions may be propagated it should not be made impossible to contradict them." The

16. Paul Eidelberg, *The Philosophy of the American Constitution* (New York, 1968), pp. 35–39, attributes the secrecy rule to a desire for candor, but his analysis ignores its duration. J. R. Pole has presented a detailed history of legislative secrecy in the seventeenth and eighteenth centuries in *The Gift of Government* (Athens, Ga., 1983); see especially chapter 5, "Telling the American People."

delegates followed Wilson, and Washington got the papers; but they also seem to have shared King's fears. When Washington specifically asked "whether copies were to be allowed to members if applied for," the Convention instructed him to "retain the Journal and other papers, subject to the order of Congress" (2:648).[17]

On the same day, however, McHenry of Maryland recorded cryptically, "Injunction of secrecy taken off" (2:650). His notes are so brief that it is unlikely that he would have made this entry without some substantive basis in the Convention. The Maryland delegates, whose instructions required them "to report the Proceedings" to the state legislature (3:586), had alone voted against giving the journals to Washington, and it seems most probable that they explained the basis for their vote. This may have resulted in some formal or informal statement or action releasing them from the secrecy rule so that they could make their reports. A more general interpretation of McHenry's note would be contrary to the Convention's response to Washington's query, and would also leave less well explained the fact that neither Madison nor the *Journal* mentions any form of release. Yet if such a special exception was made, or even if not, this would have been an appropriate time for Madison, whose position after the long summer of note taking was also somewhat special, to ask permission to use his notes in the interest of the ratification. Wilson's argument that the journals would be needed to contradict "false suggestions" pointed in that direction. But Madison let the opportunity pass in silence.

Again, why?

An explanation emerges from a close study of the *Records* of the Convention—which, it is hoped, will be made clear. In summary, the argument is this: A majority of the delegates, rejecting the extremes after long debate, arrived at an unprecedented form of dual federalism, deliberately avoiding the subject of sovereignty, national or state. The strong nationalists of the Convention, including Madison, were quite dissatisfied with the Constitution as it reached final form. They knew it to be very different from what they had hoped to achieve, yet much closer to their desires than the existing Articles of Confederation, so they resolved to work for the Constitution's ratification. But they also resolved, in case it should be adopted, to keep a free hand for its implementation, so that they could, in the establishment of

---

17. This conspiratorial psychology infected William Jackson, the secretary of the Convention. Before presenting the journals and papers to Washington he apparently burned what he called "all the loose scraps of paper which belong to the Convention," which may have included the original Pinckney Plan and other documents that have never come to light (3:82).

the system and the interpretation of the Constitution, bend it toward their own views. Hamilton, of course, has long been recognized as entertaining this perspective, but Madison and others also did. This required the suppression of his notes so that the basically different orientation that had prevailed in the Convention could not be easily and authoritatively argued against the nationalists on the basis of his own records.

Ratification and Implementation

The subsequent history of this nationalist effort will be pursued in part in chapter 6. In the immediate struggle against the Antifederalists, the nationalists had to make virtues out of some provisions of the Constitution that they had fought tenaciously to exclude, such as the equality of states in the Senate. About such structural features not much could be done, but regarding the powers there was room for interpretation. Ratification achieved, the nationalists proceeded to read the Constitution and to shape the new government, not according to the thought patterns that had prevailed in the Convention, but according to their own unreconstructed patterns. The early efforts under Washington, Hamilton, and Adams were very successful. Yet they overreached themselves—in the excise, the Bank, Jay's treaty, and their attacks on their critics. At the same time, the French Revolution sharpened issues concerning the people's role in government, driving the Federalists toward Britain and further from their own revolutionary heritage.

Madison, already in the Convention less extreme than Hamilton, was repelled by the sectional and class biases of the Secretary of the Treasury. Under the influence of Jefferson, he reoriented his position until he could defend state sovereignty in the Virginia Resolutions. Yet this split between the chief authors of *The Federalist* was itself symptomatic of their common rejection of the integrative position worked out in the Convention by the state federalists. The Republicans backed off somewhat from the drive for central power, but John Marshall on the Supreme Court continued the Federalist trend. Gradually the country became polarized, locked in a struggle over the locus of sovereignty, and the effort of the Convention to build the states into the new system as constituent (but not subordinate) parts was submerged in this struggle.

A New and Unexpected Form of Federalism

The Convention must be seen, therefore, as much more than a step in the efforts of the old ruling class to thwart the "new men." It was more, both in what it prevented and in what it promoted. As a negative force, it was, first, a successful effort to reverse a trend that had gathered momentum since the conclusion of the war, the trend toward balkanization of the Union. Sectional interests and attitudes were so divergent and seemingly irreconcilable that the creation of separate confederacies (eastern, southern, etc.) had serious advocates. Besides those possibilities, the existing states tended to rank their separate interests ahead of those of the Union (or of their neighbors), generating antagonisms and fears that a collapse of the existing confederation would lead to European interventions and armed conflicts. The Convention was also, second, an effort to prevent a reaction to the frustrations of republican government at the state and national levels that might lead to monarchy. Those who were scared by Shays's Rebellion and those who feared the democratization of the state legislatures were a numerous gentry; and we must not forget that nearly all countries were then monarchies and that the large-scale American republics were a new and unique experiment in history.

On the positive side, the Convention displayed remarkable originality. It was the architect of an entirely new scheme of government for a vast territory: a republic of republics but also of individuals. It erected a new central government on the hitherto unheard-of dual foundation of the states as integral political entities *and* the people as the ultimate constituent source of power. It designed a powerful government and yet one with legally enforceable limits on its powers. It conceived a strong but limited, unified yet nonmonarchal, executive, periodically elected, separated from but not quite independent of the legislature, and explicitly removable from office for cause. And it conceived the document by which it did these things, the Constitution, as a permanent standard, standing above and controlling all parts of the system (even the electorate), a standard that could be changed, yet only with great difficulty, and that could be enforced by a bench of judges well insulated from transitory political influences. It thus proposed an elaborate and unique embodiment of the old desideratum, a government of laws rather than of men.

These achievements were the result of an unusual degree of mutual respect and restraint, a result reached through a recognition that some issues were not amenable to solutions by a majority vote. Had a similar recognition and restraint prevailed in the First Congress, the interpretations fastened upon the new system in its implementation might have produced a different balance of the elements of consensus and coercion. The new system was potentially better than the Federalists made it: American politics need not have become a zero-sum game.[18]

Not all of the subsequent disasters can be blamed on Federalist implementation, however. If the Convention is to be admired for its achievements, it must also be accountable for the mistakes and myopias that the acceptance of its handiwork almost rigidly fixed upon posterity. Its most obvious error, the omission of a bill of rights—which almost stopped the ratification—could be at least partially corrected by the amending process. But the very success with which the Constitution established the value structures of the delegates has meant inflexibility in adaptation to changes in values, so that the nation, which was then the world's leader in innovative political solutions, has become a dangerous defender of the world's conservatives and a miscellany of petty tyrants.[19]

In structuring their defenses against the threats of popular majorities, the Framers used complicated modes of indirect elections, fragmented electorates, special majorities, multiple approvals, and long terms of office. Their ultimate defense, however, lay in their conception of a higher law, written surely by human hands, but elevated beyond the reach of ordinary legislative hands, and interpreted finally by a tiny group of professional lawyers seated on the Olympian heights of the Supreme Court.

This conception of written constitutional law, differentiated from statutory law, may well be an effective method for keeping the ship of state on a fairly even keel as it navigates the turbulent waters of republican politics. There are, however, many methods of implementing it. Those chosen by the Convention, motivated as it was by a desire to restrain the influence of popular opinion, primarily in the interest of protecting property, entailed also a pervasive protection of the status quo in general, not only against the people but also against the evolving conceptions of future elites—whether civic-minded or selfish.

To adumbrate the dimensions of this problem the question may be asked,

18. A critical review of the deterioration of the system down to the present, from a different point of view, is elaborated in Russell L. Hanson, *The Democratic Imagination in America* (Princeton, 1985).

19. For the repudiation of its innovative role, beginning with the Washington administration, see David Brion Davis, *Revolutions: Reflections on American Equality and Foreign Liberations* (Cambridge, Mass., 1990).

Cannot the Constitution be altered, by interpretation or amendment, to accommodate any change of values accepted by the American people? The answer perhaps is twofold. First, the institutional arrangements massively distort the public mind toward competitive and against cooperative, toward antagonistic and against civic values. While large parts of the world experiment with various collective solutions to public problems, the Americans work instead to extend their already exaggerated individualism. The growing use of the adversary processes of the law and the glaring injustices of the medical system well illustrate the resulting difficulties. Second, the technical requirements of the amending article place some types of change effectively beyond its reach. The current issues of abortion and equal rights for women seem to illustrate this, but the convincing example is slavery. When public opinion turned against that institution, the amendment process was so clearly not available to solve the problem that it was not even tried.[20]

The view seems inescapable, therefore, that the Founding Fathers, in the Convention, produced a highly original system of government that has vindicated their belief that durable large-scale republican government was possible; but that they, in defending property against anticipated majorities of the propertyless, entailed upon their posterity a system insufficiently flexible to adapt—in time—to changes in the values present in the political environment, both national and international.

Let us see how this came about.

---

20. If it be argued that public opinion had not changed sufficiently by 1860, that, given sufficient time and goodwill, an amendment could have abolished slavery, one may respond that the war itself proves that the degree of patience required by the amending article is not always available.

2

Ideas from England

During and after the Revolutionary War the problems of representative government continued to accumulate. The failure of various efforts to strengthen the central government, and the outbreak of Shays's Rebellion in Massachusetts, stimulated a widespread rethinking of the easy acceptance of republicanism that had characterized the 1770s. Those like Alexander Hamilton, who did not "think favorably of republican government," were anticipating the prospect that "excesses" of democracy would bring a public revulsion that would destroy it (Farrand, 1:424, 288). Others, who were less pessimistic about republicanism, still searched for ways to reduce its seeming tendency toward dangerous volatility. Such searches perhaps inevitably led to a revival of interest in, and appreciation for the merits of, the British system of government.

There were, of course, obvious and formidable obstacles to the application of British solutions to American problems. The vast size of the American continent, occupied and unoccupied, had already led to a greater number of firmly rooted political entities, the states, than Britain had known since Saxon times. No state among them was dominant as England was in Britain. This was a circumstance that favored federalism rather than the unitary system of Britain. The heritage of America as a haven for minority religious groups made the moral and political influence of religion very different from that of the established Church of England. And aside from the residual rancor of the revolutionary experience, the absence of a titled aristocracy and any embryo of monarchy made it impossible to apply, without radical modifications, the basic British concept of balanced government—the restraint of arbitrary power by institutional separation of the three estates.

Nevertheless, the Americans had clearly borrowed much from the mother country; might they not borrow still more? Might they not learn from a closer study of the political and administrative methods of the British ministers? After all, for more than a century a succession of ministries had demonstrated remarkable skill in keeping the people in their place, in avoiding the sort of popular influence that threatened property through the state legislatures.

By 1787 the revival of appreciation for the British system had proceeded apace, yet unevenly among political leaders, and selectively with regard to the elements of the system. Opposition Whig opinions continued to predominate among most Americans, but various amalgams of them with Court Whig ideas were gathering strength. To understand how these circumstances influenced the Convention of 1787, it is necessary to touch briefly on some of the complexities of the English background and on the gradual emergence in England of the elements that led to such a vigorous love-hate relationship of the colonists toward the mother country.

This chapter will examine some aspects of the dialectic in the development of English liberty and authority. From the earliest legal writings we shall see that the heritage of the Roman law, which stressed imperial authority in both church and state and gradually supplanted the "barbarian" codes on the continent, encountered successful resistance to kingly power from the common law of England. These two tendencies, toward unrestrained monarchal power and toward its restraint by "immemorial" customs and the common law, resulted in three great conflicts in the seventeenth and eighteenth centuries, the resistance to Charles I and to James II and the Revolution in America. In each case a Court party defended central authority and a Country party resisted the innovations introduced by central power.

In emphasizing the influences of the Court and Country traditions from England, there is no intention to deny the influences of continental experience and thought. Such thinkers as Montesquieu, Beccaria, and Pufendorf were frequently read and quoted; and the English traditions themselves carried important elements, both political and religious, of continental origin—Calvinism, for example. Yet (aside from the Bible and classical authors) the common language, the special British forms of religion, and the customs of the English common law made England the predominant source of political ideas in America both during and after the revolution.[1]

We shall see, in looking at these English developments, the conflicting roles of reason and will, of tradition and innovation, of power and restraints on power, and the perennial struggles of the House of Commons for independence from the king and his ministers. We shall also see that the interrelations of liberty, property, and power, continually evolving, generated conflicting interpretations of the sources and meaning of a regime of law.

Through these conflicts strode the specters of republics past—those of Greece and Rome, of the Italian city-states, and of Cromwell. In spite of the Stuarts the British staunchly supported monarchy, while, after Yorktown, most Americans saw no alternative to republicanism. Yet by the time of the Convention in 1787 some American leaders were eager to adapt the English model as the best defense against democracy.

The ambiguities of the English heritage, endemic to the American colonies from the beginning, thus remained influential, expressing themselves most clearly in the struggle for and against additional central power under the Articles of Confederation.

England's Ambivalent Medieval Heritage

The Roman law, revived in the schools of the late middle ages, was both republican and imperial. On the continent it gradually superseded the

1. See Donald S. Lutz, "The Relative Influence of European Writers on Late Eighteenth-Century American Political Thought," *American Political Science Review* 78 (March 1984): 189–97. His table 3 shows Montesquieu as the most frequently cited author; but (omitting five Greeks and Romans) there were twenty British names among the thirty-one most cited modern thinkers.

various Germanic customary codes, but it did not immediately lead to an emphasis on its elements of despotic power. During the long struggles of the princes against the centralized power of the popes, however, its imperial aspect contributed to the development, especially in France, of doctrines of unrestrained secular power.

In England, on the contrary, the common law proved stronger. Justinian's *Digest* itself (I, 3, 32) endorsed customary laws, saying that they "are binding on us for no other reason than that they have been received by the judgment of the people." The earliest commentators on the English law used parts of the civil law of Rome in explaining English institutions. Glanvil in the twelfth century used Ulpian's key phrase, "what has pleased the prince has the force of law," and applied it to England's unwritten laws, which were "promulgated on doubtful points after determination by the leading men in the [king's] council and acceptance by the king's authority." Hugh de Bracton in the thirteenth century quoted the same phrase, but immediately interpreted it in a manner that distinguished English kingship from the unlimited Roman imperium. The king, he said, was under no man, but under God and the law. He also drew on the basic Roman distinction between private and public law in distinguishing the king's absolute power to govern from his limited role in matters of private right covered by the common law.[2]

Yet Bracton himself, or a very early copyist, inserted an addition in his book saying that, if the king failed to bridle himself with the law, the magnates should "put a bridle on him." This was, no doubt, a response to the prolonged conflicts of the nobles with Henry III, and may have reflected the religious component of medieval government. The king had a duty to govern justly, and, as his advisers, the magnates shared that duty and might incur God's punishment if they failed to restrain the king from ruling unjustly.[3]

2. Ranulf de Glanvil, *Tractatus de Legibus et Consuetudinibus Regni Angliae*, ed. John Rayner (London, 1780), Prologue, quoted in R. W. and A. J. Carlyle, *A History of Medieval Political Theory in the West* (Edinburgh, 1915, 1950), 3:46n.; Hugh de Bracton, *De Legibus et Consuetudinibus Angliae*, ed. George E. Woodbine (New Haven, 1922), folios 5, 54, 107–107b, also quoted in Carlyle, *History of Medieval Political Theory*, 3:67, 69, and 2:58–67 for a general discussion; cf. Justinian, *Digest*, I, 3, 32, and I, 4, 1, and his *Institutes*, I, 2, 6. For Bracton's Latin and careful analysis see Fritz Schultz, "Bracton on Kingship," *English Historical Review* 60 (May 1945): 136–76.

3. The *addicio* is translated in full in Ewart Lewis, *Medieval Political Ideas* (London, 1954), 1:280. Charles M. Radding, "The Origins of Bracton's *Addicio de Cartis*," *Speculum* (April 1969): 239–46, suggests that the Roman law of partnerships was another source of the nobles' ideas of collective responsibility.

Succeeding legal authorities—among them the author of *Fleta* (who repeated the addition to Bracton), Sir John Fortesque, Sir Thomas Smith, and Sir Edward Coke—continued Bracton's distinction of the two spheres of kingly power, the one limited and the other not. The ways in which they used quotations from the Romans, however, coupled with the ambiguities attending the practical application of this distinction, led to what has been called "a two-fold tradition, one constitutional, the other absolutist."[4]

By temperament the Stuart monarchs lacked the subtle abilities of the Tudors to integrate this twofold tradition. Impressed with notions of divine-right monarchy, they tried to reinforce the absolutist principle by expanding the prerogative; they thereby stimulated extreme efforts to protect the constitutional limitations on absolutism.

It is important to keep in view the religious dimensions of the situation. In medieval thought, power entailed moral responsibilities, and the magnates, as sharers in power, also shared the king's responsibility to God. Divine punishment for his injustices might fall not only on the king but also on those who failed to restrain him—hence Bracton's bridle. Culminating in the Magna Carta, this view also saw the Charter, not as a kingly grant nor as a collective enactment, but as an expression of God's justice in England—and therefore not subject to change by human authority.

As the Protestant Reformation gradually disseminated the idea of unmediated moral responsibility of the individual to God, two contradictory political results (among others) transpired. On the one hand, the king's responsibility to rule justly evolved into the notion that he was exempt from all human judgment or restraint. On the other hand, the magnates' role as sharers of power and responsibility was assumed, especially under Puritan influences, by the members of the House of Commons. The resulting turmoil, which filled most of the seventeenth century, can be seen to have (for some participants, at least, on all sides) deeply conscientious motivations that made it so intractable.

This turmoil can also be seen as struggle for and against the conversion of old moral and legal limitations, which required the king to exercise self-

---

4. Charles H. McIlwain, *Constitutionalism: Ancient and Modern*, rev. ed. (Ithaca, 1947), p. 73. This little book is an excellent summary of these developments. McIlwain's sharp distinction of the king's standing above the law in his *gubernaculum* and under the law in his *jurisdictio* has been accepted by Hermann and Ernst Kantorowicz, Fritz Schulz, Paul Bridsall, Margaret Judson, and others, but challenged by Brian Tierney, Francis Oakley, and by Ewart Lewis, who insists that Bracton's king was always under the law. These differences among such competent scholars serve to underline the ambiguity of the English heritage.

restraint and which the Stuarts chose to ignore, into new political and institutional restraints or controls, which could be imposed upon the king without his agreement.[5]

In this struggle the old tradition of common-law protection for private rights against all parts of the government was confronted with the claims of the new notion of sovereignty. Imported from France toward the end of the sixteenth century, sovereignty had been first well expounded by Jean Bodin, who defined it as "supreme power over citizens and subjects unrestrained by law." Bodin did not mean *all* law, for he carefully placed his sovereign under the laws of God and nature and under certain fundamental laws, *leges imperii*, which he could not change, and also under some restraints regarding the subjects' property.[6] The Stuart apologists, however, tended to forget such refinements or to reject them as illogical—as did Hobbes.

The idea of supreme power residing in the king, lords, and commons was an old one in England; but in theory, and in law as expounded by Sir Edward Coke—from the bench (1606–16), in his *Reports* and his *Institutes*, and in the House of Commons—this power was limited by certain customs and great charters. When the House of Commons prepared the Petition of Right, the Lords wanted to add a clause "to leave entire" the king's "sovereign power." But Coke was vehement against this: "Sovereign Power is no Parliamentary word. In my opinion, it weakens Magna Charta, and all our Statutes; for they are absolute without any saving of Sovereign Power. . . . Magna Charta is such a Fellow, that he will have no Sovereign." Sir Thomas Wentworth followed with an identical view: "These laws are not acquainted with Sovereign Power."[7]

5. This is a major theme of McIlwain, ibid., pp. 90–135. Margaret A. Judson, in the lucid last chapter of her *Crisis of the Constitution: An Essay in Constitutional and Political Thought in England, 1603–1645* (New Brunswick, N.J., 1949), remarks that the king's supporters "claimed more absolute power for him than had ever in previous centuries been accorded the English monarch," but also that, by 1642, "the parliamentary opposition had become patently aggressive, claiming and exercising powers which law and precedent clearly gave the king" (p. 386).

6. *De la République* (1576) and *De Republica* (1586), book I, chapter 8, p. 84 H 6–7. Bodin's book was translated by Richard Knolles from both French and Latin and published in London in 1606. His Latin clearly said "unrestrained by law" (*legibusque soluta*), but his French had omitted that phrase in the definition, as did Knolles's English, although a few pages later Knolles gives ". . . an absolute power, not subject to any law" (88 K 3). See Julian Franklin, *Jean Bodin and the Rise of Absolutist Theory* (Cambridge, 1973), and the reprint of the Knolles translation edited by Kenneth D. McRae (Cambridge, Mass., 1962).

7. John Rushworth, *Historical Collections* (London, 1659, 1682), 1:562. Similar opinions came from Eliot, Selden, Pym, and others, and both the Lords and the king eventually backed down. On Coke see Jean Beauté, *Un grand juriste anglais, Sir Edward Coke, 1552–1634: Ses idées politiques et constitutionnelles* (Paris, 1975), and Stephen D. White, *Sir Edward Coke*

Coke spoke of the "artificial reason" of the law: the common law embodied the accumulated wisdom of experience, and its practitioners had special abilities in applying that wisdom in the pursuit of justice. An act of Parliament "against common right and reason," he held in Bonham's Case, was void. In this tradition law was found, not made; justice was a matter of right reason and could not be defined or determined by an act of will. The courts, including Parliament, might refine and make explicit the wisdom of the law, a process of ratiocination, not of volition, of *jus dicere*, not of *jus dare*. But in the seventeenth century Stuart claims to sovereignty and the resulting conflicts led to the intrusion of will into the area of law; the *making* of law became the prime mark of sovereignty. Parliament was gradually converted from a court, where collective wisdom of experience was applied to public and private conflicts, into a legislature, consciously making rather than finding the law. Issues came to be decided, not by judgments regarding customs, God's moral law, and right reason, but by the interplay of wills. [8]

Over time also a doctrine had grown up, similar to the ancient idea of the emperor as a "living law," by which the king could, when he felt it to be in the public interest, dispense with a penal law. However, as used by King Charles this prerogative power to dispense with law convinced the parliamentary leaders that law alone could not limit the king without power. Older constitutional ideas of supreme but limited power were converted into political doctrines of unlimited sovereignty—on the one hand of the divine-right monarch, and on the other a counterclaim of sovereignty in the two houses of Parliament as the institutional equivalent of the people themselves, from whom the whole structure derived. [9]

---

and *"The Grievances of the Commonwealth," 1621–1628* (Chapel Hill, 1979). On the "common-law mind" see J.G.A. Pocock, *The Ancient Constitution and the Feudal Law*, 2d ed. (New York, 1987), 30–69, 255–80.

8. 12 *Coke's Reports* 65 (1607); 8 *Coke's Reports* 118a (1609). For an analysis of reason versus will based on Coke see John Underwood Lewis, "Sir Edward Coke (1552–1633): His Theory of 'Artificial Reason' as a Context for Modern Basic Legal Theory," *Law Quarterly Review* 84 (July 1968): 330–42.

9. Henry Parker clearly claimed sovereignty for the two houses of Parliament in 1642 (*Observations upon Some of His Majesties Late Answers and Expresses*, reprinted in *Tracts on Liberty*, ed. William Haller [New York, 1933], 2:167–213). A less extreme claim for a joint sovereignty of king, lords, and commons was expressed by Charles Herle (*A Fuller Answer to a Treatise Written by Doctor Ferne* [London, 1642]) and by Philip Hunton (*A Treatise of Monarchie* [London, 1643]). Sovereignty in the king alone was argued in 1642 by John Spelman, answering Parker (*A View of a Printed Book, Intituled Observations* . . . [Oxford, 1643]), and further elaborated the next year (*The Case of our Affairs, in Law, Religion, and other Circumstances briefly examined, and Presented to the Conscience* [Oxford, 1644]). These and other tracts dealing with sovereignty are carefully analyzed in Corinne C. Weston and Janelle R. Greenberg, *Subjects and Sovereigns: The Grand Controversy over Legal Sovereignty in*

This notion of the community as the ultimate source of political power was not yet used to claim continuing sovereignty in the people themselves in the modern style. It was, instead, a claim that the "ancient constitution" had been structured by the whole community and the king's place in that structure thus determined. This led to much antiquarian research on both sides, with ambivalent results; but for those who believed that the king's power came directly from God, any argument for a human source of his power was dangerous doctrine leading quickly to Leveller attacks on property and privilege and to the chaos of war and republicanism.

Much of this controversy hinged on a document disseminated in June 1642 by King Charles himself. The king, following ill-digested advice, gave his enemies three weapons. Using the old Polybian balance of monarchy, aristocracy, and democracy, he proclaimed that "the experience and wisdom of your ancestors hath so moulded" English government "out of a mixture of these" as to avoid "the inconveniences of any one, as long as the balance hangs even between the three estates." Charles then balanced his statement of the lawmaking process: "The laws are jointly made by a king, by a house of peers, and by a house of commons chosen by the people, all having free votes." Aside from the derogatory coloring of the words "mixture" and "jointly," the phrase "your ancestors" instead of "our ancestors" countenanced the community as the originator of the constitution; and the coordination of three "votes" in lawmaking undercut the royalist interpretation that the laws were made by the king with the advice and consent of the two houses. Moreover, in his description of the "balance," the king clearly set himself in the role of one of the estates instead of standing above them—the most serious strategic error.[10]

Stuart England (Cambridge, 1981). That the royalists learned little from the turmoil is indicated by the views of Sir Philip Warwick, who sat in the Long Parliament and wrote about 1670 of the king: "His houses pray a law, but he enacts it; for authority must be single . . ." (quoted in Weston and Greenberg, *Subjects and Sovereigns*, p. 95).

10. *His Majesty's Answer to the Nineteen Propositions of Both Houses of Parliament*, text in J. P. Kenyon, ed., *The Stuart Constitution, 1603–1688*, 2d ed. (Cambridge, 1986), pp. 18–20. Recent discussions of the *Answer* are in J.G.A. Pocock, *The Machiavellian Moment: Florentine Political Thought and the Atlantic Republican Tradition* (Princeton, 1975), pp. 361–66, and Weston and Greenberg, *Subjects and Sovereigns*, chapters 3 and 4; but the most thorough analysis of the concepts of estates, reaching back to the early fifteenth century and stressing the importance of the religious conflicts, is Michael Mendle, *Dangerous Positions: Mixed Government, the Estates of the Realm, and the Making of the "Answer to the xix Propositions"* (University, Ala., 1985).

Both versions of the trinity of estates—lords temporal, lords spiritual, and the commons, and king, lords, and commons—were current long before 1642 but were not used in issues of the king's power. See S. B. Chrimes, *English Constitutional Ideas in the Fifteenth Century*

The king's supporters tried to extricate him from the damaging implications of this document and to restore the claim of royal sovereignty. They hardly succeeded, but the pamphlet warfare of the time clarified the alternative readings of the constitution. The republican experiments of the era were even less successful, in effect casting a permanent shadow over any application of popular sovereignty in the form of republican government. The Stuarts were restored in 1660, to the accompaniment of a national sigh of relief.

Force had been able to kill a king but it had not been able to limit a monarchy. No new conditions had been imposed upon Charles II.[11] He, however, still claiming divine appointment and power to make and dispense with laws, gradually dissipated the public goodwill with which he started. In 1673 he made an issue of his prerogative; the two houses stood firmly against him and defeated him. The prevailing view had come to be that sovereignty resided, not in the king nor in the two houses, but in king, lords, and commons, a view that was seen as a middle position between two obnoxious extremes.

If the supreme power was thus divided, was it still "unrestrained by law" because it was the source of law? There remained a body of public opinion that was still Cokeian, still suspicious of all claims to unlimited power. The fabric of thought regarding supreme power was interwoven of four elements, a woof of the traditional versus the rational and a warp of the religious versus the secular—all with roots in the Middle Ages. Two patterns run through this fabric, the notion of sovereignty (from Bodin through Hobbes, Filmer, Brady, and Blackstone to John Austin) and the notion that all power is limited (from Hooker, Coke, Lawson, and Locke to Camden, James Wilson, and other American revolutionaries).

In this second pattern it was not enough to balance the three estates so that the people through the House of Commons could restrain the king. It was also necessary to maintain a balance between the power of government and the rights of the citizens. Among the great difficulties in the doctrine of sovereignty, from such a viewpoint, was this: neither liberty nor property would be immune to invasion by the unlimited power of king, lords, and

---

(Cambridge, 1936), pp. 100–126; Weston and Greenberg, *Subjects and Sovereigns*, pp. 42–46, 282–84; and Mendle, *Dangerous Positions*, pp. 21–96.

11. The Parliament, on May Day 1660, resolved that "according to the ancient and fundamental laws of this kingdom, the government is, and ought to be, by King, Lords, and Commons." *Parliamentary History of England*, ed. William Cobbett (London, 1806–), vol. 2, cols. 24–25.

commons. Those who valued liberty above order, and traditions and customs above the logic of Hobbes—the "Country" opposition—continued to believe that, even if the House of Commons should fail in this duty, customary legal and moral restraints should bar the path of government against any invasion of traditional English rights. Popular control, therefore, could supplement but never entirely supplant the older idea of limitations on the power of government.

In its practical application this line of thought came to focus primarily on the independence of the House of Commons. There were three dimensions of this independence: free collective decision making, uncontrolled by the crown and its ministers; freedom of the members as individuals to express and vote their convictions; and the independence, both political and economic, of the electors at the grass-roots level. Such independence required personal security and economic resources protected by law. The possession and legal protection of property were thus essential for eligibility to participate in the political process.

An easy corollary of this requirement of independence was the exclusion of the poor from the political decision process. They could not be independent; they did not have the leisure or the education to understand issues of public policy; and they were in no position to appreciate the role of property as a guarantor that decisions would be genuinely independent. And, in practice, they would be easily swayed, they would sell their votes, and their numbers would overwhelm the independent property holders.[12]

It is also easy to dismiss this pattern of thought as the rationalization of class prejudice, a form of elite selfishness. No doubt it did contain an element of prejudice; but it contained as well an element of sincere public spirit that made property holders, especially landed property holders, confident of their own virtue, suspicious of manipulating ministers and standing armies, and antagonistic to the growing influence of the "monied interest" of the City of London.

England's Second Revolution

The Glorious Revolution of 1688 was a very ambivalent phenomenon, but on the whole conservative. The earlier view that it represented a triumph of

---

12. Henry Neville, one of the most prominent of the commonwealth men, in his best-known work, *Plato Redivivus* (1681), wrote against "admitting (in the beginning of a government, or afterwards) the meaner sort of people, who have no share in the territory, into an equal part of ordering the commonwealth: these being less sober, less considering, and less careful of the public concerns; and being commonly the major part; are made the instruments oft-times of the ambition of the great ones, and very apt to kindle into faction." Caroline Robbins, ed., *Two English Republican Tracts* (Cambridge, 1969), p. 102.

the ideas of John Locke on popular sovereignty and the social contract has been exploded by recent scholarship.[13] The dilemma of either ejecting King James or accepting a restoration of Catholicism was so traumatic that most participants sought security in the preservation of institutions.

Several anonymous writers, hurriedly publishing advice to the Convention Parliament,[14] used contract theory to argue that the king's departure from England dissolved the old arrangements and left the people or the Convention free to create new ones, even republican ones. The author of *Advice Before It Be Too Late* was very clear in distinguishing the constituent power of the Convention from the power that the King-in-Parliament would have afterward, which would be limited to whatever rules the Convention established: "A parliament makes laws for the administration, but the people, as in a community make laws for the constitution."[15]

In the Convention itself, however, these views had little support. In the debates of January and February 1689 a few men, such as Sir Robert Howard, held that "[t]he Constitution of the Government is actually grounded upon pact and covenant with the People."[16] Most members, on the contrary, preferred to admit contract thinking only in the attenuated form expressed by the coronation oath and the oaths of fealty. The Whig leaders, conscious

13. Peter Laslett, "The English Revolution and Locke's 'Two Treatises of Government,' " *Cambridge Historical Journal* 12 (no. 1, 1956): 40–55; John Dunn, "The Politics of Locke in England and America in the Eighteenth Century," in John W. Yolton, ed., *John Locke: Problems and Perspectives* (Cambridge, 1969), pp. 45–80; M. P. Thompson, "The Reception of John Locke's *Two Treatises of Government*, 1690–1705," *Political Studies* 24 (June 1976): 184–91; and Richard Ashcraft, *Revolutionary Politics and Locke's "Two Treatises of Government"* (Princeton, 1986), who places Locke among the radicals who were dissatisfied with the Glorious Revolution.

14. This appellation arose from the irregularities of its assembly in the absence of a call by a king. James had twice issued and twice rescinded the call. On February 23, 1689, William accepted a bill converting the Convention into a Parliament.

15. The author may have been the Presbyterian John Humfrey. He named five powers that should be exercised only with Parliament's consent, but two of them, the power of the sword and that of appointments, as sufficient to deliver the nation "from all slavery for ever." *A Collection of Scarce and Valuable Tracts . . . of the Late Lord Somers*, ed. Walter Scott, 2d ed., vol. 10 (London, 1813), pp. 198–202. The attribution to Humfrey is in Edmund Calamy, *An Abridgement of Mr. Baxter's History of His Life and Times*, 2d ed., vol. 2 (London, 1713), p. 621.

16. Anchitel Grey, *Debates of the House of Commons, 1667–1694* (London, 1763), vol. 9, p. 20. Robert Ferguson, the Rye House plotter, who also saw all civil authority as derived from "some Grant of the people," still saw cause to reject a republic: "To dream of reducing *England* to a Democratical Republick, is incident only to persons of shallow Capacities. . . . For as the Mercurial and Masculine Temper of the English people, is not to be moulded and accomodated to a Democracy; so it is impracticable to establish such a Common-wealth, where there is a numerous Nobility and Gentry, unless we should first destroy and extirpate them." *A Brief Justification of the Prince of Orange's Descent into England* (London, 1689), p. 23 (40-page edition published anonymously).

of the need to carry the House of Lords with them and to avoid alienating the Tories (who might defect to King James) or William of Orange (who might give up his venture in England if displeased with limits on his power), chose to establish a Protestant king rather than to clarify the constitution.[17]

To protect the "ancient" constitutional balance of king, lords, and commons the Convention refused to assert its own supremacy, yet it declared the throne vacant by construing James's departure as an abdication. It carefully avoided any assertion that he had been deposed. To prevent its actions from becoming precedents for future revolutions, it stressed the unique nature of circumstances and insisted that in setting up a new dynasty it was preserving the old constitution against absolutism and a restoration of Catholicism by King James. It wrote a Declaration of Rights, much watered down, which was presented to William and Mary at their coronation; this was not a condition of their tenure, however, so that the major changes— such as the Protestant succession, the independence of judges, triennial elections, and annual sessions of Parliament—were left for later.[18]

In establishing a Dutch king, however, the Convention involved the nation in continental wars and in Dutch methods of financing them. This required an army that was supported by borrowed money, leading to a new role for public creditors, to the mortgaging of the tax revenues, and to increasingly sophisticated and successful efforts to control Parliament through patronage. The new king, to avoid too great dependence on the Whigs, even brought into his ministry the Tory lords Danby, Halifax, and Nottingham, who had served King James to the end. These empirical developments impinged upon the ideological differences of interpretation of the Revolution, and thus led to the division of the Whigs into a Court group holding power with William III and opposition groups that believed the revolution was going astray.

17. The public and parliamentary debate is concisely presented in J. P. Kenyon, *Revolution Principles: The Politics of Party, 1698–1720* (Cambridge, 1977), pp. 5–34. Of the vast literature, see J. R. Jones, *The Revolution of 1688 in England* (New York, 1972); J.G.A. Pocock, ed., *Three British Revolutions: 1641, 1688, 1776* (Princeton, 1980); and David S. Lovejoy, *The Glorious Revolution in America* (New York, 1972).

18. For activities and interpretations of the interregnum winter see: Henry Horwitz, "Parliament and the Glorious Revolution," *Bulletin of the Institute of Historical Research* (University of London) 47 (May 1974): 36–52; Robert J. Frankle, "The Formulation of the Declaration of Rights," *Historical Journal* 17 (June 1974): 265–79; J. P. Kenyon, "The Revolution of 1688: Resistance and Contract," in Neil McKendrick, ed., *Historical Perspectives* (London, 1974), pp. 43–69; and Ashcraft, *Revolutionary Politics*, pp. 555–601. Lois G. Schwoerer, *The Declaration of Rights, 1689* (Baltimore, 1981), believes the Declaration contained new restraints.

All factions continued to adhere to the notion of balanced government, but they differed as to how completely separate and independent the three parts should be. All agreed that financial restraints on the king were necessary and legitimate.[19] The ministry always opposed place bills (excluding those holding crown patronage positions from sitting in the Commons) on the ground that the House of Commons should not be entirely independent of the crown. Yet the ministry introduced in 1719 a Peerage bill that was roundly defeated in the Commons on the ground (among others) that it would make the House of Lords too independent. The three branches, therefore, should be interdependent, not independent; but Court and Country disagreed on how best to achieve this.[20]

They differed also as to the source of danger to balanced government. The Court Whigs, now in office, became convinced that the constitutional balance was threatened not by the monarch but by the growing power of the House of Commons. Balance could be preserved only by increasing the influence of the king and his ministers in Parliament through the management of elections and the granting of pensions and positions to its members. Sir Robert Walpole and his successors became wonderfully adept at such methods.[21]

From the beginning of William's reign the need for borrowed money to fight his wars gave a new importance not only to the financial interests of the City of London but also to the Treasury ministers. An ability to manage taxes and credit, even more than military or diplomatic skill, became the key to political leadership and power. Walpole's supposed financial skill in carrying the country through the South Sea Company collapse in 1720 led to his appointment as First Lord of the Treasury and Chancellor of the Exchequer, the foundation of his power until 1742. His skills failed him only twice—at the end, of course, and in 1733, when he had to withdraw his

19. Clayton Roberts, "The Constitutional Significance of the Financial Settlement of 1690," *Historical Journal* 20 (March 1977): 59–76.

20. For a good analysis of the theory of the balanced constitution in the seventeenth and eighteenth centuries, see M.J.C. Vile, *Constitutionalism and the Separation of Powers* (Oxford, 1967), pp. 51–75.

21. "The king must have his real power, as well as the other parts of the legislature," Walpole's *London Journal* said on October 5, 1734, "and . . . he can have no real power (now that the crown lands are gone, and he depends absolutely upon the people for money), but by those dependencies, which his power of disposing of all places, civil, military and ecclesiastical, creates." Quoted in H. T. Dickinson, *Liberty and Property* (New York, 1977), p. 155. Reed Browning gives a friendly analysis of Court Whigs and their ideology in his *Political and Constitutional Ideas of the Court Whigs* (Baton Rouge, 1982), calling them "Ciceronian" in contrast to the inflexibility of Cato of Utica and their opponents.

proposed excise, which had aroused deep fears of tax collectors invading and searching private homes.[22]

King William's involvement in land wars on the Continent brought standing armies, including foreign mercenaries, that were not disbanded in the intervals of peace. It also brought increasing numbers of military officers into the Commons, and increasing fears among backbenchers that these developments were part of a deep design to destroy the liberties of England. Recent experience in England, France, and other countries was expounded by Country journalists to show that standing armies had been used in that way. The Court Whigs denied the parallel, of course, since some control had been instituted with the first annual Mutiny bill in 1689.[23]

From Limited to Unlimited Power

There is no doubt that, in spite of the wars, England under the Court Whigs did achieve a remarkable prosperity and stability, the Augustan Age, which contrasted sharply with the vicissitudes and violence of the Stuart era.[24]

With their continued success, the Court Whig interpretation of the Glorious Revolution of 1688 underwent a metamorphosis. The emphasis on preserving the constitution, as the embodiment of the wisdom of immemorial custom, evolved into an emphasis on the precarious balance of the old regime and the sovereign power of Parliament in converting it into an established, stable system.

22. Stephen B. Baxter, *The Development of the Treasury, 1660–1702* (London, 1957); Jeremy Black, *Robert Walpole and the Nature of Politics in Early Eighteenth-Century Britain* (New York, 1990); John Brewer, *The Sinews of Power: War, Money, and the English State, 1688–1783* (Cambridge, Mass., 1990); P.G.M. Dickson, *The Financial Revolution in England: A Study in the Development of Public Credit, 1688–1756* (London, 1967); Paul Langford, *The Excise Crisis: Society and Politics in the Age of Walpole* (Oxford, 1975); and Henry Roseveare, *The Treasury, 1600–1870: The Foundations of Control* (London, 1973), a summary with documents. A fine brief summary of Walpole's methods is Evaline Cruickshanks, "The Political Management of Sir Robert Walpole, 1720–42," in Jeremy Black, ed., *Britain in the Age of Walpole* (London, 1984).

23. See Lois G. Schwoerer, *"No Standing Armies!" The Anti-Army Ideology in Seventeenth-Century England* (Baltimore, 1974).

24. This is well described in J. H. Plumb, *The Growth of Political Stability in England, 1675–1725* (London, 1967). But see also W. A. Speck, *Stability and Strife: England, 1714–1760* (Cambridge, Mass., 1977); Geoffrey Holmes, "The Achievement of Stability: The Social Context of Politics from the 1680s to the Age of Walpole," in John Cannon, ed., *The Whig Ascendancy* (New York, 1981); and Ian R. Christie, *Stress and Stability in Late Eighteenth-Century Britain* (Oxford, 1984).

Nothing shows more clearly the nature of this change than the way in which Walpole's writers in the 1730s revived and used the Tory reading of history expounded by the extreme royalist Robert Brady in the 1680s.[25] Brady had defended the Stuart claims to royal power as a direct inheritance from a centralized feudalism established by William the Conqueror in 1066: all laws and liberties were concessions by the royal grace and favor.

Accepting this extreme version of the past, the Whigs could claim that freedom began only with the revolution and that they were its creators and its guardians. The Court Whigs hoped by this argument to deprive their critics of all support from notions of the "ancient" constitution. But it is clear that this line of thought also denigrates tradition and custom in favor of positive law and undercuts all restraints on central power. The active role of Parliament in the Glorious Revolution had made questionable, moreover, the old notion of limits on its power.[26]

The exponents of Parliamentary sovereignty (Atkyns, for example) sometimes were very explicit that they included in it king, lords, and commons; but the actions of the Convention Parliament had shown equally clearly that lords and commons could act in the absence of a king. When the royal veto ceased to be used, early in the eighteenth century, Parliamentary sovereignty came tacitly to mean the two houses. But those who insisted on it were eager to use it, not so much against absolute monarchy (which had been abandoned even by the Jacobites), as against a doctrine of the ultimate sovereignty of the people.

Repeatedly—not only in the revolution of 1688, but in establishing the Hanoverians, in the Septennial Act of 1716, and in amending the Act of Settlement—the majority in Parliament changed things thought to be fundamental parts of the constitution. Thus eroded in practice, the idea of limited parliamentary power, restrained by the "ancient" constitution, was entirely abandoned among the Court Whigs by 1765. In volume one of his *Commentaries*, published that year, Sir William Blackstone even cited Sir Edward Coke as authority for the doctrine that Parliament "hath sovereign

25. *London Journal*, August 8, 1730, September 1, 1733, March 16, 1734, and November 16, 1734. For penetrating analysis of Brady's work and its uses see Pocock, *The Ancient Constitution*, pp. 182–228, 335–57; Weston and Greenberg, *Subjects and Sovereigns*, 182–221; and Isaac Kramnick, *Bolingbroke and His Circle: The Politics of Nostalgia in the Age of Walpole* (Cambridge, Mass., 1968), pp. 127–36.

26. Sir Robert Atkyns, one of the legal advisers to the Convention Parliament, published in 1689 an earlier legal brief in which he held that "[t]he Parliament is of an absolute and unlimited power in things temporal within this nation." *The Power, Jurisdiction and Privilege of Parliament: And the Antiquity of the House of Commons Asserted* (London, 1689), p. 50.

and uncontrollable authority . . . this being the place where that absolute despotic power, which must in all governments reside somewhere, is intrusted by the constitution of these kingdoms."[27] The Glorious Revolution was now seen as the foundation of secure English freedom. The following year (1766, the year of the Declaratory Act, which reasserted power over the American colonists) Lord Chancellor Northington told the House of Lords, "I seek for the liberty and constitution of this kingdom no farther back than the Revolution: there I make my stand." Another Court Whig elaborated the point: "It is absurd to apply records from the earliest times to our present constitution; because the constitution is not the same . . . there are things even in Magna Charta which are not constitutional now. . . . The constitution of this country has been always in a moving state."[28]

The Country Opposition

While these developments were taking place the Country ideologists, who included Tories as well as Whigs, continually criticized the Court Whigs' methods of governing. Such methods, they argued, far from protecting the balance of the constitution as the Glorious Revolution had intended, were building dangerous standing armies, were mortgaging the tax revenues for unprecedented public debts, were filling both houses of Parliament with members dependent upon the executive, and were thus eroding the independent power of Parliament to protect the people against arbitrary government.

The Whigs under Shaftesbury in the 1670s had started as an opposition group, had reached a crescendo in the Exclusion crisis, and some at least, like him, had fled abroad in the 1680s. Returning in triumph with William, they soon found it necessary to make various compromises with the Tories that some of them could not accept. As the new regime was established without what some considered adequate safeguards against the evils of the

27. Book I, chap. 2, sec. 3 (London, 1811, p. 160) citing Coke's *Fourth Institute*, p. 36. This illustrates clearly the "two-fold tradition" noted by McIlwain (above, p. 21), for Coke had there said, "Of the power and jurisdiction of the Parliament for making laws in proceeding by Bill, it is so transcendant and absolute, as it cannot be confined either for causes or persons within any bounds" (London, 1644 edition, p. 36). But J. W. Allen, quoting this, held it to be "certain that Coke never really believed that Parliament's power of making law could not be confined." See his *English Political Thought, 1603–1660* (London, 1938), 1:37.

28. Cobbett, *Parliamentary History*, vol. 16, cols. 171, 197.

old, and as the Whigs in office gradually abandoned "revolution principles" in favor of executive power, the opposition mind-set reemerged to divide the party.[29]

In Parliament the Country members were the congenital backbenchers, without ambition for office and suspicious of all officeholders. They saw their role in national politics as one of protecting the ancient liberties and property of the subject against the greed and ambitions of the new moneyed and military interests. Many were country squires, mostly Tories, troubled by the "decadence" of the Court and the City of London. A minority were Whigs, mostly representing the larger boroughs, including London—which accounts for a lack of cohesion among them. Theirs were the voices and the votes that carried on the Cokeian tradition of reasonable and constitutional limits on the exercise of power.[30]

Against the Court policies the Country opposition deployed many arguments, both logical and empirical. Drawing on Machiavelli and on recent continental experience, they opposed the employment of foreign mercenaries as both dangerous to liberty and unreliable in war. A well-disciplined militia, they believed, would promote civic virtue and responsibility, would cost less, and would fight more courageously in defense of their homes. Drawing on England's own recent experience of repeated ministerial corruption and public scandals like the South Sea Bubble, they argued that the pursuit of exorbitant wealth and luxury was undermining the morals of the people and eroding their respect for political authority.

But the primary concern of the Country ideologists was the growth of central power. The increasing scale of foreign war led inevitably to more fighting men and matériel, more contractors and creditors, more taxes and tax collectors, all used politically to increase the dependents of the executive branch in Parliament until they threatened to outnumber the independent members. Against this threat the opposition mounted two types of defense: the idea of constitutional limitations on what Parliament could legally do,

29. Mark Goldie has shown a vigorous continuity of opposition thought and action centering around John Wildman, a veteran of the Putney debates in Cromwell's army: "The Roots of True Whiggism, 1688–94," *History of Political Thought* 1 (June 1980): 195–236. The period 1670–1690 is convincingly elaborated in Ashcraft, *Revolutionary Politics*. Also see Robert Zaller, "The Continuity of British Radicalism in the Seventeenth and Eighteenth Centuries," *Eighteenth-Century Life* 6 (January 1981): 17–38.

30. The difficulties attendant upon efforts to identify the Country members are well described in David Hayton, "The 'Country' Interest and the Party System, 1689–c.1720," in Clyve Jones, ed., *Party and Management in Parliament, 1660–1784* (Leicester, 1984), pp. 37–85.

and the effort to apply practical limits through place bills and members' relations with the electorate.[31] The first of these had little success in England but became a prime ingredient in American government at all levels. The second, after many failures and modifications, eventuated in the Reform acts of 1832 and 1867 and the modern parliamentary system.

The Country leadership encountered difficulties in defending limits on the powers of Parliament. The logic of Hobbesian sovereignty demanded an unlimited power to be located somewhere. If they accepted this logic and still wished to limit Parliament, they were caught conceptually between the twin terrors of the alternatives: absolute monarchy and popular sovereignty. Determined to avoid both, the Country leaders rejected the logic in favor of an Aristotelian faith in the wisdom of custom and the subordination of power to morals. William Shippen, Tory member for Newton and a Jacobite, gave a concise statement of this attitude in the debate on the Septennial bill in 1716: "The supreme legislature," he said, "is restrained from subverting the foundations on which it stands; and . . . ought not, on any pretence whatsoever, to touch or alter those laws, which are so far admitted into the constitution, as to become essential parts of it."[32] Similar, usually unsuccessful, struggles on this basis were also repeatedly mounted against standing armies from the 1690s, modifications of the Act of Settlement in 1705, the Peerage bill in 1719, Jewish Naturalization in 1753, and the Stamp Act and the Declaratory Act in the 1760s—a long train of examples showing the continuity of American revolutionary ideology and doctrines of limitations on government with English ideas of the seventeenth century and earlier.

Country efforts to preserve the independence of Parliament through place and pension bills frequently failed, but they did succeed in barring some categories of crown employees. Efforts to repeal the Septennial Act also failed, but they displayed clearly the expected role of terms of office in eighteenth-century politics. The seven-year term went far toward emancipating the member from his constituents, reducing the influence of the electorate. Long tenure of the opportunities of office, moreover, quickly resulted in more expensive campaigning, effectively pricing a seat in Parlia-

31. See Geoffrey S. Holmes, "The Attack on 'the Influence of the Crown,' 1702–1716," *Bulletin of the Institute of Historical Research* 39 (May 1966): 47–68.

32. Cobbett, *Parliamentary History*, vol. 7, col. 317, quoted in Dickinson, *Liberty and Property*, p. 187. In America similar arguments were more successful. Having no representatives, the colonists had more to fear from an omnipotent Parliament. An extended debate on the British constitution appeared in the *Maryland Gazette* (Annapolis), February 10 to June 4, 1748. It is briefly summarized in Lawrence H. Leder, *Liberty and Authority: Early American Political Ideology, 1689–1763* (Chicago, 1968), pp. 90–92.

ment beyond the means of many of the rural gentry. Attacks on the Septennial Act, therefore, had to do with money in politics: the independent-minded squirearchs felt themselves being squeezed out by the "monied men." But such attacks also, at a more fundamental level, expressed the conviction that frequent elections were necessary to make effective the idea that the power of office was a continuous public trust and not a carte blanche between elections.

Deprived of frequent elections, the Country opposition resorted to well-managed campaigns of instructions to members of the House of Commons from their constituents—most successfully against the proposed excise in 1733. The Court Whigs, of course, attacked instructions as a violation of the responsibility of each member to the whole country, not only to his constituents; but they were even more offended by the involvement of the electorate in policy issues. In employing this tactic the opposition had no wish to encourage the notion of popular sovereignty. Their proposals for electoral reform were all aimed at a redistribution of seats and not at an expansion of the franchise.[33]

The Country Whigs, like those of the Court, were committed to elitist views of the political process. The idea of the people as the ultimate source of political authority was fairly prevalent among them; but, at the same time, they shared the general fear of the masses and contempt for the poor. Even John Trenchard and Thomas Gordon, the relatively radical authors of *Cato's Letters*, so widely read in the colonies, wrote of the "Herd of Mankind," of the "Dregs of the People," and of servants as a "Sort of idle and rioting Vermin."[34] They believed, under the influence of James Harrington, that "[t]he first Principle of all Power is Property . . . it is foolish to think, that Men of Fortunes will be governed by those who have none." Hence it followed that, for the Country as well as for the Court Whigs, political power

33. From the 1730s Bolingbroke and others advocated the redistribution of seats according to tax contributions; but not until the 1780s did the radicals use tax payments to justify widening the franchise. These developments are well summarized in Dickinson, *Liberty and Property*, pp. 190–231. "The support either for absolute monarchy or for the sovereignty of the people was eventually reduced to negligible proportions. . . . [N]one of those who can be termed a radical Whig was in fact a genuine democrat." Ibid., p. 93; see also pp. 57, 116.

34. *Cato's Letters: or, Essays on Liberty, Civil and Religious, and Other Important Subjects* (6th ed., London, 1755; repr. New York, 1971), vol. 4, pp. 241, 244, 245 (no. 133, June 15, 1723). "Cato" shared Robert Ferguson's view of republicanism (above, p. 27, n. 16): "it is impossible to settle a Commonwealth here" unless enough power can be concentrated "to turn all the Possessions of *England* topsy turvy, and throw them into Average"—a republic would not be stable without an equal distribution of property. Ibid., vol. 3, p. 160 (no. 85, July 14, 1722).

should be in the hands of property holders and should be used to protect property.[35]

The Religious Dimension

The rural gentry being largely Tory, the Country opposition in Parliament was usually also largely Tory, although its ideological spokesmen were frequently Whig. The Tories had grudgingly accepted the Glorious Revolution more to defend the Church of England than for political reasons, and the strongly secular, even Erastian, bias of the Court Whigs led the Tories frequently to raise the cry, "the Church in Danger." Their motives may have been political, but they struck a popular note, kept the ministers on the defensive on Church issues, and long delayed the legal habilitation of Dissenters, Jews, Quakers, and others. Although Puritanism lost ground rapidly after the Restoration in 1660, recent scholarship has shown the continuing importance of religious influences and issues in eighteenth-century England.[36]

The word "corruption," constantly used by the Country ideologists in a political sense, also carries moral and religious connotations. The earlier Whig critics of the Court Whigs, unlike their Tory counterparts, laid little emphasis on the religious dimension of moral virtue; but after 1750 their secular concerns were increasingly supplemented with a concern for a decline of public and private morality brought on by growing luxury and private selfishness stimulated by the financial interests. The Tories were supplanted as carriers of the nation's religious vigilance by a number of dissenting divines and leaders of dissenting academies—James Burgh, Joseph Priestly, Richard Price, and others—who persistently criticized the ministries of George III from that point of view, both for their domestic policies and for their treatment of the colonies. They revived the early dynamic of the Glorious Revolution as a moral crusade against the corruptions of the Stuart regime that had threatened to destroy the balance of the English constitution and with it the virtues and liberties of England. The

35. Ibid., vol. 3, p. 151 (no. 84, July 7, 1722).
36. See G. V. Bennett, *The Tory Crisis in Church and State, 1688–1730: The Career of Francis Atterbury, Bishop of Rochester* (Oxford, 1975); John Seed, "Gentlemen Dissenters: The Social and Political Meanings of Rational Dissent in the 1770s and 1780s," *Historical Journal* 28 (June 1985): 299–325; and J.C.D. Clark, *English Society, 1688–1832: Ideology, Social Structure, and Political Practice during the Ancien Regime* (Cambridge, 1985), chapters 5 and 6, together with the critique by Joanna Innes, "Jonathan Clark, Social History, and England's 'Ancien Regime,' " *Past and Present*, no. 115 (May 1987): 165–200.

Georgian regime, with its claims of unlimited power in Parliament, was using its power to promote the pursuit of wealth, they believed, when it should be encouraging the people toward piety and civic virtue.

The dissenters spoke a language congenial to the Puritan strain among Americans and were widely read in the colonies. The Americans were well aware, as Gordon Wood has emphasized, that the vices of luxury and selfishness were not unknown in the colonies, yet they believed that an escape from the corrupting influence of England would bring a rebirth of public and private virtue. "Revolution, republicanism and regeneration all blended in American thinking."[37]

As military and political experience accumulated from 1775 to 1785, however, it became increasingly apparent that a pragmatic aspect of affairs could override the moral aspect. Even more important, perhaps, the conversion of moral aims into public policies generated deep, and deeply conscientious, differences of view.

English Ambivalence Imported

This brief review has indicated a profound ambivalence in the English traditions reaching back into the Middle Ages, with strong components of central power on the one hand and of private rights protected by law on the other. The two revolutions of the seventeenth century eliminated republicanism in favor of a mixed and balanced monarchy. All the "political nation" agreed (until the 1780s) that the dependent classes should be excluded from the mixture, but the parties, and Court and Country wings within each, disagreed on how the balance should be maintained. By the use of wars, armies, debts, bribery, pensions, and places, the ministries generally kept the Crown and the Commons working in tandem, while the Country ideologists kept alive the Cokeian view that just government required restraints on power. By the 1760s the Court leaders were prepared to assert the unlimited sovereignty of Parliament, which provoked a triumph of Country influences in the American Revolution.

37. Wood, *Creation of the American Republic*, pp. 107–24, quotation on p. 117. The dissenters are treated at length in Isaac Kramnick, *Republicanism and Bourgeois Radicalism: Political Ideology in Late Eighteenth-Century England and America* (Ithaca, 1990). See also Sydney E. Ahlstrom, *A Religious History of the American People* (New Haven, 1972), p. 362, and Ellis Sandoz, *A Government of Laws: Political Theory, Religion, and the American Founding* (Baton Rouge, 1990), chapter 5.

As the fighting began, Lord Chatham, more friendly toward the Americans, believed that the Declaratory Act was unconstitutional, that there were limits to Parliament's authority; but he was no more able than the ministry to forego insisting on Parliamentary supremacy or to accept the Americans as equal subjects, enjoying all the rights of Englishmen. Back in 1764, James Otis had accepted Parliamentary supremacy in the faith that Parliament would repeal its own acts when convinced of their injustice. A dozen years of argument, however, brought few repeals. They brought, instead, much clearer understanding that estimates of injustice were matters of opinion, easily distorted by points of view, and therefore that all claims to unlimited power were incompatible with freedom.[38]

In trying to learn from their experience and to write its lessons into their new constitutions, the Americans were well aware that their heritage from England contained many healthy elements. The colonial perspective enabled them to see more clearly than most of their British contemporaries the basic point that the rule of law—perhaps the finest element of their heritage—required a clearer distinction between statutes and the fundamental constitution, so that the rights of the people could not be invaded by ordinary statute. This required a rejection of the doctrine of the sovereignty of Parliament and all similar doctrines of unlimited governmental power.

Colonial experience also led to a reassessment of the available alternatives to Parliamentary sovereignty—absolute monarchy and popular sovereignty. By denying Blackstone's requirement of an unlimited power lodged somewhere in all governments, the way was opened for practical republicanism without any felt need to derive it from a doctrine of popular sovereignty. Having enjoyed effective self-government for generations under the benign neglect of Britain, the colonists had accumulated very different impressions of republican government from those generated in England by the brief Cromwellian episode. With the final revulsion against King George in 1776 they quickly embraced the republican alternative, so that in no colony was serious consideration given to monarchy as the form of the new state government.[39]

These new governments, reflecting the separate and different histories of the old colonies, quickly became laboratories for republican experiments— with results to be borrowed or to be avoided. They also formed an indestructible foundation for federalism, an insurmountable obstacle to the establish-

---

38. Cobbett, *Parliamentary History*, 18:203–4 (February 1775). James Otis, *Rights of the British Colonies Asserted and Proved* (Boston, 1764), p. 47.
39. See pp. 130–32 on some later revivals of monarchism.

ment of a unitary system of government. This meant that political ideas imported from the unitary states of Europe might experience something of a sea change. Without losing its primary focus on the dangers of concentrated power, the Court versus Country conflict took on a special national versus local emphasis. The Country antagonism toward central power gradually became a much more radical justification for revolution. It also became a claim to sovereignty for each state—which was, in fact, accepted as Article 2 of the Confederation. On the other hand, an accumulation of wartime experiences, followed by postwar failures of cooperation, stimulated a yearning for central power, particularly among army officers and urban commercial leaders who entertained a vision of empire in which the states were only provinces. This developing polarization among the American patriots came to a head in the movement for changes in the Articles of Confederation. However, as will be seen, the potential conflict between the Court-Country extremes was forestalled by a third group, the state federalists, who occupied at the Convention some middle ground made available by the existence of the separate states.

While the American leaders might thus easily accept the republican notion of the people as the theoretical source and foundation of their governments, they had no wish to attribute unlimited power to the people— even when they spoke of popular sovereignty. They did not forget the Country Whig tradition, which said that the sovereign was under the law. They proceeded to write constitutions (which the Convention Parliament had failed to do) and to append bills of rights to them, thus limiting their governments at the same time that they were establishing them. In these frames of government they applied Country Whig ideas by curtailing the powers of the executive branch, by requiring frequent elections, and by using property qualifications in various ways. In their bills of rights, drawing on Magna Carta and on English and colonial experience, they tried to prevent the worst abuses of censorship, prerogative courts, standing armies, and the like. But this whole structure fixed limits on the people's agents, not on the people themselves. English experience had shown that kings could be limited, but it provided no guidance for the limitation of a sovereign Parliament or a sovereign people. Yet the Cokeian rejection of sovereignty and the continual efforts of the Country opposition to find constitutional restraints on Parliament did provide evidence of long-standing awareness of the problem of unlimited political power. Was it not as dangerous in the hands of a sovereign people as in those of a king or a sovereign Parliament?

By 1787 there were those who were satisfied that the problems of representative government derived from the people themselves and not from their agents. The search for American substitutes for the estates that were "balanced" in the English government had led men like John Adams, Alexander Hamilton, and Gouverneur Morris to emphasize a distinction between the rich and the poor.[40] This in turn led them to expect growing conflicts about property and to see each local instance of debtor legislation as part of a long-term trend undermining the very foundations of civil peace. It had been thought that a wise deployment of property qualifications for voting and for office would prevent such attacks on property, but they had proved insufficient. In searching for further solutions it was perhaps inevitable that these men would be attracted by English methods, which, after all, had successfully contained such conflicts for a century. Thus the attitude that government should not be influenced by the "lower orders," that election districts need not be equal, that the electors and the officeholders should be manipulated by financial inducements—the whole Walpolean system—found adherents who believed that it could be adapted to the American context. The Revolutionary War debts, in particular, seemed to parallel the English situation after 1688, and the financial genius of Robert Morris and Hamilton enabled them to see how the parallel could be exploited both to unite the country and to retard, perhaps even to stop, the slide of republicanism toward democracy.

Of course, by 1787 not all the political leaders had reached this level of skepticism regarding popular government. Not all of them were so clear-sighted about the distinction of statutory from constitutional law, nor about the problems of unlimited power. Not all the state constitutions contained bills of rights, and not all the legislatures felt themselves limited by their constitution, which, in several cases, had been drafted and promulgated by earlier legislatures.

When the Philadelphia Convention assembled in May 1787, therefore, it brought together men of very diverse economic, political, and ideological backgrounds, who were further differentiated by contrasts of geography, wealth, wartime experience, and a half-century in age. They may all have been members of a state's elite (no dirt farmers or journeymen were there), far better educated and more au courant than most of the people of their states, and this degree of social cohesion no doubt expedited understanding

40. On Adams see p. 6, n. 10; for Hamilton see Farrand, *Records*, 1:288 (June 18); for Morris, see 1:512–14 (July 2) and 2:202–3 (August 7).

and provided a certain unity of purpose; but they brought with them a variety of agendas and value structures that made the achievement of agreement doubtful until July 17.

In the analysis that follows primary reliance will be placed on the debates in the Convention itself, read in relation to the external contexts of the different delegates. It is not assumed that the speakers were always candid or meant what they said; after all, they were engaged in persuasion, not in confession. Yet their closed doors and the secrecy rule probably brought a closer correspondence of what they said with what they believed than is usual among politicians, and thus justifies taking their words seriously.

3

Political Motivations

Was the purpose of the Convention primarily political or was it economic? Was it to strengthen and preserve the integrity of the recently independent confederacy or was it to defend and perpetuate the special advantages of property owners? Were the delegates more afraid of disunion and foreign intervention, or of the growing numbers and influence of less wealthy citizens?

I believe, and shall argue, that the priority concerns of the Convention, although clearly and consciously carrying economic implications, were fundamentally political.

The nature of the problems, and the proper solutions, were seen by different delegates from several divergent and often conflicting perspectives. The special circumstances and interests of the separate states strongly influenced these perspectives but did not always determine them—hence the divided votes within state delegations.

The nationalists were eager to arrest two interrelated postwar trends, moving toward "excessive" democracy and toward a breakup of the Union. For both purposes an increase in central power seemed required. Those from the large states were also determined that, in the exercise of this power, their states must have influence proportional to their size. Those from the smaller states, however, were even more determined to preserve their long-standing advantage, the equal vote by states in national decision making. These seemingly irreconcilable motives, had they been shared by all the delegates, might well have broken up the Convention; but we shall see that, for a number of delegates, these motives were not irreconcilable and that these men were able to work creatively to construct a government that could avoid the twin extremes of state sovereignty and internal national sovereignty.

The Problems as the Nationalists Saw Them

First, and perhaps far ahead of all other concerns, the nationalists wanted to arrest the trend they saw toward state particularism and the fragmentation of the Union. This problem had been debated in Congress in 1777 when state sovereignty had been inserted into the Articles of Confederation, a debate in which several members of the Convention had participated. Each failure to obtain an import duty for Congress and each failure of a state to meet its quota added to the fears that the wartime unity was slowly but surely eroding. It cannot be assumed that such fears were unfounded or were exaggerated for other purposes. The example of South America, to say nothing of the Balkans after their war of independence against Turkey, argues against that assumption. Moreover, it is not irrelevant that, in spite of the best efforts of the nationalists, the Union did break apart in 1860.[1]

Second, the delegates, or most of them, desired to arrest the trend toward democracy. This trend is less easy to document, but their antagonism to it is very clear. The responsiveness of the state legislatures to popular demands had taken the form of economic legislation, arousing the ire and apprehension of the creditors. Had the Convention been composed solely of creditors, and had they expressed the same antagonism to democracy, one might presume that the debtors' laws had shaped their attitude; but the presump-

---

1. Calvin C. Jillson has shown that a sharp North-South polarization existed in Congress from October 1783: pp. 19–20 in his "Political Culture and the Pattern of Congressional Politics under the Articles of Confederation," *Publius* 18 (Winter 1988): 1–26.

tion would still be unproven. For the same responsiveness that tried to relieve debtors also tried to reduce taxes by refusing to pay the quotas of Congress, for various local reasons. The democratic trend, from the point of view of the nationalists, thus tended to undermine national unity and strength in response to separate state interests. It was highly undesirable on political grounds, therefore, entirely apart from its effects on creditors.

Third, the states with large populations (either actual or anticipated) wanted to escape from the equal vote by states as provided in the Articles of Confederation. The great importance they attached to proportional representation (or PR) was made explicit on June 9, when Wilson referred to it as "the object of our meeting" (1:183). The debates of 1774 and 1776–77 had served notice that this provision was regarded by them as temporary. At the same time, it had been so firmly secured by the unanimity rule for amendments that there was no way to escape from it short of subverting the Articles. Virginia had the greatest interest in PR,[2] but it was supported in this by the states to the south and by Pennsylvania and Massachusetts. The planters of the South thus joined the commercial men of Philadelphia and Boston in common cause against the Articles and, incidentally, against the small states. The third concern could not, of course, be shared by the small-state delegates, which led to the incomplete success of the nationalists in achieving their aims on this point. Its importance to them, however, is evident in the bitterness with which they accepted their defeat on the Connecticut compromise.

The connection of the third of these problems with the first, and the urgency of their solution, had been forcefully presented the year before by John Jay's negotiations with the Spanish envoy, Gardoqui. In order to secure some commercial advantages, Jay was willing to concede the temporary closing of the Mississippi River, as demanded by Spain, and requested from Congress a change in his instructions to permit this. In the debate it became evident that northern delegates wanted the river closed, not only to obtain the commercial advantages but to retard the growth of population in the West and South. In the summer of 1786 eleven roll call votes were taken in Congress on Jay's negotiations, all of them decided by a straight North-South split. Had Delaware been present, and had Maryland (which had no direct interest in the Mississippi) supported the North as it was to do in May

2. Virginia had fought almost alone for PR in Congress in 1777. See *Journals*, vol. 9, pp. 779–82. This is summarized in Merrill Jensen, *The Articles of Confederation: An Interpretation of the Social-Constitutional History of the American Revolution, 1774–1781* (Madison, 1940), p. 145.

1787, the nine votes required to ratify such a treaty would have been there, so Jay's project was far from chimerical. No other issue displayed the sectional antagonisms so sharply, or flashed so clear a warning of the instability of the Union under the Articles. The equality of states was seen as a clear and present danger to the South; and the New Englanders especially were suspected of a desire to drive the slave states out of the Confederation.[3]

For each of these concerns the nationalists saw the same solution: the establishment of a strong, centralized, autonomous government, as far removed from popular and state influence as possible. Merrill Jensen has argued that this movement for a strong central government, far from being a result of postwar problems under the Articles, actually antedated the Revolution itself. Franklin had been advocating centralization since the 1750s, and in 1775 he proposed a plan of confederation based on PR.[4] Many of those who, like John Dickinson and Joseph Galloway, opposed the break with Britain were fearful of its effects on the social structure. Gouverneur Morris, for example, in the secrecy of a letter to his friend Richard Penn (May 30, 1774), predicted, "with fear and trembling, that if the disputes with great Britain continue" the aristocracy would lose all power and "be under the dominion of a riotous mob." He preferred, therefore, "reunion with the parent state" since "the spirit of the English constitution . . . will give the wealthy people a superiority" in the colonies.[5] The Dickinson draft of the Articles of Confederation, drawn up in June 1776, was strongly centralistic and was intended to replace the authority of Britain, since independence had become unavoidable. The localists, however, rejected any such replacement, revised the draft in 1777, inserted a statement of state sovereignty, and reserved to the states all powers not "expressly delegated."

The nationalists, in response, developed two theories of central power:

3. The conflict over Jay's negotiations is summarized in H. James Henderson, *Party Politics in the Continental Congress* (New York, 1974), pp. 387–407. See also James Monroe to Patrick Henry, August 12, and to Madison, September 3, 1786, in *Letters of Members of the Continental Congress*, ed. Edmund C. Burnett (Washington, 1921–36), 8:424–25, 461, and the exchange among them in the Virginia ratifying convention on June 13, 1788, in Jonathan Elliot, ed., *The Debates in the Several State Conventions on the Adoption of the Federal Constitution* (2d ed., Philadelphia, 1888), 3:332–65 (hereafter cited as Elliot's *Debates*).

4. See the *Journals of the Continental Congress*, vol. 2, pp. 196–97.

5. Peter Force, ed., *American Archives*, fourth series, vol. 1 (Washington, 1837), pp. 342–43; also in full in Jared Sparks, *The Life of Gouverneur Morris*, vol. 1 (Boston, 1832), pp. 23–26.

the devolution of British sovereignty upon Congress, and the idea of inherent powers of Congress.

In the devolution theory, the lands beyond the Ohio played an important part.[6] The speculators whose claims did not derive from Virginia, among whom James Wilson was prominent, argued that Congress should assume the power of Britain over such lands. William Trent of the Walpole (Vandalia) Company, for example, presented to Congress in 1779 a memorial declaring that "all the Rights and all the obligations of the Crown of Great Britain respecting the lands and governments devolve upon the *United States* and are to be claimed, exercised and discharged by the United States in Congress Assembled."[7] Aside from the lands, however, it could be and was argued that the action of the Continental Congress in declaring independence was a national one, not thirteen separate state actions, and resulted in one new sovereign nation, not thirteen. "As to those matters which are referred to Congress," Wilson held in 1776, "we are not so many states; we are one large state. We lay aside our individuality whenever we come here." John Adams and Benjamin Rush expressed similar views.[8]

With or without national sovereignty certain inherent powers could be claimed for Congress. In his long letter (September 3, 1780) to James Duane, who was then in Congress, Hamilton proposed the calling of a convention to establish a "solid coercive union" with sovereignty, but he also argued that Congress "should have considered themselves as vested with full power *to preserve the republic from harm*" and should exercise "undefined powers" that were "discretionary powers," limited only by their object, "the independence and freedom of America."[9] Similarly, the Hartford Convention, meeting in November of that year and representing five

6. The role of land claims in the politics of the era is cogently analyzed in Peter S. Onuf, *The Origins of the Federal Republic: Jurisdictional Controversies in the United States, 1775–1787* (Philadelphia, 1983).

7. Papers of the Continental Congress, no. 41, X, folios 79–86, quoted in Merrill Jensen, "The Idea of a National Government during the American Revolution," *Political Science Quarterly* 58 (1943): 356–79, at p. 365. Recently Jerrilyn Marston has argued convincingly that Congress was primarily an executive body, not a legislature, and exercised powers that had been held by the Crown, while the legislative powers of Parliament were taken up by the state legislatures. See her *King and Congress: The Transfer of Political Legitimacy, 1774–1776* (Princeton, 1987), especially chapter 10.

8. *The Papers of Thomas Jefferson*, ed. Julian P. Boyd (Princeton, 1950–), 1:327; John Adams, *Works*, 2:499.

9. *The Papers of Alexander Hamilton*, ed. Harold C. Syrett (New York, 1961–87), 2:401, 407. At that time Hamilton reserved to the states all internal taxing power and "the rights of property and life among individuals" as exceptions to the proposed "complete sovereignty" of Congress. Ibid., pp. 407–8.

states, found a "necessarily implied compact" among the states for the
Revolution, from which it "may be certainly inferred that Congress was
vested with every power essential to the common defence and which had
the prosecution of the war, and the establishment of our General Liberties
for its immediate object."[10] And Madison, as draftsman for a three-man
committee of Congress (1781) to prepare plans to implement the Articles of
Confederation, which had just been ratified, declared that the Confederation gave Congress "a general and implied power" to "enforce and carry [the
Articles] into effect against any of the States."[11] It remained, however, for
Wilson to develop this doctrine most completely. From the states, he
admitted, Congress derived only those powers expressly delegated, but

> [i]t does not thence follow, that the United States in congress have
> *no other* powers. . . . The United States have general rights, general
> powers, and general obligations not derived from any particular
> states, nor from all the particular states, taken separately; but result-
> ing from the union of the whole. . . . To many purposes, the United
> States are to be considered as one undivided, independent nation;
> and as possessed of all the rights, and powers, and properties, by the
> law of nations incident to such. Whenever an object occurs, to the
> direction of which no particular state is competent, the management
> of it must, of necessity, belong to the United States in congress
> assembled.[12]

These theories continued to be embraced only by a minority, however.
The nationalists, in a more practical vein, attempted on many occasions to
persuade Congress to exercise unexpressed powers, hoping to establish
precedents. The radicals, well aware of this tactic, usually defeated them—
the chartering of the Bank of North America being an outstanding exception.

With the end of the war, which was the strongest force holding the states
together, the nationalists feared a gradual dissolution of the union. Almost
in desperation some of them, including Hamilton and Gouverneur Morris,
tried to manipulate Washington and his army, then encamped at Newburgh

10. "A Hartford Convention in 1780, Proceedings" [November 8–14], *Magazine of American History* 8 (October 1882): 688–98, at p. 696.

11. *Journals of the Continental Congress*, vol. 20, pp. 469–71.

12. "Considerations on the Bank of North America" [1785], in *The Works of James Wilson*, ed. Robert G. McCloskey (Cambridge, Mass., 1967), vol. 2, p. 829. His use of plural verbs with "the United States" should be noted.

on the Hudson, in an effort to push Congress and the states toward effective central power. But Washington was not a Cromwell nor a Napoleon, so the effort was a fiasco.[13] This was followed by a renewed attempt to secure an impost revenue for Congress, which again failed, and by a more general set of amendments prepared by a committee of Congress of which Pinckney* was chairman. The unanimity rule for such amendments, however, made the prospect hopeless. Both the military and the legal paths to change seemed to be closed; only a convention held any promise.

In working for a convention the nationalists were consciously building a machine for the overthrow of the Articles of Confederation. As Jensen phrased it, "The nationalist leaders had no intention of merely revising the Articles of Confederation. They wanted to create a government free from subordination to and control by the state legislatures; one which, in contrast, would have the power to control both the states and their citizens."[14] Yet when they got their convention it was limited explicitly by its terms of reference to "the sole and express purpose of revising the Articles of Confederation." What to do?

It is conceivable that the Constitution, as it ultimately emerged from the Convention (but without the ratification article), might have been adopted under the unanimity rule. After all, the Articles themselves were pending longer between their submission to the states in 1777 and the last ratification in 1781 than was the Constitution between its submission and its ratification by Rhode Island in 1790. The nationalists, however, were unwilling to risk this. Being intent upon changes, such as PR, which would be more drastic than those already rejected and especially disadvantageous to the small states, they could not expect approval by all states—particularly by Rhode Island, which had already refused to participate.

Early in the Convention Wilson made it clear that departure from the

*Unless C. C. Pinckney is named, all references are to Charles Pinckney.

13. There are sharp differences of interpretation of this episode. Richard H. Kohn, "The Inside History of the Newburgh Conspiracy: America and the Coup d'Etat," *William and Mary Quarterly* 27 (April 1970): 187–220, finds a real threat of mutiny to shake Congress; Paul D. Nelson, "Horatio Gates at Newburgh, 1783: A Misunderstood Role," *William and Mary Quarterly* 29 (January 1972): 143–58, and C. Edward Skeen, "The Newburgh Conspiracy Reconsidered," *William and Mary Quarterly* 31 (April 1974): 273–98, take it less seriously. Congress, however, was sufficiently impressed to act on the 1780 promise to the officers of half pay for life: it now promised them full pay for five years.

14. Merrill Jensen, *The Making of the American Constitution* (New York, 1964), p. 36. The literature on the intentions of the Framers is voluminous and growing. For essays on the varying views see Jack N. Rakove, ed., *Interpreting the Constitution: The Debate over Original Intent* (Boston, 1990).

unanimity rule was contemplated, that a new union of the large states alone might be necessary (1:123, 179). Believing it to be expedient, perhaps essential, to abandon the established constitutional framework in ratification, they abandoned also the form of amendments to the Articles in favor of a new, entirely separate document.

Thus in matters of procedure, as well as in the content of their new system, the nationalists led the Convention into territory quite outside its terms of reference and quite beyond public expectations. Adopting a rule of the strictest secrecy, it worked diligently for months, six days a week, erecting a structure unlike any then in existence. But was it such a structure as the nationalists planned? Were its leading principles the ones the nationalists had brought to Philadelphia?

The Virginia Plan

The Virginia Plan is usually seen as the early outline of the final Constitution, yet the fact that two of the delegates who drafted it refused in the end to sign the Constitution should alert us to the possibility that the essence of the Plan had been changed.[15] I shall argue here that it had been, that what emerged at the end was not intended in the beginning. It may be that the extreme nationalists wanted even more centralization than the Plan provided. But it will be argued that the nationalists as well as the state-sovereignty men fundamentally failed to achieve their aims. To support these contentions it will be necessary to examine in detail certain parts of the debate, noticing the choice of words by means of quotations and the evolution of thought by means of dates.

The Original Orientation

Let us first see what Randolph, as spokesman for the Virginians, had in mind. Having presented the fifteen resolutions of the Plan, Randolph (according to Yates) "candidly confessed that they were not intended for a federal government—he meant a strong *consolidated* union, in which the idea of states should be nearly annihilated" (1:24). Only Yates reports these

15. Michael P. Zuckert finds six different federalisms in the Convention debates; see his "Federalism and the Founding: Toward a Reinterpretation of the Constitutional Convention," *Review of Politics* 48 (Spring 1986): 166–210.

remarks, but they are supported by three new resolutions Randolph introduced on May 30. Suggested by Gouverneur Morris, these resolutions were
a response to the "necessary and preliminary inquiry" raised by Hamilton
just before adjournment the previous day. Having heard the Plan, Hamilton
pointed out that, before considering it, the delegates must first of all decide
"whether the United States were susceptible of one government, or required
a separate existence connected only by leagues offensive and defensive and
treaties of commerce" (1:27). Taking unequivocally the former position,
Randolph proposed: "1) that a Union of the States merely federal will not
accomplish the objects [of the Confederation and of paragraph 1 of the Plan];
2) that no treaty or treaties among the whole or part of the States, as
individual sovereignties, would be sufficient; 3) that a *national* Government
ought to be established consisting of a *supreme* Legislative, Executive and
Judiciary" (1:33).

Not a federal but a unitary government was thus clearly expressed, a
supreme government, in no manner hampered by separate state sovereignties.

From the Virginia Plan itself it further appears that Randolph and his
colleagues wanted the "rights of suffrage in the National Legislature" no
longer to be based on the international-law principle of the equality of
states, but "to be proportioned to the Quotas of contribution, or to the
numbers of free inhabitants. . . ." This legislature "ought to be empowered"
as Congress had been,

> and moreover [1] to legislate in all cases to which the separate States
> are incompetent, or in which the harmony of the United States may
> be interrupted by the exercise of individual Legislation; [2] to
> negative all laws passed by the several States, contravening in the
> opinion of the National Legislature the articles of Union; and [3] to
> call forth the force of the Union agst. any member of the Union failing
> to fulfill its duty under the articles thereof. (1:21)

The members of the first branch should be directly elected "by the people
of the several States" for fixed terms, subject to rotation and recall. The
members of a second branch should be elected by those of the first from
among persons nominated by the state legislatures, with no mention of
rotation or recall. A "National Executive" to be chosen by the legislature
"and to be ineligible a second time," a "National Judiciary" of "one or more
supreme tribunals, and of inferior tribunals to be chosen by the National

Legislature, to hold their offices during good behaviour," and a council of revision (with a conditional veto), composed of the executive and part of the judiciary, were also provided. A complete government was thus proposed, making, executing, and adjudicating its own laws through its own officers, and overriding legally and by force if necessary any law or action of a state that the legislature found unconstitutional.

Was this proposal designed to "abolish the State Governts. altogether," as Charles Pinckney asked on May 30? Randolph's reply was ambivalent, and certain ambiguities of the Virginia Plan should be noted. The guarantee to each state of its territory and a republican government seems clear enough as evidence that the states were to continue; but the fact that Pinckney felt impelled to ask his question shows that the matter was not so clear to those who heard Randolph. Yet the absence of any mention of a power to tax individuals, coupled with the use of the words "Quotas of contribution" and the nomination of senators by the "individual Legislatures," indicate that the Virginians had not yet conceived their new government as completely independent of the states, acting only on individuals. This indication is reinforced by the use of the phrase "member of the Union" in reference to the states. It is, however, disparaged by the reference to the "collection of the National revenue" in the jurisdiction of the proposed courts.

Later statements by Randolph, Madison, and others may shed additional light on the intentions embodied in the Virginia Plan and will be used in their proper places, but as debate progressed the delegates' opinions may also have progressed and thus diverged from those they held when the Plan was prepared.

Now, how were these ideas received by the other delegates? Madison, having not yet hit his stride as a reporter, omits much that was said on May 30, but he is well supplemented by McHenry and Yates. Only McHenry records the uneasy silence that greeted Randolph's three resolutions that day: "Mr. Whythe [sic] presumes from the silence of the house that they gentn. are prepared to pass on the resolution and proposes its being put" (1:41). The men of South Carolina recovered first. Charles Pinckney's question was noted above. C. C. Pinckney doubted that the Convention, commissioned to revise the Articles, could continue if it determined the Confederation to be incapable of improvement. Butler was "open to the light which discussion might throw" (1:34), but, impressed as were others with the difficulties the Pinckneys had raised, he moved that Randolph's first two resolutions be passed over and discussion be centered on the third. After debate the third resolution was accepted by six of the eight states present—only Ellsworth and Sherman of Connecticut and Yates of New York being recorded against it (1:35).

In the course of this discussion Gouverneur Morris undertook to distinguish a federal and a national government, "the former being a mere compact resting on the good faith of the parties; the latter having a compleat and *compulsive* operation" (1:34). No one disputed his distinction, but Elbridge Gerry saw the situation in a different light: "We ought not to determine that there is this distinction for if we do, it is questionable not only whether this convention can propose an government totally different or whether Congress itself would have a right to pass such a resolution as that before the house" (1:42–43). Build a government, in other words, that will be national in substance, but be prepared to call it federal. The devious nature of this procedure perhaps only gradually took possession of the delegates. The immediate attempt by Read of Delaware to implement Gerry's idea—his amendment of the third resolution to read "a more effective Government" instead of a "national Government"—was lost on a tie vote. The majority still wanted the word "national"; not until June 20 did they begin to accept substitute phrases.

Removal of the Federal Features

In the meantime the remnants of federalism were removed from the Virginia Plan.[16] Already on May 30 Mason insisted that "such a Govt. was necessary as could directly operate on individuals" (1:34), and King took the Virginia proposals to be intended "to act upon the whole people" (1:43). A week later Mason said that the acts of the national legislature "will not be on states, but on individual persons" (1:141), and Madison reminded the delegates that "when we agreed to the first resolve of having a national government, consisting of a supreme executive, judicial and legislative power, it was then intended to operate to the exclusion of a federal government" (1:141). Similarly, Randolph, speaking against the New Jersey Plan, said that "[t]he resolutions from Virginia must have been adopted [by the Committee of the Whole] on the supposition that a federal government was impracticable" (1:262). On June 25 Wilson was even more explicit: "The Genl. Govt. is not

16. Cathy D. Matson and Peter S. Onuf argue that "the *nationalists* who met at Philadelphia became *federalists* as they sought to translate their vision of national power and prosperity into a politically acceptable constitutional design." See their *Union of Interests* (Lawrence, Kans., 1990), p. 101. However, the nationalists first overextended themselves in the opposite direction, and they later at least partially succeeded in redefining federalism to mean nationalism.

an assemblage of States, but of individuals for certain political purposes—it is not meant for the States, but for the individuals composing them" (1:406). By July 14 King could say that "[h]e considered the proposed Government as substantially and formally, a General and National Government over the people of America. There never will be a case in which it will act as a federal Government on the States and not on the individual Citizens" (2:6). And Madison challenged the delegates to name a single such case (2:9).

A similar progression of opinion took place regarding the matter of taxation. King early objected to the quotas of contribution as a measure of representation because, he said, "the revenue might hereafter be so collected by the general Govt. that the sums respectively drawn from the States would not appear" (1:36). He later added the point that if an import duty were used, the nonimporting states "wd. have no representation" (1:197). On June 11 Williamson of North Carolina supposed that "there will not be any Assignment or Quotas to States; the Governmt. to operate individually, and not on States" (1:207), and Gerry said, "The Taxes must be drawn by the natl. Governmt. immediately from the People; otherwise will never be collected" (1:208). By the end of the month Madison assumed a consensus that the new government would "have the power, without the consent of the State Legislatures, to levy money directly on the people themselves," and he was not contradicted (1:464).

The Problem of Sovereignty

The matter of state sovereignty, which Randolph had left ambiguous, was clarified. Article 2, which had been inserted into the Dickinson draft of the Articles of Confederation on the initiative of Thomas Burke of North Carolina, expressly stated, "Each state retains its sovereignty, freedom and independence. . . ." Burke had held that "all sovereign power was in the States separately."[17] On June 9 Paterson argued against attempting to draft a national government on the ground that "[a] confederacy supposes sovereignty in the members composing it and sovereignty supposes equality" (1:178). He was answered by Wilson, whom Madison quotes as saying, "If N. J. will not part with her Sovereignty it is in vain to talk of Govt." (1:180). Yates gives this as "If no state will part with any of its sovereignty, it is in vain to talk of a national government" (1:183), a rather different statement.

17. Burnett, *Letters of Members*, vol. 2, p. 346.

In either case, Wilson implied that the states were sovereign, and, in Yates's version, that sovereignty was divisible.

Ten days later, however, state sovereignty was expressly denied by Rufus King.

> The States were not 'sovereigns' in the sense contended for by some. They did not possess the peculiar features of sovereignty. They could not make war, nor peace, nor alliances, nor treaties. . . . Congs. can act alone without the States—they can act & their acts will be binding agst. the Instructions of the States. If they declare war, war is de jure declared, captures made in pursuance of it are lawful. No acts of the States can vary the situation, or prevent the judicial consequences. If the States therefore retained some portion of their sovereignty, they had certainly divested themselves of essential portions of it. (1:323–24)

Following King, Wilson deduced from the Declaration of Independence that the states had become independent "not *Individually* but *Unitedly*" (1:324). Yet another ten days and the tone of argument became derogatory: "The States and the advocates for them," Elbridge Gerry said, "were intoxicated with the idea of their *sovereignty*. . . . It appears to me that the states never were independent—they had only corporate rights" (1:467, 474). Madison too, according to Yates, held that "[t]he states never possessed the essential rights of sovereignty. These were always vested in congress. Their voting, as states, in congress, is no evidence of sovereignty. The state of Maryland voted by counties—did this make the counties sovereign?" (1:471).[18] And King spoke of the "phantom of *State* sovereignty" as a "wonderful illusion" (1:489–90).

These mutually reinforcing statements by spokesmen from the three large states did not, of course, go unchallenged. The strongest voices supporting state sovereignty were those of Luther Martin, William Paterson, and John Lansing. "At the separation from the British Empire," Martin* said on June 20, "the people of America preferred the Establishment of themselves into

---

*Unless Alexander Martin is named, all references are to Luther Martin.

18. Some forty-six years later Madison impugned the accuracy of Yates's record as being "incredible" in view of the second Article of Confederation; yet his own report of his speech said that state laws "in relation to the paramount law of the Confederacy were analogous to that of bye laws to the supreme law, within a State." Madison to W. C. Rives, October 21, 1833; see Farrand, *Records*, 3:521–22; 1:464.

thirteen separate sovereignties instead of incorporating themselves into one" (1:340). They had refused to grant unnecessary powers to Congress "lest the powers should prove dangerous to the sovereignties of the particular States which the Union was meant to support" (1:341). On the same day Lansing pointed out that "[i]t could not be expected that those possessing Sovereignty could ever voluntarily part with it. It was not to be expected from any one State, much less from thirteen" (1:337). Yet the drift of ideas was so pronounced that, by June 29, when Lansing's motion to establish the equality of states in the first branch of the new legislature came to a vote, it lost by 4 to 6, with Maryland divided. Martin lamented that "the language of the States being *Sovereign & Independent*, was once familiar and understood; though it seemed now so strange & obscure" (1:468).

In the course of these discussions the nationalists revealed the depth of their antagonism toward the states. Randolph, in his opening description of the sad plight of the Union, did not directly criticize them. He found "our chief danger" in democracy, but it was clear that he referred to democracy in operation in the state legislatures; by inference, then, the danger lay in the states. On June 6 George Read of Delaware, who stood closest to Hamilton in his views, began the denigration of the states. "We must," he said, "look beyond their continuance. A national Govt. must soon of necessity swallow all of them up" (1:136). "We must come to a consolidation," he averred. "The State Govts must be swept away—We had better speak out" (1:143). In this he was supported by Pierce Butler of South Carolina (1:144). Three days later Paterson, in notes for his speech, put Randolph's name beside these sentiments: "We ought to be one Nation—etc. The States as States must be cut up, and destroyed—This is the way to form us into a Nation." In his long speech of June 18 Hamilton, as reported by Yates, said, "we must establish a general and national government, completely sovereign, and annihilate the state distinctions and state operations" (1:297). King, on the following day, "proved" that "the States are now subordinate corporations or Societies and not Sovereigns" (1:331). The nationalists were frequently accused of planning to abolish the states, and Wilson, King, and Hamilton thought it desirable to deny the charge. Yet their denials tended to confirm the accusation, since they made it clear that they would preserve the states for "local purposes," in a "subordinate" role. "*As States*," Hamilton said, "they ought to be abolished." "Even with corporate rights the states will be dangerous to the national government, and ought to be extinguished, new modified, or reduced to a smaller scale" (1:323, 328). But, as we shall see, it was not until they were faced with the Connecticut compromise some three weeks later that Gouverneur Morris expressed the most vehement antagonism toward the states (1:530).

Others who were ready for a newly structured national government, Mason and the Pinckneys in particular, were impressed with the necessity for the states to retain a substantial part in the governmental system. On June 6 Charles Pinckney, seconded by Rutledge, moved the election of the first branch "by the State Legislatures, and not by the people" (1:132). Supporting him, Sherman argued that "[i]f the State Govts. are to be continued, it is necessary in order to preserve harmony between the national & State Govts. that the elections to the former shd. be made by the latter" (1:133). And C. C. Pinckney "wished to have a good national Govt. & at the same time to leave a considerable share of power in the States. . . . The State Legislatures . . . would be more jealous, & more ready to thwart the National Govt. if excluded from a participation in it." He added, according to Pierce, "If the people choose[,] it will have a tendency to destroy the foundation of the State Govts" (1:137, 147).[19] On June 7 Mason believed that "[w]hatever power may be necessary for the Natl. Govt. a certain portion must necessarily be left in the States. It is impossible for one power to pervade the extreme parts of the U.S. so as to carry equal justice to them" (1:155). On the 20th he reiterated, "I will never consent to the Abolition of the State Govts. [T]here never can be a Genl. Govt. that will perform their offices—I will go a proper length in favor of the Genl. Government but I will take equal care of the State Govts" (1:349). The following day C. C. Pinckney was "for making the State Govts. a part of the General System" (1:360). His young cousin, Charles Pinckney, echoed these views on the 25th, adding that consolidation had been "found impracticable" before independence and that "it would necessarily place the power in the hands of the few, nearest the seat of government" (1:412). The general government "cannot effectually exist" without the states: "they are the instruments upon which the Union must frequently depend for the support & execution of their powers, however immediately operating upon the people, and not upon the States" (1:404). He was supported by Ellsworth, Johnson, and Williamson, the first arguing that, without the states, "it would be impossible to support a Republican Govt. over so great an extent of Country" (1:406).

19. Both the Pinckneys and Sherman were influenced in these opinions by a desire to minimize the role of the people in the new system, as well as to preserve the states. Pinckney's motion carried only Connecticut, New Jersey, and South Carolina (1:137–38).

Clearly the nationalists' designs on the states were arousing a new opposition.

In these discussions no one used the term "sovereignty" in the sense of unlimited power. It was used for state equality and for state autonomy, and the latter was confined to the area of internal affairs. Foreign relations were not in dispute. No one argued the theoretical notion of the indivisibility of sovereignty; on the contrary, these practical men seemed generally satisfied that experience had proved divisibility.[20]

We should not forget that the controversies of the 1760s and 1770s were still fresh in the minds of many delegates. During the period before the armed conflict, an important element of the colonial argument had been a distinction between those functions and objects (such as taxation) that were appropriate to the separate colony governments and those appropriate to the imperial power in London. The application of this distinction varied as the dispute developed, but in the end the Revolution came because the central government insisted on its power and right to legislate and to tax within the colonies.

In joining together to resist that claim the new states had been careful, in instructions to their delegates and in the Articles of Confederation, to retain autonomy in their internal affairs. Now, in a new attempt to create a better central government, the relation of the existing state governments to it was a crucial issue. For many members of the Convention the thrust of the more ardent nationalists toward a unitary system was a threat to the internal autonomy for which the Revolution itself had been fought. Yet some reduction in that autonomy seemed to be required—more, in fact, than the authors of the New Jersey Plan had conceded.

A conception was needed that would provide firm ground for a new form of government that would neither reduce the states to the level of counties, as Madison wanted to do (1:449), nor permit them to claim sovereignty, as the Articles provided.

20. See, for example, Wilson (1:183), King (1:324), Johnson (1:355), Williamson (1:445), Bedford (1:491), etc. Peter S. Onuf, distinguishing the Americans' notion of sovereignty from that in England, called the latter "indivisible" and "institutional," a "synthesis of the branches in Parliament," while American sovereignty was "extra-institutional, outside the government," residing in "the people of the new states." "Toward Federalism: Virginia, Congress, and the Western Lands," *William and Mary Quarterly* 34 (July 1977): 353–74, at 360–61. In fact, he believed, sovereignty was an unmanageable concept in American politics, appropriate only in foreign policy. "In other respects, early American constitutional history . . . may be read as an evasion of, and retreat from, the sovereignty concept." *Maryland and the Empire, 1773* (Baltimore, 1974), Introduction, pp. 4–12.

The State Federalists

Lansing had said, in introducing his motion for state equality (above, p. 56), that it would "determine the question of a federal or national government" (1:455). The issue, however, was not decided on that vote. The state-sovereignty extremists had been repelled, but the states had defenders of other and more resourceful kinds. From their ranks came the movement that robbed the large-state men of their victory. Culminating in the Connecticut compromise, it was a matter not only of mutual concessions but of a quite different set of principles.

Rejecting both the unitary and the federal systems in their pure forms, the architects of this new conception consciously sought a form of compound government or mixed state, combining not only the ancient ingredients—monarchy, aristocracy, and democracy—but also the modern unitary and federal systems. They were gradually brought to this conception, hitherto unknown, by the interaction of their knowledge of the American realities with the debates at Philadelphia.

The nationalists, although they generally held that the government under the Articles was strictly federal and therefore beyond redemption, occasionally found it convenient to argue that it was partly national. Madison on July 19, for example, suggested that neither the existing Articles nor Paterson's proposals conformed to the strict requirements of federalism since in some cases the government operated directly on individuals, not on states, and since in Connecticut and Rhode Island the delegates to Congress were directly elected by the people (1:314). King also said that the Articles "are partly federal & partly of the nature of a constitution or form of Govt. arising from & applying to the Citizens of the US. & not from the individual States" (1:331). Yet these views, intended to make the nationalist proposals seem less radical, were based on the Articles themselves and made no reference to the underlying American society. The society itself, however, when conceived as being both national *and* federal—not to be pushed to either extreme—became the basis for a new conception of governmental structure.

The Nature of American Society

The earliest statement of this orientation came from John Dickinson, who had the special advantage in perspective gained by serving in the Continental Congress from the large state of Pennsylvania and in the Convention from the small state of Delaware. On May 30, while the Convention was struggling to distinguish federal and national systems, Dickinson said, "We are a nation altho' consisting of parts or States—we are also confederated" (1:42). The realities of the situation, he already saw, were both federal and national, so that the Convention should not attempt to prepare either system in its pure form. "The accidental lucky division of this country into distinct States" was a "principal source of stability," whereas a consolidated government would soon share the fate of earlier republics (1:86–87). Therefore, he "hoped that each State would retain an equal voice at least in one branch of the National Legislature" (1:87).

William Pierce of Georgia held similar views on May 31, the day of his arrival. The influence of the states, he thought, must be eliminated from some part of the new government, which should "carry at least some of its principles into the mass of the people. . . . But in my opinion it will be right to show the sovereignty of the State in one branch of the Legislature, and that should be in the Senate" (1:59). On the same day, Richard Spaight of North Carolina moved the election of the second branch by the state legislatures (1:51, 58). And Butler of South Carolina, Gerry of Massachusetts, and Sherman of Connecticut thought that the legislatures should elect the first branch as well (1:48, 50, 57–58).

When the Convention debated methods of choosing the legislators, Dickinson considered it "essential" that one branch be elected by the people and "expedient" that the other be chosen by state legislatures (1:136). In this he was supported by Pierce, who said that thus "the Citizens of the States wd. be represented both *individually* and *collectively*" (1:137).[21] When Dickinson moved (June 7) that members of the second branch be chosen by the state legislatures, he was seconded by Sherman on the ground

---

21. Forrest McDonald, in his acute analysis of the Convention, *Novus Ordo Seclorum* (Lawrence, Kans., 1985), credits Dickinson, on June 6, with proposing a "mixed system," "an approach that was theoretically sound, practically sound, and tailored to American realities" (pp. 213, 215). He also credits Spaight, along with Pierce, as the only two delegates "to see the merits of Dickinson's perception." Spaight, however, favored PR and withdrew his motion of May 31 when King objected that it would require the Senate to be too large if Delaware elected one member (1:52). There is no evidence that he spoke in support of Dickinson. On July 16 he voted against the Connecticut compromise (2:15).

McDonald's chapter 6 contains a valiant effort to group the delegates into categories, using their later actions in Congress and other sources as well as their Convention remarks and votes. He begins with "the absolutely central issue" of the role, if any, that the states would play in the new system, which leads him to a list of ten "court party" nationalists (p. 186), and thirteen country "republican ideologues" (pp. 200–201). He also found an overlapping group of six "foederalists," who wanted a system based on the state governments (p. 214), and other groupings, but they all differ substantially from mine on p. 62 below.

that the states "would thus be interested in supporting the National Governmt. and that a due harmony" would obtain (1:150). Only Wilson, Read, and Madison spoke against this, and it was carried unanimously (1:149). To Wilson's objection that state interests might oppose the national government Dickinson replied that, on the contrary, "Safety may flow from this variety of Interests" (1:158–59). "It will produce that collision between the different authorities which should be wished for in order to check each other" (1:153). This was very different ground from that of Sherman, ground that Mason also took on June 20 (1:346–47). This view clearly implied that the states would remain as coordinate parts of the governmental structure. They could not be effective checks if they were to become subordinate to the central power. At the same time Dickinson supported the Congressional veto of state laws, which, of course, the state-sovereignty men opposed vehemently (1:167–68)

Dr. William Johnson of Connecticut was another who clearly grasped the bases for a dual federal and national system. After noting on June 21 the need for direct and equal representation of the states in the second branch (1:355, 363), he gave on the 29th a reasoned argument for it:

> The controversy must be endless whilst Gentlemen differ in the grounds of their arguments; Those on one side considering the States as districts of people composing one political Society; those on the other considering them as so many political societies. The fact is that the States do exist as political Societies, and a Govt. is to be formed for them in their political capacity, as well as for the individuals composing them. . . . On the whole he thought that as in some respects the States are to be considered in their political capacity, and in others as districts of individual citizens, the two ideas embraced on different sides, instead of being opposed to each other, ought to be combined; that in *one* branch the *people*, ought to be represented; in the *other*, the *States*. (1:461–62)

This reasoning impressed even Madison, who "agreed with Docr. Johnson, that the mixed nature of the Govt. ought to be kept in view," but thought that the states did not rank very high as political societies (1:463–64).

The decision for PR in the first branch of the legislature had just been taken, June 29, when Ellsworth set forth another summary of the argument, in moving for state equality in the second branch: "We were partly national;

partly federal. The proportional representation in the first branch was conformable to the national principle & would secure the large States agst. the small. An equality of voices [in the second branch] was conformable to the federal principle and was necessary to secure the Small States agst. the large" (1:468). In Yates's report of this speech Ellsworth said the effect would be "to make the general government *partly federal and partly national*" (1:474). It appears that he stressed the compromise nature of his proposal as well as its conformity to the dual aspects of American society.

This suggestion, far from deriving from the defeat of the New Jersey Plan, had been advanced as desirable in itself by Dickinson and Pierce in May and again formally by Sherman on June 11, before the small states prepared their plan (1:196). "As the States would remain possessed of certain individual rights," Sherman had said, "each State ought to be able to protect itself: otherwise a few large States will rule the rest" (1:196).[22] On June 28 he had added a comparison with rich and poor citizens: "In society, the poor are equal to the rich in voting. . . . This arises from an equal distribution of liberty amongst all ranks; and it is, on the same grounds, secured to the states in the confederation" (1:457).

William Davie of North Carolina went beyond the idea of protection for the small states, as expressed by Ellsworth and Sherman. Using Ellsworth's phrase, he said, "We were partly federal, partly national in our Union," but, like Dickinson and Johnson, he stressed the nature of the underlying society. Rejecting the "extremes on both sides," he thought that the nature of the society could be reflected in the operation as well as in the structure of the new government. "He did not see why the Govt. might not in some respects operate on the States, in others on the people" (1:488).

Some fifteen delegates can thus be identified as state federalists. There were six (Dickinson, Mason, Pierce, C. C. Pinckney, Sherman, and probably Johnson) who were state federalists by June 7, and two more (Ellsworth and Davie) who expressed such views by the end of June. Five others, who rejected Madison's negative on state laws and who were neither state-sovereignty men nor strong nationalists (Gerry, Randolph, Williamson, Rutledge, and Baldwin), also spoke for the appointment of the Connecticut-compromise committee on July 2 or served on it. Although less dependable, Butler and Spaight can also be included, since they defended state legislatures, opposed Madison's negative, and usually voted with their state

22. The same six states voted against Sherman's proposal on June 11 and against Lansing's on the 29th. Sherman made the same argument (but no motion) on June 20 (1:343).

colleagues. With the exceptions of Mason and Davie, the southern supporters of state federalism were influenced by the southern economy of export staples and slavery, and wanted to preserve the states more as a protection against the northern majority than as reflecting the dual nature of American society.

The Connecticut Compromise

Ellsworth's motion for state equality in the Senate split the Convention evenly, Luther Martin being enabled by the absence of Jenifer to add Maryland to the bloc of small northern states, and Georgia being divided. To break this deadlock a committee of one delegate from each state was chosen by ballot on July 2 (1:509). Strangely enough, it included not one of the most outspoken nationalists, while the opposite camp was well represented by Bedford, Martin, Paterson, and Yates. Six of the eleven members were state federalists. The composition of this committee indicated that the nationalists had lost control of the Convention. It indicated also that the main provision of the committee's report was already anticipated; there was no need for strong nationalists on the committee to carry on the struggle.[23]

Even before the committee was decided on, Franklin, sensing an erosion of support for the hard line against the states, tried to classify certain types of questions on which the states could protect themselves by equal votes in the Senate (1:489). Another possibility was suggested by King. Noting that the "fundamental rights of individuals" were secured by "express provisions" in the state constitutions, "why may not a like security," he asked, "be provided for the Rights of States in the National Constitution?" (1:493). But neither Franklin nor King made a motion, and these ideas were not pursued.

On July 5 the committee reported in favor of an equal vote for each state in the second branch, balanced by PR in the first branch and certain restrictions on money bills (1:524). Gerry as chairman, in his explanations of the report, said, "We were however in a peculiar situation. We were neither the same Nation nor different Nations. We ought not therefore to pursue the one or the other of these ideas too closely" (1:532).

The nationalists, furious that they had been outflanked, were not yet prepared to abandon the pursuit of their ideas. Wilson made the surly

---

23. Only Madison and Wilson spoke against appointment of a committee. They would not have done so if there had been any likelihood that it would report in favor of PR in the Senate (1:515). For detailed analysis see Jack N. Rakove, "The Great Compromise: Ideas, Interests, and the Politics of Constitution Making," *William and Mary Quarterly* 44 (July 1987): 424–57.

response that the committee "has exceeded their powers." And Madison restrained himself "from animadverting on the report" (1:535). But Morris* wrapped himself in the mantle of "a Representative of America" and "in some degree as a Representative of the whole human race" in delivering his Gallows and Halter tirade, in which he admitted that "we cannot annihilate" the states, "but we may perhaps take out the teeth of the serpents" (1:530).

The next day Gerry, in conciliatory tone, remarked that "[a] Govert. short of a proper national plan if generally acceptable, would be preferable to a proper one which if it could be carried at all, would operate on discontented States" (1:550). Sherman, who also had served on the committee, made the point (July 7) that "[i]f they vote by States in the 2d. branch, and each State has an equal vote, there must be always a majority of States as well as a majority of the people on the side of public measures" (1:550). On the other hand, he went on, "If a Majority of the lesser states be agt. the Laws of the national Governmt.; those Laws cannot be executed—There must then be a Branch immediately from the States" (1:555).

Sherman had held this conception of a dual majority for many years. John Adams records that on August 1, 1776, when Congress was debating the Articles of Confederation, Sherman proposed that "the vote should be taken two ways; call the Colonies, and call the individuals, and have a majority of both."[24] Yet it was not his role on the committee alone that gave to its report the name Connecticut compromise. This was the primary structural provision by which the state federalists wrote their conceptions into the Constitution, and Connecticut was the only state from which the whole delegation were state federalists.[25] This circumstance may not be unrelated to the fact

---

*Unless Robert Morris is named, all references are to Gouverneur Morris.

24. *The Works of John Adams*, 2:499; also in Worthington C. Ford et al., eds., *Journals of the Continental Congress, 1774–1789* (Washington, 1904–37), 6:1081. Sherman's conception seems to have impressed his colleagues. When Congress was debating the Articles again in 1777, Jefferson, who probably had heard Sherman, wrote to John Adams from Williamsburg on May 16 urging him to use in the debate "the proposition I formerly made you in private . . . that any proposition might be negatived by the representatives of a majority of the people of America, or of a majority of the colonies of America." Boyd, *The Papers of Thomas Jefferson*, 2:18–19. And on May 5 in that debate, Thomas Burke of North Carolina, who had not heard Sherman, elaborated the idea into a proposal for a bicameral Congress, one house with proportional representation and the other with "one Delegate from every State." Ford, *Journals*, 7:328.

25. The unique voting pattern of Connecticut in the Convention was brought to my attention by Susan M. Stoudinger, who first isolated the "Connecticut Factor" in her M.A. thesis, "An Analysis of Voting Behavior in the Constitutional Convention of 1787," at the University of Maryland in 1968, p. 43. It is confirmed in more detail by Calvin Jillson, who has greatly

that experience with federalism went back much further in that state than elsewhere, to the Fundamental Orders of Connecticut in 1639; that document, interestingly enough, could be read as an anticipation of state federalism. Three towns of the Connecticut valley joined together "to be as one Publike State" (a unitary concept?), and also entered "into Combination and Confederation together" (clearly a federal concept).[26] In any event, the three Connecticut delegates had been vigorous in promoting the combination of equality in the Senate with PR in the House.

The equality of states was retained tentatively on July 7 by a vote of 6 to 3, with Massachusetts and Georgia divided (1:549). On July 10 Randolph gave Madison a suggested list of types of questions on which the states would have equal votes in the Senate.[27] Like Franklin and King, however, he made no motion.

These suggestions from the three large states were not attractive to the state federalists, it seems, and for good reasons. Each was predicated on PR in both branches of the new legislature on most matters, not on the use of the two branches to balance the national and the federal aspects of American society.

The nationalists continued their opposition to the compromise through July 16, when it was confirmed finally by 5 to 4, New York having departed, Massachusetts still being divided, and Georgia voting "no" (2:15). Even then, Madison reports, "a number of members from the larger states,"

---

increased the sophistication of the procedures in his *Constitution Making: Conflict and Consensus in the Federal Convention of 1787* (New York, 1988), pp. 73, 114–15. Although we both make extensive use of factor analysis, Jillson carefully examines the Convention as a laboratory for the testing and refinement of coalition-realignment theory, while I am more concerned with ideological continuity and am more critical of the Framers.

26. The original towns had equal representation in the one-house legislature, but the legislature was empowered to proportion the representation of any additional towns "to the number of Freemen." Donald S. Lutz and others he cites have recognized a continuity in Connecticut federalism: the Royal Charter of 1662, which became the state's constitution in 1776, was "essentially a ratification of the Fundamental Orders," retaining its federal structure. See his *Origins of American Constitutionalism* (Baton Rouge, 1988), pp. 35–49, 64–66, and his "Connecticut: Achieving Consent and Assuring Control," pp. 117–37 in *Ratifying the Constitution*, ed. Michael A. Gillespie and Michael Lienesch (Lawrence, Kans., 1989), especially p. 118.

27. Randolph handed his proposal to Madison on July 10 but did not mention it on the floor until the 16th. It provided, among other things, that the states would have an equal vote in the second branch in thirteen specified types of decisions. Why was this elaborately thought-out proposal never introduced? The tone of Randolph's remarks on the 16th (2:17–18) indicates that the nationalists, having defeated the state-sovereignty advocates with the help of the South, were still expecting also to defeat the state federalists without a compromise—even after the Connecticut compromise had been voted.

dissatisfied with the decision, met to coordinate their further strategy. They were split, however, between those who wanted "the principal States, and a majority of the people" to propose a scheme "in a firm opposition to the smaller States" and those who "seemed inclined to yield to the smaller States" and to propose "an Act however imperfect & exceptionable" on which the whole Convention could agree. This split, Madison concluded bitterly, satisfied the small-state men who attended the meeting that "they had nothing to apprehend from a Union of the larger [states], in any plan whatever" against state equality in the second branch (2:19–20).[28]

The most divisive of all issues in the Convention was thus resolved. The solution had been achieved by a coalition of men representing four quite different lines of thought. There were those, like Dickinson, Johnson, and Davie, who started from the dual conception of American society as both federal and national, so that each house of the legislature reflected positively a basic aspect of the society. There were those, like Ellsworth and Sherman, who saw the matter largely in terms of protection for the continued existence of the states. There were those from the large states, like Gerry and Mason, who were impressed by the reasoning of the first two groups and who saw that the PR program of the nationalists would not go down either in the Convention or with the public. And there were, of course, the state-sovereignty men, like Bedford and Luther Martin, who had voted for state equality in the first branch. The Connecticut compromise thus resulted from a coincidence of divergent views, not from majority acceptance of the dual nature of American society.

Of these four groups only the last had opposed the creation of a strong central government, so it should occasion no surprise that, once the equality of the states in the Senate had been accepted, the nationalists, so sorely yet narrowly defeated on this, gained the support of the other three groups in pushing many of the remaining parts of their program.

Reactions of the Nationalists

What, in the opinions of the nationalists, would be the effects of state equality in the Senate? Their first reactions to the committee report were noted above (pp. 63–64), but what were their judgments during the lengthy debate as to the results that would flow from the compromise, if approved?

28. It is most probable that Madison and Wilson were among those who wished to continue the drive for PR, while Gerry and Mason were "inclined to yield."

The committee report was debated for nine days, the equality provision itself on Saturday, July 7, and again the following Saturday. On the 7th Morris opposed the report "because it maintained the improper Constitution of the 2d. branch. It made it another Congress, a mere whisp of straw" (1:551). "What hopes will our Constituents entertain," Wilson asked on the 14th, "when they find that the essential principles of justice have been violated in the outset of the Governmt." (2:4). They will say, he went on, "We sent you to form an efficient Govt and you have given us one more complex indeed, but having all the weakness of the former Governt." (2:11). King was "sure that no Govt. could last that was not founded on just principles. He preferred doing nothing, to an allowance of an equal vote to all the States. It would be better he thought to submit to a little more confusion & convulsion, than to submit to such an evil" (2:7). Madison also "expressed his apprehensions that if the proper foundation of Governmt was destroyed, by substituting an equality in place of a proportional Representation, no proper superstructure would be raised" (2:8). He denied categorically that the government would be partly federal and partly national, and therefore denied that there was any "true ground of compromise." He catalogued the objections to equality, saying that "the evil . . . would increase with every new State," since all must come in on "the principle of equality." And he held up before the southern states the specter of "the perpetuity it would give to the preponderance" of the North (2:8–9). Wilson then added a more general terror: "A vice in the Representation . . . must be followed by disease, convulsions, and finally death itself" (2:10).

These views were colored, of course, by the intensity of feeling while the issue remained unsettled. But to the extent that they expressed opinions— were not pure rhetoric—they may be compared with the views set forth during ratification, since the basic feature to which they here objected remained in the final document.

The Compromise in Relation to Sovereignty

Since the Connecticut compromise was the prime structural element in resolving the dispute over the continuing role of the states in the new system, this may be an appropriate point at which to look more closely at the Convention's treatment of sovereignty.

The use of this word never involved a claim to unlimited power. It involved instead two things: the equality of the states, and the distribution of powers and duties between the central government and the state governments.

In the two weeks of debate on the compromise, some of it quite acrimonious, sovereignty was never mentioned. The architects of the new mixed system were satisfied to build the states as political societies into the new government, and to erect adequate safeguards for their continuing role, without attempting to argue the abstract issues of sovereignty. Yet the solution through silence resulted in a tragic and perhaps unnecessary ambiguity in the relations of the states to the nation.

This ambiguity, of course, had long existed in various forms. It may even be said to have antedated the Revolution. The colonial period had been sufficiently long to fix firmly the habits of thought and action in separate political societies, which made no claim to sovereignty; but when the colonies began acting together the issue of equality immediately arose. The First Continental Congress adopted a decision rule (September 6, 1774): "That in determining questions in this Congress, each Colony or Province shall have one Vote, the Congress not being possess'd of, or at present able to procure proper materials for ascertaining the importance of each Colony."[29] The practical effect of this rule, as it was continued under the Articles and in the Convention itself, was the equality of states; but the explanatory clause pointed clearly away from the international-law rule of equality and toward some future form of union reflecting the "importance of each Colony."

When independence was declared—seemingly a moment of great psychological unity—the ambiguity was not resolved but enshrined in the document. The plural word "states" was chosen over "provinces" to replace "colonies"; the phrase "Free and Independent States," not "a Free and Independent State," was used and repeated; and the phrase "thirteen united States of America" clearly referred to separate states and not to one political entity, the United States. Yet this clear and consistent phrasing was clouded by the joint preparation and promulgation of the Declaration. As Wilson said, they acted "unitedly," not in thirteen separate declarations; and those who signed it claimed to act by the authority of "the good People of these Colonies," not of the "good Peoples."

If there was a devolution of imperial authority involved in the Declaration, the new repository might be the new Congress, as representing the American people, or it might be the new state governments being created in the

29. *Journals*, vol. 1, p. 25.

old separate colonies, each representing its own people. In practice, however, there was less ambiguity: Congress took charge of external affairs and the states of internal; but the exigencies of the war soon blurred this distinction. In any event, there was no devolution of unlimited power. At both levels the revolutionaries diligently set to work on constitutional documents designed to establish and at the same time to limit legitimate power.

The reader will recall that the Revolution itself had developed from ambiguities in the British constitution that had provided support for diametrically opposite interpretations.[30] The war had been fought against a claim of indivisible, unlimited sovereignty. The British claim, from the 1760s, threatened the colonists in two ways: a distant Parliament in which they were not represented was reaching into the territory of their local legislatures, and worse, this claim undercut all rights, immunities, privileges, and customs in favor of unlimited power. The counterclaim by the colonists to constitutional immunity from internal taxation by Parliament was clearly incompatible with any conception of Parliamentary sovereignty, and, perhaps less clearly, it was predicated on the view that sovereignty could be divided—in contradiction to Hobbes, Blackstone, and King George's ministers. From that prolonged conflict the states, and the older Convention delegates, retained a very wary attitude toward central power and a strong preference for local and limited government.

The Articles of Confederation tried to end the ambiguity by an explicit statement of state sovereignty. The circumstances in which the Articles were drafted and ratified, however, had led to a definite division of powers between the Congress and the states. The latter, by turning foreign relations over to Congress, clearly did not claim full sovereignty; in spite of Article 2, the Articles were ambiguous. The Convention was planning to set aside the Articles, with their explicit statement, and, unless care was taken, the result might be even more ambiguous. Given the balance of opinions, within the Convention and among the public, what might have been done?

An explicit statement of state sovereignty could not be made; the votes were not there. An unambiguous statement of national sovereignty, if it could be made, would create difficulties, perhaps insuperable ones, for the ratification. But were there other possibilities? Could a clear statement of divided sovereignty have been written? Or a clear denial of internal sovereignty, state and national?

30. See chapter 2, pp. 22ff. and 30ff. on English conflicts regarding sovereignty.

The Cokeian strain of the Country ideology, with which the resistance to Britain was defended, spoke more against the unlimited aspect of the notion of sovereignty than against the indivisible aspect; but the two are easily connected, since an obvious means to restrain power is to divide it—the foundation of doctrines of balanced government.

By undertaking an enumeration of national powers, and by laying prohibitions on both the nation and the states, the Convention denied both the indivisible and the unlimited aspects of the notion of sovereignty. This denial was not thought to be contradicted by either the "supremacy" clause or the "necessary and proper" clause, as the paucity of debate on those clauses clearly shows.

This insight of the Convention, this rejection of sovereignty, was stressed by Hannah Arendt a generation ago: ". . . the great and, in the long run, perhaps the greatest American innovation in politics as such was the consistent abolition of sovereignty within the body politic of the republic, the insight that in the realm of human affairs sovereignty and tyranny are the same."[31] Yet this conception, excluding internal sovereignty, was never expounded in theoretical terms in the Convention. It was too clear a corollary of the opposition Whig heritage, and of the motives of the Revolution itself, to need exposition.

The nationalists, however, were closer to the views of the Court Whigs. When Sherman tried, toward the end of the Convention, to get another layer of protection for the "internal police" of the states (parallel to the protection of slavery) in the amending article, he was defeated (below, pp. 157–58). At the same time he succeeded on the equality of states in the Senate. This is the best evidence we have that the Convention, with a near balance of forces, was not willing to make more explicit its rejection of internal sovereignty.

The state federalists wanted the Constitution to reflect the dual aspects of American society through the acceptance of the states as essential constituent parts of a single governmental fabric. Even before the Convention, Sherman had worked out his conception of the proper relations and roles of the central and the state governments. He recognized that their roles were not properly balanced under the Articles. Drawing on the old and widely held colonial view by which external affairs belonged to the imperial government while internal affairs in each colony were the domain of the colony government, Sherman believed the new central government should

31. *On Revolution*, p. 152.

have power to bind the people and the officials of the states "in all cases which concern the common interests of the United States: but not to interfere with the government of the individual states, in matters of internal police which respect the government of such states only, and wherein the general welfare of the United States is not affected."[32] Such national laws should be "carried into execution by the judiciary and executive officers of the respective states" (3:616). The work of the Convention carried Sherman and the other state federalists toward a more independent role for the proposed government than he had wanted earlier, but still in collaboration with the state governments. They had the optimism and confidence to conceive that the differences that might arise could be resolved by men of good will without the command of a supreme authority—that political societies, as well as men, could govern themselves. From the beginning, and unanimously, the states had accepted the conduct of external affairs by the central government. They had also insisted upon internal autonomy. Neither government, therefore, held the full panoply of sovereign power; each was incomplete and dependent on the other. Like the English system of the joint power of King-in-Parliament, this system could work effectively only through mutual forbearance and restraint, not through command and coercion. Nor would it be possible to settle disputes in any other way without changing the system—as Philip Hunton had said regarding the English system in 1643.[33] "If the United States and the individual states will quarrel," Ellsworth told the Connecticut ratifying convention, "if they want to fight, they may do it, and no frame of government can possibly prevent it."[34]

The nationalists, on the other hand, believing that the states, like men,

32. Sherman moved this on July 17, was seconded by Wilson, and, according to Madison, "in explanation of his ideas read an enumeration of powers" (2:25–26), which was probably his Plan (3:615–16). The date of this document is uncertain; it seems to lie between April 1783 and June 1787. See William W. Crosskey and William Jeffrey, Jr., *Politics and the Constitution*, vol. 3 (Chicago, 1980), pp. 102–3, 528.

33. Hunton expounded a doctrine of corporate sovereignty, located in the King-in-Parliament, which could be exercised only when the three "*incomplete* independent powers" concurred and acted as "one *integrall* mixt power." This was a doctrine of organic unity, and he admitted that, if the unity was lost and the powers could not agree, there was no constitutional judge to decide their dispute. When the people establish such a government, "it is evident they reserve to themselves, not a Formall Authoritative Power, but a morall Power, such as they had originally before the Constitution of the Government; which must needs remaine, being not conveyed away in the Constitution." Quoted in Charles H. McIlwain, "A Forgotten Worthy, Philip Hunton, and the Sovereignty of King in Parliament," in his *Constitutionalism and the Changing World* (Cambridge, 1939), pp. 206, 202.

34. *Elliot's Debates*, 2:196.

must be governed, thought in terms of supremacy and subordination. On June 30 Ellsworth accused them of "razing the foundations of the building. When we need only repair the roof." Agreeing that a national government would provide general security, he went on to summarize well the state-federalist position: "What he wanted was domestic happiness. The Natl. Govt. could not descend to the local objects on which this depended. It could only embrace objects of a general nature. He turned his eyes therefore for the preservation of his rights to the State Govts." And it was not enough that these be preserved "in a subordinate degree," as King phrased it; "No, small states must possess the power of self defence or be ruined" (1:484, 492, 496).

Self-defense for state governments did not require an insistence on state sovereignty.[35] On the contrary, the two levels of government must work together in harmony (Sherman's idea, pp. 60–61 above) and at the same time check and balance each other (Dickinson's idea, p. 61)—which could not be done if either the nation or the states could assume a sovereign posture against the other.

In the absence of any explicit denial of internal sovereignty, however, the road was open for the nationalists, once in power in the new government, and armed with the "supremacy" clause and the "necessary and proper" clause, to push for national sovereignty.

The Powers of Government

The structure of the new government and its relations to the states, as we have seen, were fundamentally changed from the conceptions of the Virginia Plan. How did the nationalists fare with their other conceptions—in partic-

35. There are several indications that the state federalists did not want an express recognition of state sovereignty. For one, they did not propose this, nor did they couch their arguments in terms of sovereignty. Second, on June 19, the only state they then controlled, Connecticut, voted against the New Jersey Plan, which would have continued the Articles provision for state sovereignty (1:322). Third, looking further back, in drafting the Articles of Confederation Dickinson had inserted equal votes by states but not state sovereignty, and in describing himself to Madison as a friend of "a good National Government" on June 15, he again insisted, not on state sovereignty, but on "an equality of suffrage" in at least one branch (1:242). And, fourth, they accepted the article on amendments, which was incompatible with state sovereignty, as will be discussed below, p. 161. Dickinson and Read may also have voted against the New Jersey Plan; all five Delaware delegates were present on June 19.

ular, their conceptions of the powers to be exercised by the national government?

General or Specified Powers

After a false start on Monday, still unadjusted to the equality in the Senate, the delegates began on Tuesday, July 17, to empower the new legislature. The Virginia Plan included the powers already in Congress and a power "to legislate in all cases to which the separate States are incompetent, or in which the harmony of the United States may be interrupted by the exercise of individual Legislation" (1:21). Broad as this may seem, Bedford proposed to add "to legislate in all cases for the general interests of the Union."[36] This struck Randolph as "a formidable idea indeed. It involves," he objected, "the power of violating all the laws and constitutions of the States, and of intermeddling with their police" (2:26). Bedford, on the other hand, thought his proposal no more "extensive or formidable" than the clause without it. This exchange indicates that to Randolph the Virginia Plan would leave the bulk of legislative activity in the hands of the states, with the national legislature filling the gaps between them and overriding the conflicts among them, while to Bedford the new legislature should come first, providing for all general interests and leaving to the states only the remaining local affairs. The Convention followed Bedford six states to four, Connecticut, Virginia, South Carolina, and Georgia dissenting (2:27).

Did the other delegates understand the clause as Bedford did? The previous day, when Butler objected to the "vagueness of the terms," Gorham had said that "the vagueness of the terms constitutes the propriety of them. We are now establishing general principles, to be extended hereafter into details which will be precise & explicit" (2:17). Yet back in May, when Butler had raised a similar objection, and Randolph had responded that his "opinion was fixed" against giving "indefinite powers to the national Legislature," Sherman had said (according to Pierce) that "it would be hard to define all the powers by detail." And Sherman had been echoed by Wilson: "it would be impossible to enumerate the powers which the federal Legislature ought to have," and by Madison, who had brought to the Convention

36. Made the day after the Connecticut compromise was approved, this motion displays dramatically the impact of their victory on the small-state men. From an emotional advocate of state sovereignty who contended on June 30 "that there was no middle way between a perfect consolidation and a mere confederacy of the States," Bedford had come to feel secure enough to go beyond the Virginia Plan.

"a strong prepossession for the defining of the limits and powers of the federal Legislature," yet had become "convinced it could not be done" (1:59–60). It would thus appear that some delegates, probably including Bedford and Wilson, and certainly Hamilton (1:323), saw the vague and general grant of power as sufficient and desirable without further specification, while other delegates, including Randolph and Gorham, saw it only as a "general principle" to be refined in a detailed enumeration of specific powers.

Randolph, Gorham, and Wilson, along with Ellsworth and Rutledge, composed the Committee of Detail chosen on July 24 to which the general grant of power was referred. Adhering still to his "fixed opinion" against indefinite powers, Randolph prepared a draft enumerating particular powers and entirely eliminating the phrases about "the general interests" or "the harmony of the United States" and "all cases to which the separate states are incompetent" (4:43–45). This draft was worked over by Rutledge as chairman; into it he inserted, among other additions, "a right to make all Laws necessary to carry the foregoing Powers into Execu——" (4:45). The Committee refined and rearranged the resulting list of powers but did not substantially expand it. The revenue clause, however, was transformed: Randolph had named only "taxation," which became "taxes, duties, imposts and excises"; he had stated a limiting purpose, "for the past or future debts and necessities of the union," which was eliminated; and his "establish rules for collection," which might accommodate state collection, became "lay and collect," purely national. There is no evidence that Wilson attempted to retain or revive the concept of general powers. A late committee draft in his handwriting, however, contains, as the last of the particular powers, the "necessary and proper" clause, already full-blown in all its radiant ambiguity (2:168).

The documents surviving from the Committee of Detail provide some evidence that the state-federalist conception of federalism was leavening its work. Randolph's early draft, in discussing the problems of a preamble, expressed the view that a general statement of the "ends of government and human politics" was inappropriate "since we are not working on the natural rights of men not yet gathered into society, but upon those rights, modified by society, and (supporting) interwoven with what we call (states) the rights of states" (2:137). Randolph had crossed out "supporting" and "states" and inserted "interwoven with" instead. Farther along, where Randolph had used simply "The executive" to introduce that branch, Rutledge wrote "Governor of the united People and States of America" (2:145 and 4:46).

This change did not survive, but it shows that Rutledge grasped the state-federalist distinction and agreed that they were uniting both the people and the states. In Wilson's first draft the preamble began "We the People of the States of New-Hampshire &C," indicating that even a strong nationalist did not see the Constitution as arising from a union of individuals who composed a single national group (2:150). His second draft is even more interesting. It started "We the People of and the States of New Hampshire . . ."; the "and" was an insertion later crossed out. Yet the first paragraph read: "The Stile of this Government shall be the 'United People and States of America' "—no insertion and no crossing out (2:152; see also 160). Both the "and" and the "People" disappeared in the final committee report, but the names of the states remained until September 12, when the Committee of Style omitted them. It is unfortunate that no debate on that omission is recorded since it set the stage for the later denial, by Marshall, Webster, and others, of any agency on the part of the states.

The Committee of Detail having reported an enumerated list of powers, other delegates, especially Pinckney and Madison, advanced additional powers that were also referred to the Committee. Some of these, such as bankruptcies, patents and copyrights, the militia, Indian affairs, and jurisdiction over a seat of government, survived to become parts of the Constitution. Others, such as charters of incorporation (proposed by both Madison and Pinckney), although discussed and rejected by the Convention, were subsequently discovered to be hidden in the "necessary and proper" clause. One provision of the original report of the Committee, a power to emit bills of credit, was attacked and killed by the Convention, yet similarly was found alive much later under the healing hand of the Supreme Court.

The Army

Two of the new powers, the army and taxation, were extended far beyond the original expectations of the Virginia Plan. Madison, it is true, interpreting the Plan on June 28, said it included "a compleat power of taxation," although neither a power to tax nor a standing army had been mentioned by Randolph.

Under the Articles, neither Congress nor the states could keep up "any body of forces" in time of peace except what Congress "deemed requisite to garrison the forts" (Article 6). The Committee of Detail, nevertheless, reported a power "to raise armies," with no restrictions of times or numbers. This was approved, 11 to 0, on August 18 over strenuous objections from

Gerry; and his and Martin's attempt to limit the numbers of troops in time of peace was defeated by the same vote (2:329–30). Even Mason's attempt, supported by Madison and Randolph, to mention "the danger of standing armies in time of peace" in the militia clause was approved only by Virginia and Georgia (2:616–17). In England in the 1690s the Country opposition had fought hard to reduce William's armies in time of peace; in the Convention of 1787, on the other hand, the Court view had overwhelming support.

Taxation

The Pinckney Plan probably included an "exclusive Power" of "levying Imposts" (2:135 and 3:607). The New Jersey Plan included, in addition to import duties, stamps on paper and postage, and a power "to make rules and regulations for the collection thereof" (1:243). The Committee of Detail considered an "exclusive power" of "rating and causing public Taxes to be levied" and "of levying Duties"—a distinction that seems to retain some state agency in taxes; but it came finally to the broadest possible statement, with no limits whatever (2:158, 181).[37] The Convention accepted this, Gerry alone voting "no" (2:308); but gradually it attached restrictions: no export duty (over the opposition of Madison, Morris, and Wilson) (2:305–8, 363); indirect taxes to be uniform (2:418, 481, 614); and certain limiting purposes were named (2:414, 497, 499). Two other restrictive efforts failed, however. Mason, mindful of English experience, initiated a clause against "the danger of perpetual revenue which must of necessity subvert the liberty of any Country" (2:326). This was reported by the Committee of Detail on August 22 (2:366), but the report was never considered. Martin proposed, August 21, that direct taxes be collected only after a state failed to comply with a requisition. This also was not debated; only New Jersey supported it (2:359).

The Elastic Clause

When the "necessary and proper" clause from the Committee of Detail came up for consideration Madison and Pinckney tried to insert "and establish all offices" after "laws." They were assured by Morris, Wilson, Rutledge, and Ellsworth that this amendment "could not be necessary," yet

---

37. Direct taxes were to be proportioned to population by earlier decision; but Morris, who had originated the idea, already foresaw that it would be little used and wanted to eliminate it (2:106, 223).

they did not withdraw the motion (2:345). By bringing it to a vote, and losing 2 to 9, they effectively put the Convention on record as holding that the power to make necessary laws implied the power to establish necessary offices. No one is recorded as having used the phrase "implied powers," and the gambit about offices, instead of stimulating a question as to what else might be implied, seems to have satisfied the delegates, who then, without further discussion, passed the clause 11 to 0. This brief debate is hardly ground on which to argue that the delegates understood and accepted this as an "elastic clause" containing many, if not all, of the powers to legislate for the "general interests of the Union" that Bedford had proposed. Yet it must be noted that no motion or even suggestion was made, either before or after this, that the powers of the national legislature be limited to those "expressly delegated." This phrase, prominent in Article 2 of the Confederation as a requirement for powers of Congress, is so easily associated with the idea of enumerating powers that some delegates seem to have assumed that it was somehow included. C. C. Pinckney, for example, told the South Carolina House of Representatives that "[t]he general government has no powers but what are expressly granted to it" (3:256), and Washington wrote to Lafayette (April 28, 1788) that the people "retained every thing they did not in express terms give up" (3:298). Its connection with the proclamation of state sovereignty in Article 2, of course, may have influenced the convention, but it is not to be supposed that all of the delegates were oblivious to its absence in the new document, or to the implications.

Concurrent or Exclusive Powers

Were these enumerated powers given exclusively to the national government, or could they be exercised concurrently by the states? Some were obviously exclusive; others, such as taxation, were probably concurrent (assuming the states were to continue); but still others were quite ambiguous. Strangely enough, this problem was not discussed until September 15, when the Maryland delegates moved an amendment that no state be prohibited from laying tonnage duties "for improving their harbors and keeping up lights . . . subject to the approbation or repeal of Congress" (2:633). Morris thought "the States are not restrained from laying tonnage as the Constitution now Stands. The exception proposed will imply the Contrary," perhaps in other matters. Madison, on the other hand, thought the terms of the commerce clause "are vague but seem to exclude this power of the States." He was "more & more convinced that the regulation of

Commerce was in its nature indivisible." The clear-minded Sherman then suggested, "The power of the U. States to regulate trade being supreme can controul interferences of the State regulations when such interferences happen; so that there is no danger to be apprehended from a concurrent jurisdiction" (2:625). Still, Langdon of New Hampshire insisted, "the regulation of tonnage was an essential part of the regulation of trade," and the states "ought to have nothing to do with it" (2:625). This discussion hardly clarified the general question of concurrent authority, but it pointed toward two things—first, there was a tendency to deal with each power by its own characteristics rather than to apply a single rule to all, and, second, there were quite divergent views among the delegates.

From this brief analysis we can see that the nationalists encountered little opposition in their efforts to confer extensive powers on the proposed government. The desire of Madison and Wilson for a broad and general grant was supplanted by Randolph's and Gorham's approach through detailed specification, yet the word "expressly" was carefully avoided. Rutledge and Wilson, in the "necessary and proper" clause, found a way by subterfuge to expand the content of the specified powers. Many of these powers had been held expressly by the existing government, but the meanings of some (for example, to make treaties, borrow money, raise naval forces) were transformed by the new powers over commerce and revenue.

Restricting State Power

The converse of the process of empowering the new government was that of restricting the powers of the states. To "take out the teeth of the serpents" (Morris's phrase), the nationalists began by proposing a blanket veto on state laws—Madison's favorite brainchild. Since it was so clearly derived from the king's veto over colonial laws, the debate on it well illustrates both the strength and the weakness of Court Whig ideas in the Convention. This plan was still on Madison's mind in 1836 (3:549).

The Legislative Negative

The Virginia Plan included a power in the national legislature "to negative all laws passed by the several States, contravening in the opinion of the National Legislature the articles of Union" (1:21). This clause was approved on May 31—Madison says "witht. debate or dissent," but Pierce says reservations were expressed by Sherman (1:54, 60).

This quick victory was not enough for some of the nationalists. A week later Pinckney moved a reconsideration (1:150) with a view to making the clause still more comprehensive: to negative "all Laws which they shd. judge to be improper" (1:164). Madison seconded this, regarding "an indefinite power . . . as absolutely essential to a perfect system" (1:164). He thought it the "mildest expedient," the alternative to the use of force against a state. But these arguments stirred up opposition. Gerry replied that "such a power may enslave the states" and that it had never been projected in any pamphlet or paper and would "never be acceded to" (1:165). Sherman suggested that the cases might be defined in which the negative could be used, but Wilson and Dickinson regarded this as "impracticable" or "impossible" (1:166–67). By then they had overreached themselves, however. Bedford, raising a series of practical objections, spoke of the "impossibility of adopting such a system as that on the table" and of the "enormous & monstrous influence" that Pennsylvania and Virginia seemed to want (1:167). Butler was "vehement agst. the Negative," and Madison further riled Bedford by asking him how the small states would fare in the dissolution of the Union, "wch. seemed likely" (1:168).

After this heated exchange, the Pinckney proposal was rejected, only the three large states supporting it, with Delaware divided. Mason and Randolph voted against it, Madison records, and "Genl. W. not consulted" (1:168). The vote left the earlier version of the negative intact, and it was reported by the Committee of the Whole as part of the Virginia Plan on June 13; but the opposition had been aroused and had quickly found the strength to turn back this extreme form of central power.

Another extreme form was included by Hamilton in his plan of June 18: all state laws contrary to the Constitution and laws of the United States "to be utterly void," and the governor of each state to be appointed by the central government with an absolute veto on *all* laws of his state (1:293). He did not formally propose this and it was not discussed.

With the continuing resistance of the small states, the situation gradually changed. Knowing how intensely the negative was disliked by them, Randolph included a modification of it in his unpresented compromise proposal of July 10 (above, p. 65). Yet his modification indicates how little the nationalists wanted to yield: he provided only that "any State may appeal to the national Judiciary against a negative," which in the meantime would block the state law (3:56).

When the Convention reached this part of the Virginia Plan on July 17 it was decisively rejected, only Massachusetts, Virginia, and North Carolina voting for it. Madison and Pinckney tried to defend it, the former holding it to be "essential" and "at once the most mild & certain means of preserving the harmony of the system." He again drew the parallel with the British control of colony legislation before the Revolution—an argument that probably cost him some votes. But by that time five counterarguments had turned the delegates away from their snap judgment of May 31: first, the impossible mass of state legislation (Bedford, Lansing, Martin); second, the almost certain refusal of the states to accept such control (Gerry, Lansing, Martin, Morris); third, the incompetence of the national legislature to judge local laws (Lansing); fourth, the dangerous and oppressive possibilities of such a power (Gerry, Butler); and, fifth, the alternative method through judicial review of state legislation (Sherman, Morris). The last, which now seems so obvious as a solution, was inadequate for Madison; the state judges could not, he thought, be trusted, and review by the national courts would be too slow (2:27–28).

Even this defeat, however, did not end the matter of the legislative negative. The fertile mind of young Pinckney realized that still another possibility remained: the negative exercised by "two thirds of the members of each House." He moved this on August 23 and was supported by Broom, Madison, Wilson, and Langdon (2:390). Wilson "considered this as the key-stone wanted to compleat the wide arch of Government we are raising. . . . The firmness of Judges is not of itself sufficient[.] Something further is requisite—It will be better to prevent the passage of an improper law, than to declare it void when passed." Rutledge, on the other hand, said, "If nothing else, this alone would damn and ought to damn the Constitution," and Ellsworth brought up the issue of appointed state governors, with veto powers, in the style that Hamilton had suggested. This question was in no way involved in Pinckney's proposal, but he "declared that he thought the State Executives ought to be so appointed with such a controul" (2:391). Madison had proposed that the motion be referred to a committee, and the vote taken on this (it lost 5 to 6), while not unambiguous, shows surprising vitality in the idea of the legislative negative. It did not come up again in the Convention, but Madison remained so enamored with it that, as late as September 12, he held to his opinion that the courts would be "insufficient" as protection against "injurious acts of the States" (2:589). Dissatisfied to the end, he defended it elaborately in a letter to Jefferson in October (3:133–35).[38]

38. In "The Negative on State Laws: James Madison, the Constitution, and the Crisis of Republican Government," *William and Mary Quarterly* 36 (April 1979): 215–35, Charles F.

The "Supremacy" Clause

While the legislative negative was thus being eliminated, its purposes were in part at least being covered by other provisions.

The first of these was the "supremacy" clause, Article VI, Section 2. Its first appearance was in the New Jersey Plan on June 15 (1:245). A month after that Plan had been rejected, an almost verbatim version of it was moved on July 17 by Martin (2:28–29), who was probably the originator of it in the first place. It is perhaps strange that a state-sovereignty man should author such a clause. In his version the "Legislative acts of the U. S." properly made, and treaties, "shall be the supreme law of the respective States" and their "Judiciaries . . . bound thereby, . . . any thing in the respective laws of the individual States to the contrary notwithstanding" (2:28–29). As Martin pointed out after the Convention, its meaning had been subtly yet radically changed during passage. The "Judiciaries of the several States" had become "judges in the several States," making room for national judges not bound by state constitutions; and the state constitutions had been inserted alongside state laws in the last part of the clause. He professed that he had omitted the constitutions so that, while subordinating state law to national law and treaties, the state judges would still uphold their constitutions and bills of rights (3:287). Yet if he saw the distinctions as clearly in June 1787 as he made them in March 1788, he surely used strange words not only in the Paterson text but in his own version of July 17. Is it credible that he conceived a "supreme law" subordinate to the state constitutions? In any event, the Committee of Detail reported a less ambiguous clause on August 6 that, prima facie, left little room for state sovereignty. This version was slightly amended, but it encountered no further opposition. It is amazing that this clause, so vigorously debated during the ratification struggle, was approved by the Convention unanimously and without discussion on four separate occasions.

Specific Restrictions

A second group of provisions substituted for the legislative negative was the specific prohibitions on the states, Article I, Section 10. Randolph at the beginning, according to McHenry, suggested that Congress should have power to prevent the states from emitting bills of credit (1:26). His Plan,

---

Hobson has argued convincingly that Madison regarded this negative as equally essential with extended size as a "republican remedy for the diseases most incident to republican government." Only thus could the central government adequately restrain the state legislatures, where most of the ills originated.

however, did not mention this, it being embraced in the proposed general negative on state laws. Pinckney also may have included some specific prohibitions, borrowed from the Articles of Confederation, in his original Plan (3:607). Yet no attention was given to this approach until the Committee of Detail seized upon it and reported, August 6, a long list of prohibitions (2:187). With a few exceptions these dealt with military and foreign affairs, came from the Articles, and had been included, in fact, in the Dickinson draft of the Articles, so they went back to June 1776. The exceptions were all concerned with money and commerce: the coining of money was absolutely prohibited to the states and, "without the consent of the Legislature of the United States," also bills of credit, tender laws, and imposts or duties on imports. Three weeks later, when this article was debated, the prohibitions on bills and tender laws were made absolute after Sherman suggested that, if the legislature "could authorize emissions of it, the friends of paper money would make every exertion to get into the Legislature in order to license it" (2:439). King then moved to add a prohibition on interference in private contracts (which will be discussed in chapter 4, p. 107), in which he ultimately succeeded. Madison and Williamson tried to make absolute the prohibition against state imposts and duties, but failed; King tried to add "or exports" after the word "imports," and succeeded. Sherman also succeeded in sending "the proceeds of all State duties on imports and exports, into the common Treasury" (2:441–42). The prohibitions as amended were then approved.

The General Result

The political motivations of the delegates, to preserve the Union and to restrain democracy by strengthening the central government, gave the nationalists an opportunity to set the agenda with their Virginia Plan. Their thrust for a new system, a near replication of England's relation to the colonies, with general powers and a blanket veto over the states, was at first accepted by the Convention. Their uncompromising attitude and their summary rejection of the New Jersey Plan, however, alerted the other delegates to the danger that the Convention might vitiate its own work by proposing a departure from established political customs too radical for the people to accept. Moreover, the nationalists' denigration of the states seemed too extreme, both unnecessary and unrealistic. For the state federalists the dual nature of American political society, as both one nation and several nations, required the recognition, the preservation, and the utilization of the states in the new system. Some older delegates especially, such as Dickinson, Sherman, Gerry, Mason, and Rutledge, who had been active in the conflicts of the 1760s and 1770s, remembered the dangers of central power against which the Revolution had been fought. Under these influences the Convention moved back from its early extremism, defeated the nationalists in the Connecticut compromise, and provided an important role for the states.

This accomplished, and the threat of dissolution obviated, the state federalists and several exponents of the New Jersey Plan joined with the nationalists in building a strong central government. But it was not to take the Court Whig form. General powers were replaced by enumerated powers; the branches of government were more clearly separated; most offices were given fixed terms; and both the central and the state governments were limited by numerous restraints. Yet the powers enumerated were very broad; the word "expressly" was carefully avoided, leaving room for implied powers; no restraints were laid on reelections or on standing armies; and no bill of rights was included.

Madison's Congressional veto of state legislation was rejected, but so also was Sherman's special protection for the "internal police" of the states. Internal sovereignty was thus excluded, and the only supremacy mentioned was vested in written national law. The foundations were laid for an unprecedented role for the judicial branch in the preservation of a rule of law, both against the other branches and the states and against the people themselves, as chapter 5 will explain.

4

Economic Motivations

The Annapolis Convention, forerunner of the Philadelphia gathering, had been called for commercial purposes. If the nationalists of 1783–84, centered around Robert Morris, were clearly commercial, was this also true of the more broadly based movement of 1786–87? There can be no doubt that the Founding Fathers were very aware that political and economic forces and motives were closely intertwined. James Harrington had told them so. Experience with the state legislatures also had taught them—both that power follows property and that political power could be used to redistribute property. May it not be that they were more impressed with the political problems and possibilities than with the potency of economic power? May it not be that the Marxian idea of the primacy of economics is anachronistic when applied to them? After all, an economic effect of an action, or even the expectation of an economic effect as suggested by Charles A. Beard, does not establish that effect as the primary motive for the action.

So much has been written on the economic backgrounds and motivations of the men at Philadelphia that the ennui of historians with the subject is eminently justified; yet the economic drama refuses to leave the stage. Started by Madison and others at the time, this interpretation was stressed by Richard Hildreth and by Martin Van Buren long before Beard made it his central theme.[1] And even now it occupies the attention of both scholars and textbook writers.

In 1956 Robert E. Brown went after Beard like an ancient Fury, tracking him almost line by line through every chapter, including the fine-print thickets of the footnotes, and wounding him in every vulnerable spot.[2] Two years later, a monumental research effort on the economic origins of the Constitution, while differing from Beard, nonetheless found that "no historian who followed in studying the making of the Constitution has been free from Beard's view of it." Forrest McDonald believed that Beard's "account as history gradually came into almost universal acceptance," hence his own great effort—to show that the "economic interpretation of the Constitution does not work."[3] But Jackson Turner Main, reviewing the book, found that "Beard has survived the attack."[4] Very shortly both Brown and McDonald were subjected to devastating attacks, methodological and substantive, by (among others) Lee Benson, who opted to "extend Beard's original ideas" and to outline a "social interpretation" that did not "dismiss as irrelevant to ideology and opinion the amount and kind of property owned and occupation held," but regarded them as less influential than "the nature of men's participation in the economy and the character of their over-all social environment."[5]

"Beard's major thesis that the Constitution was the handiwork of the classes . . . possessing status and property," while not his alone, according to E. James Ferguson, "is a theme of historical interpretation supported by the testimony of the founding fathers and sustained on the whole by historical scholarship."[6] Yet he agreed with Staughton Lynd that Beard's

1. Richard Hildreth, *The History of the United States of America* (New York, 1851), 4:349–50, and *The Theory of Politics* (New York, 1853), pp. 49–53, 151–57; Martin Van Buren, *Inquiry into the Origin and Course of Political Parties in the United States* (New York, 1867), pp. 180–81.

2. Robert E. Brown, *Charles Beard and the Constitution* (Princeton, 1956).

3. Forrest McDonald, *We the People* (Chicago, 1958), pp. vii, ix.

4. "Charles A. Beard and the Constitution," *William and Mary Quarterly* 17 (January 1960): 86.

5. Lee Benson, *Turner and Beard, American Historical Writing Reconsidered* (Glencoe, Ill., 1960), pp. 95–233, quotations from 224, 228.

6. E. James Ferguson, *The Power of the Purse*, p. 338. See also Stuart Bruchey and E. James Ferguson, "Forces Behind the Constitution," *William and Mary Quarterly* 19 (July 1962): 429–38.

great emphasis on the role of "personalty," as distinguished from real
property (an important element in Brown's attack), must be abandoned; but
this "does not require abandoning an economic approach to the period.
Beard's drama for villainous capitalist and virtuous farmer must make room
for a more complex scenario which preserves his sense of the role of
economic power."[7] Gordon S. Wood, on the other hand, held that "Beard's
interpretation of the origins of the Constitution in a narrow sense is
undeniably dead." He made a bow to Benson's view (above), however, and
went on: "the general interpretation of the Progressive generation of historians—that the Constitution was in some sense an aristocratic document
designed to curb the democratic excesses of the Revolution—still seems to
me to be the most helpful framework for understanding the politics and
ideology surrounding the Constitution."[8]

The delegates, of course, were property holders to varying extents. The
difficulty is in assessing the degree to which their holdings may have
conditioned their thinking and acting in the Convention. In this assessment
it is desirable to bear in mind a distinction between views of private property
as a general social institution and views reflecting the delegates' individual
holdings. A delegate might, for example, take the Whig view of property as
a bulwark against corruption (above, p. 26) without himself being wealthy.

To assess the role of property it is necessary to look closely at the
Convention debates on economic issues, without assuming that a delegate's
opinions were determined by his individual economic position. Through
Beard's influence, it is almost customary to expect a consistent bias among
them in favor of wealth. Yet the bias may not be consistent, and its most
blatant expressions may not be supported by the Convention as a whole.
Without denying the influences of property holdings and considerations,
however, it is suggested that they may have been exaggerated and that their
expression in the final document was both subtle and indirect.

This chapter will not deal with the property holdings of individual
delegates. It will examine economic attitudes and their influences on the
Convention in terms, first, of the role, if any, which property should play in
the new government, and second, of the powers and duties which the
government should have in economic matters. We shall see that the delegates were very aware that their decisions would have implications both
political and economic; but we shall also see that their motivations, even on

7. Staughton Lynd, *Class Conflict, Slavery, and the United States Constitution* (Indianapolis,
1967), pp. 17–18.
8. Wood, *Creation of the American Republic*, p. 626.

economic issues, were based on political considerations more than Beard believed.

The Role of Wealth in the Government

Three provisions were considered that bore upon the role of wealth in the new government openly and directly: the allocation of representation on a basis of wealth; property qualifications for the suffrage; and property qualifications for office holding. Each of these had advocates, yet each was overwhelmingly rejected.

Wealth as the Basis of Representation

The Virginia Plan called for "rights of suffrage" of the states "to be proportioned to the Quotas of contribution or to the number of free inhabitants, as the one or the other rule may seem best in different cases" (1:20). The rules of wealth and numbers were thus considered as alternatives, not as joint influences upon a single rule.[9]

A preliminary skirmish came the following day, May 30, in which Hamilton, seconded by Spaight, moved to eliminate the quotas rule, leaving only "free inhabitants." Madison repeatedly tried to get approval for proportional representation, but the whole subject was postponed on request from Delaware.

On June 11 Rutledge proposed the quotas rule, and Butler, supporting him, was paraphrased as saying that "money is power; and that the States ought to have weight in the Govt.—in proportion to their wealth" (1:196). How important Butler thought this to be appears from his remark on June 6 that, if the ratio of representation "proceeds on a principle favorable to wealth as well as numbers of Free Inhabitants," he would be content "in abolishing the State Legislatures, and becoming one Nation instead of a confed. of Republics" (1:144).[10] These two men and Gouverneur Morris

9. The "different cases" contemplated were probably different objects of legislation, not different states; and the phrase "rights of suffrage," instead of "representation," suggests that the voting power of a state's representatives might differ, as the rule changed, from one bill to another. This flexible approach was not explored, however, as debate concentrated on the allocation of representatives.

10. No one responded to this by suggesting that they were already one nation.

frequently argued that property was the "main object of Society" and the "only just measure of representation" (1:533, 534, 542). Dickinson also supported Rutledge with the suggestion that, if based on actual contributions, this rule would give the states an incentive to pay their quotas.

The Rutledge proposal did not come to a vote at this time, however. Wilson and Charles Pinckney, ignoring Dickinson's idea, put forward a substitute motion, the rule in the Act of Congress for apportioning quotas—namely, free inhabitants plus "three fifths of all other persons . . ." (1:201). This plan, which was ultimately incorporated into the Constitution, was seen at the time as a rule of both wealth and numbers (perhaps primarily of wealth), as is clear from several circumstances: (1) in making his motion immediately after Rutledge had moved the quota rule, Wilson mentioned its connection with the quota system of Congress; (2) Rutledge apparently accepted the substitute; (3) Gerry objected that southern property—the slaves—would increase their representation, while northern property in horses or oxen would not; and (4) the vote of South Carolina was cast for Wilson's motion. It carried 9 to 2, with New Jersey and Delaware opposed (1:201).

This decision on how to proportion representation was still contingent on the more basic issue, whether or not to proportion it. Involved also was the question of PR in the Senate. Again the southerners took the lead in proposing a property basis for the Senate. Baldwin of Georgia, on June 29, "thought the second branch ought to be the representation of property, and that in forming it therefore some reference ought to be had to the relative wealth of their Constituents" (1:469–70). He pointed to the example of Massachusetts: "There the first branch represents the people, and the second its property" (1:475). Butler also, on July 5, when the committee of the states reported the Connecticut compromise, "urged that the 2d. branch ought to represent the States according to their property" (1:529). And Davie, the following day, expressed a view parallel to Baldwin's (1:542).

In this debate the large-state men, opposing the equality of states in the Senate, appealed to property interests. "Life and liberty were generally said to be of more value, than property," Morris argued. "An accurate view of the matter would nevertheless prove that property was the main object of Society. The savage State was more favorable to liberty than the Civilized; and sufficiently so to life. It was preferred by all men who had not acquired a taste for property; it was only renounced for the sake of property which could only be secured by the restraints of regular Government" (1:533). Rutledge agreed: "Property was certainly the principal object of Society. If numbers should be made the rule of representation, the Atlantic States will be subjected to the Western." He therefore moved the postponement of the committee report in order to take up again a pure property rule, incorporating Dickinson's point of June 11: "that the suffrages of the several States be regulated and proportioned according to the sums paid towards the general revenue by the inhabitants of each State respectively" (1:534).

The vote on this motion, which saw South Carolina standing alone against nine other states (Georgia was absent), was not a clear-cut rejection of the rule of wealth, however, since the rule adopted on June 11 and included in the committee report was regarded by some, as noted above, as itself a rule of wealth. It measured wealth by numbers, counting slaves—an inexact method at best and a dangerous one as well, according to Morris, Rutledge, King, and others, when the new states to be created in the West were considered. "I do not think numbers are a proper Index of Wealth now, it will be much less so hereafter," Rutledge said in introducing his motion (1:537). Wealth, he thought, would continue to accumulate along the Atlantic coast, while the population would grow in the West; and the additional representatives based on the slaves would not give South Carolina a voice proportional to her wealth. The following day King of Massachusetts, where there were few slaves, echoed Rutledge: "that ye. number of inhabitants was not the proper index of ability & wealth; that property was the primary object of Society; and that in fixing a ratio this ought not to be excluded from the estimate" (1:541). And Butler "contended strenuously that property was the only just measure of representation. This was the great object of Government: the great cause of war, the great means of carrying it on" (1:542). This contention was the basis for South Carolina's later vote against the Connecticut Compromise.

On the other hand, the contrary argument was well summarized by Pinckney: "The value of land had been found on full investigation to be an impracticable rule. The contributions of revenue including imports & exports, must be too changeable in their amount; too difficult to be adjusted; and too injurious to the noncommercial States. The number of inhabitants appeared to him the only just & practicable rule" (1:542). His argument was not that numbers rather than wealth should be the rule, but that wealth was best measured by numbers. This is clear from his desire to count slaves equally with other inhabitants.

A somewhat different view was expressed by Gerry, who wanted the "combined ratio of numbers of Inhabitants and of wealth, and not of either singly" (1:541). This view was reported by the Committee on Representation on July 9, using the phrase "wealth and number of inhabitants," which would seem to call for the counting of slaves equally and also for recognizing other forms of property. This paragraph of the report was accepted without debate, with only New York and New Jersey opposed (1:559–60). Paterson, however, then objected to the counting of slaves, pointing out that they were not counted by the southern states in the apportionment of their own legislatures (1:561).[11] King defended the southerners, saying "Eleven out of 13 of the States had agreed to consider Slaves in the apportionment of taxation; and taxation and Representation ought to go together" (1:562).

The committee report provided that the legislature "be authorized" and "possess authority" to make changes in representation as circumstances changed, but it was not required to make them. Randolph suspected that "a pretext would never be wanting to postpone alteration" so that power would remain in the hands that first held it—namely, the North (1:561).

The following day, when the southerners moved for the reduction of the representation of New Hampshire, Morris began to back away from them: "Property ought to have its weight; but not all the weight" (1:567). When Randolph formally moved to require the legislature to reallocate representatives periodically, Morris, depending on the committee report, "dwelt much on the danger of throwing such a preponderancy into the Western Scale, suggesting that in time the Western people wd. outnumber the Atlantic States. He wished therefore to put it in the power of the latter to keep a majority of votes in their own hands" (1:571).

On July 11 Sherman opposed and Mason supported the Randolph motion. Williamson, also supporting the mandatory approach, brought forward a substitute motion (which Randolph accepted) "that in order to ascertain the alterations that may happen in the population & wealth of the several States, a census shall be taken of the free white inhabitants" and three fifths of the others (1:579). Wealth was thus equated with slaves, and no other forms were included. Butler moved to strike out the fraction on the ground that slaves were as productive of wealth as were freemen, but only Delaware, South Carolina, and Georgia supported this motion (1:580–81). When Rutledge, also taking the mandatory approach, moved to substitute "the principles of wealth & population" instead of Williamson's proposal, however, Massachusetts and Pennsylvania joined with those three states, indicating that some delegates who opposed giving full weight to the special southern form of wealth nonetheless favored giving weight to wealth in

11. At this point Madison suggested a compromise that gained no support: free inhabitants as the basis for the first house, and, for the second, "which had for one of its primary objects the guardianship of property," the whole number, including slaves (1:562).

general (1:582, 586). The first clause of Williamson's proposal, for a census of free inhabitants, was then approved 6 to 4; but the second clause, for three fifths of the slaves, was defeated 4 to 6, with Connecticut voting for it and South Carolina against. The truncated proposal was then rejected by all states (1:586, 588).

In this debate the most divergent views were enunciated. The "great objection" of Morris to the Williamson proposal "was that the number of inhabitants was not a proper standard of wealth." Sherman, on the contrary, "thought the number of people alone the best rule for measuring wealth as well as representation." Disagreeing with both, Wilson considered wealth itself "an impracticable rule." And Madison, admitting that numbers were never "an accurate measure of wealth," nevertheless contended that "in the U. States" they were "sufficiently so for the object in contemplation." On the issue of requiring the legislature to adjust the representation, Morris, Wilson, and Read still opposed this, while Sherman and Gorham acknowledged themselves convinced by the arguments of Randolph and Mason for it (1:581–85). Madison well summarized the subject in his ridicule of Morris: "at the same time that he recommended . . . implicit confidence to the Southern States in the Northern Majority, he was still more zealous in exhorting all to a jealousy of a Western majority" (1:584).

To break the impasse, Morris took up the following day the hint that King had thrown out on July 9 (1:562) and moved that a proviso be added that "direct taxation ought to be proportioned to representation" (1:591–93). This evoked kind words from Mason, C. C. Pinckney, and Wilson and was approved unanimously. But the counting of slaves as a measure of wealth remained a stumbling block, with Davie saying that unless "at least" three fifths of them were counted North Carolina "would never confederate" and "the business was at an end," to which Morris responded that he "verily believed the people of Pena. will never agree to a representation of Negroes" (1:593).

C. C. Pinckney again made it clear that "the rule of wealth should be ascertained and not left to the pleasure of the Legislature; and that property in slaves should not be exposed to danger under a Govt. instituted for the protection of property" (1:593–94). To implement this a motion was hammered out by Ellsworth, Randolph, and Wilson. It provided that representation should be proportioned to taxation and taxation to the census of free inhabitants and three fifths of the slaves, so that representation was related to wealth only indirectly, through taxation, thus making the counting of slaves more acceptable to the North. Charles Pinckney, repeating much of

Butler's argument of the previous day, tried to amend this to count all of the slaves, but only South Carolina and Georgia voted with him (1:594–96).[12] The motion was then approved by 6 to 2, with Massachusetts and South Carolina divided and New Jersey and Delaware voting "no" just as they had done on June 11 and July 9 (1:597).

Seeing in this vote an assurance that three fifths of the slaves would be counted, the southerners on the following day made a new bid for additional power. Randolph moved to strike out wealth as a separate rule in reapportionment of representatives in order to eliminate all forms of wealth that would increase northern representation, leaving the special southern form intact (1:603). This provoked Morris into a lengthy and candid speech of opposition. "The Southern Gentlemen," he said, "will not be satisfied unless they see the way open to their gaining a majority in the public Councils." Such a transfer of power "from the maritime to the interior & landed interest" would bring on an "oppression of commerce" and war with Spain over the Mississippi—"everything was to be apprehended from their getting the power into their hands." He would even, he said, "vote for ye. vicious principle of equality in the 2d. branch in order to provide some defence for the N. States agst. it." If the distinction between northern and southern states was real (and his own attitude attested to its reality), "instead of attempting to blend incompatible things, let us at once take a friendly leave of each other" (1:604–5).

In reply Butler took advantage of a remark by Morris to deny "that N. C.[,] S. C. & Geo. would have more people than all the other States." "The security the Southn. States want is that their negroes may not be taken from them which some gentlemen within or without doors, have a very good mind to do" (1:605).

Wilson also replied, displaying the grounds for northern acquiescence in Randolph's proposal. Proportional representation in both branches of the legislature being, for him, the main point, he rejected the "vicious principle of equality" for the Senate, and generalized PR from states to geographic areas. "The majority of people wherever found ought in all questions to govern the minority." Conceiving that "all men wherever placed have equal rights and are equally entitled to confidence," he expected that, if the "interior Country" should gain a majority, "they will not only have the right, but will avail themselves of it whether we will or no." The failure of Great

12. Johnson of Connecticut and two Pennsylvania delegates also voted "ay," but Delaware, which had supported the same position the day before, now opposed it.

Britain to understand this had led to the Revolution, and "Like consequences will result on the part of the interior settlements, if like jealousy & policy be pursued on ours." Moreover, neither Congress nor any state had been able to propose a better measure of wealth than the "rule of numbers." Wilson "could not agree that property was the sole or the primary object of Governt. & Society. The cultivation & improvement of the human mind was the most noble object. With respect to this object, as well as to other *personal* rights, numbers were surely the natural & precise measure of Representation. And with respect to property, they could not vary much from the precise measure" (1:605–6).

The vote was then taken on the Randolph motion, no one, so far as the *Records* show, having joined Morris in his opposition. Delaware was divided, but the other nine states voted to strike out "wealth" (1:606).

Some part of this consensus may be attributed to the cogency of Wilson's reasoning, but the larger part came from the gradual but general acceptance of two ideas: that, as Wilson phrased it, "the rule of numbers, does not differ much from the combined rule of numbers & wealth," and that, if a division of the Union was to be avoided, three fifths of the slaves would have to be counted. Behind northern accession to this second idea lay the quid pro quo mentioned frankly by King on July 9: "If the latter [the northern states] expect those preferential distinctions in Commerce & other advantages which they will derive from the connection they must not expect to receive them without allowing some advantages in return" (1:562). It was not a consensus in favor of numbers instead of wealth. In this whole debate not one delegate stood up consistently for free inhabitants alone as the basis for representation. Wealth per se was thus overwhelmingly rejected, but only after the Convention was satisfied that the numbers rule adopted would adequately measure it.

Property Qualifications for Voting

The second of the three provisions (above, p. 88) bearing directly upon the role of wealth was property qualifications for the suffrage. It stimulated much less debate and can be covered more briefly.

Although differences among the states on this matter had been mentioned by Hamilton (1:465) and Madison (2:57), no proposal for a uniform national suffrage had been made before the Committee of Detail began its work on July 23. The Randolph draft for the Committee contained a property alternative to residence or militia service, but it was crossed out; the first

Wilson draft required "a Freehold Estate in at least fifty Acres of Land" (2:140, 151). The Committee, however, abandoned the search for a uniform rule, and its report read: "The qualifications of the electors shall be the same, from time to time, as those of the electors in the several States, of the most numerous branch of their own legislatures" (2:178).

This provision was debated on August 7 and 8, after Morris moved to delete it. Dickinson, Morris, and Madison made an effort to confine the suffrage to freeholders. Dickinson "considered them as the best guardians of liberty" against "the dangerous influence of those multitudes without property & without principle, with which our Country like all others, will in time abound." Morris went further: "Give the votes to people who have no property, and they will sell them to the rich who will be able to buy them," and thus an "aristocracy will grow out of the House of Representatives" (2:202). Madison agreed: freeholders would be the "safest depositories of Republican liberty." In the future "a great majority" of the people would be without property and would either combine against "the rights of property & public liberty" or else "become the tools of opulence and ambition" (2:203–4). They professed to think a restriction of the suffrage to freeholders would be popular, because "the great mass" (Dickinson), even "9/10" (Morris), of the people were freeholders.

These views were opposed by at least eight speakers. "The people will not readily subscribe to the Natl. Constitution," Ellsworth pointed out, "if it should subject them to be disfranchised." "Eight or nine States," Mason added, "have extended the right of suffrage beyond the freeholders." Butler and Rutledge also took up this point. Mason's main argument was "that every man having evidence of attachment to & permanent common interest with the Society ought to share in all its rights & privileges" and that "the merchant, the monied man, the parent of a number of children," as well as the landowner, shared such attachments and interests. Ellsworth also advanced the basic principle that "every man who pays a tax," which would include wealthy merchants and manufacturers, ought "to vote for the representative who is to levy & dispose of his money." Franklin drew upon British history in a more practical vein, saying that Parliament had restricted the franchise and then oppressed the nonvoters, making them less patriotic than the Americans, as the Revolutionary War had shown. "It is of great consequence that we shd. not depress the virtue & public spirit of our common people" (2:201–5).

The Morris proposal to delete carried only Delaware, with Maryland divided and New Jersey and Georgia absent (2:206). Continuing the debate briefly the next day, Gorham said, "The elections in Phila. N. York & Boston where the Merchants, & Mechanics vote are at least as good as those made by freeholders only" and recommended that the "rooted prejudices" of the people be consulted "if we expect their concurrence in our propositions." The Committee provision was then approved by all states (2:216). It was not again challenged and became part of the Constitution.

How is this brief episode to be interpreted? If consistently guided by a desire to reduce the influences of states upon their new government, the delegates might have seen a uniform national suffrage rule as a necessity. If guided by economic considerations, they might have written such a rule either in terms of property or, if personalty dominated their thinking, in terms of manhood suffrage with the idea of influencing their economic dependents. Yet they did none of these things.

Gouverneur Morris, identified with the commercial interests of Philadelphia, was a leading advocate of the freehold franchise. Could he have been serious about this? If he wanted to disfranchise "the ignorant & the dependent," as he said, he might have attracted support for his proposal by including personalty or taxpaying alternatives to the freehold—fifty acres or £50 estate, for example. He did not do this, nor, surprisingly, did anyone else.[13]

Another surprising element is the resurgence of state orientation in the plan proposed by the Committee of Detail. Of these five men (Ellsworth, Gorham, Randolph, Rutledge, and Wilson), the majority were from the large states, and four were strong nationalists. From them a uniform rule, perhaps a property rule, might be expected. Having won PR in the first house and accepted defeat on equality in the Senate, they had settled their most basic issues. The states, however, could not be excluded from the system, so it was best to use them where possible in aid of ratification. The Committee provision had the great advantage over a uniform rule that it avoided controversy in every state without leaving the matter in the hands of the state legislatures.

Those who tried to substitute a freehold provision were not unaware of its relation to ratification. They relied on the preponderance of freeholders in the voting population, Madison saying that his own view would "depend much on the probable reception" of the change "in States where the right

13. Fifty acres was mentioned in five state constitutions, and estates from £10 to £60 in six. The alternative Morris proposed (reported by King but omitted by Madison) was "to leave it to the Legislature to establish the Qualifications of Electors & Elected." This was opposed by Mason, Franklin, and Madison (2:206–7).

was now exercised by every description of people" (2:203). They differed from the Committee in trying to provide for the remote future. Dickinson foresaw, as noted above, "multitudes without property." "The time is not distant," Morris added, "when this Country will abound with mechanics & manufacturers who will receive their bread from their employers" (2:202). And Madison too (as quoted on p. 95)—they all expressed a belief that the kind of political virtue they desired would be safer, in the long run, in the hands of the landowning yeomanry than in those of the wealthy, the "aristocracy," or the plebs.

Did the Convention, in rejecting the freehold suffrage, also reject this belief? Had another uniform rule been adopted, one might answer with confidence, "yes." It seems, however, that most delegates did not view the suffrage as an important matter to be decided on the basis of principle, but rather as a matter of expediency in the coming ratification struggle. Some, like Mason and Franklin, stood on principle, but expedient arguments were more numerous. It seems probable also that some may have decided, on practical grounds, to apply property requirements to the elected rather than to the electors.

Property Qualifications for Office

The third provision bearing directly upon the role of wealth (above, p. 88) was property qualifications for office holding.

Virginia was not one of the states then using such qualifications,[14] and the Virginia Plan contained no such provision. However, it was a Virginian, Mason, who first suggested on June 26 that such a requirement would be appropriate for senators, since the Senate "was to secure the rights of property" (1:428). A month later Mason, seconded by Pinckney, moved "that the Committee of detail be instructed to receive a clause requiring certain qualifications of landed property & citizenship of the U. States in members of the Legislature . . ." (2:121).

This proposal was amended twice and accepted. The Pinckneys suggested the extension of such qualifications to the executive and the judiciary, which was agreed without debate and without opposition (2:122). Madison and Morris proposed the elimination of the word "landed," so that the Committee might consider other forms of property. Again no one spoke against this,

14. Special property requirements, increasing with the power of the office, were used in New Hampshire, Massachusetts, New Jersey, Maryland, North Carolina, South Carolina, and Georgia.

but Maryland voted "no" (2:124). The vote on Mason's motion was 8 to 3, with Connecticut, Pennsylvania, and Delaware opposed (2:125).

In this debate Morris, Dickinson, and Madison expressed the view that property qualifications "in the Electors would be much more effectual than in the elected." Dickinson "doubted the policy of interweaving into a Republican constitution a veneration for wealth." It seemed to him "improper that any man of merit should be subjected to disabilities in a Republic where merit was understood to form the great title to public trust, honors & rewards." Both Morris and King spoke of "the monied interest" being excluded if a landed property qualification were adopted. Madison, in moving to strike out "landed," argued that "[i]t was politic as well as just that the interests & rights of every class should be duly represented & understood in the public Councils." The "three principle [*sic*] classes" were the commercial, the manufacturing, and the landed. "These classes understand much less of each others interests & affairs, than men of the same class inhabiting different districts. It is particularly requisite therefore that the interests of one or two of them should not be left entirely to the care, or the impartiality of the third" (2:121–24).

The records of the Committee of Detail, however, show little effect from the Mason motion. The Randolph draft included a property qualification only for senators, but no type or amount was specified. It also had a marginal query on "landed property" for Representatives, but it was crossed out (2:141, 139; 4:41, 39). The second Wilson draft gave the legislature expressed power to set qualifications "of the Members of each House with Regard to Property," but it was silent with regard to the other branches (2:155–56). This phrasing was retained in the final Wilson draft and was reported by the Committee (2:165, 179).

When debated on August 10 this section of the Committee report was attacked from all sides. Pinckney scolded the Committee for failing to report "proper qualifications of property," so that the first legislature would meet without any and might set extreme qualifications—high or low. He was "opposed to the establishment of an undue aristocratic influence in the Constitution but he thought it essential that the members of the Legislature, the Executive, and the Judges—should be possessed of competent property to make them independent & respectable." He therefore proposed the requiring of "a clear unincumbered Estate" in a specified amount for each office. Supporting him, Rutledge admitted that the Committee had reported no amounts because it could not agree, "being embarrassed by the danger on one side of displeasing the people by making them high, and on the other of rendering them nugatory by making them low." Ellsworth, however, thought it "improper to have either *uniform* or *fixed* qualifications": if high enough to be "useful in the S. States" they would be "inapplicable to the E. States," and if "accommodated to the existing State of things among us" they might be "very inconvenient in some future state of them." Franklin, aroused to make one of his few extemporaneous speeches, pointed out that the constitution they were drafting would "be much read and attended to in Europe" and that any "great partiality to the rich—will not only hurt us in the esteem of the most liberal and enlightened men there, but discourage the common people from removing to this Country." Pinckney's motion was then "rejected by so general a *no* that the States were not called" (2:248–49).

The attack on the Committee report continued. Madison thought "the qualifications of electors and elected were fundamental articles in a Republican Govt. and ought to be fixed by the Constitution." Morris moved to strike out property "in order to leave the Legislature entirely at large" to set any requirements. This led Williamson to point out that any type of men who might control the first legislature, "lawyers for example, which is no improbable supposition," might then write requirements that only their own type could meet. Madison also opposed Morris, citing abuse of a similar power by Parliament. The amendment was defeated 4 to 7. Yet "property" was not to survive. Rutledge spoke against the legislature having this discretion; and Wilson himself, the author of the plan, agreed that "on the whole" it would be best to "let the Section go out," since the legislature would probably never establish a uniform rule "and this particular power would constructively exclude every other power of regulating qualifications." The section of property qualifications was then destroyed 7 to 3, with New Hampshire, Massachusetts, and Georgia still favoring it (2:249–51).

How is this seemingly paradoxical result to be explained? Eight states had supported Mason's original motion on July 26; why were only three supporting property qualifications on August 10? Several explanations emerge. Voting for committee consideration of such qualifications was clearly different from voting for the qualifications themselves. The delegates had become aware of the great differences of impact, from one state to another, of any specific levels of property requirements. When Pinckney indiscreetly said he "should not think of less than one hundred thousand dollars for the President" (2:248), he revealed the southern bias of his thinking and repelled all those who had an eye to ratification. The alternative, favorable to the North, of giving discretion to the legislature aroused the same fears that similar discretion with regard to reapportionment had aroused (above, pp. 91–94) and was attacked by every southerner who spoke. Because of these difficulties, many men who earlier had favored it abandoned the open provision of property qualifications.

Before this happened, however, a line of thought appeared by which such qualifications could be covertly accommodated without any risk to the prospects for ratification or any need to trust the new national legislature. Again it was Wilson who saw the solution: delete the provision so as not to "exclude every other power," namely, the state legislatures, that could then set locally significant property qualifications. By this line of thought the votes of July 26 and August 10 may be reconciled: at least five of the seven against the Committee provision may be seen as preferences for Wilson's local-option approach.

In this whole discussion, we should note, only Dickinson and Franklin spoke against property qualifications as such.

The Implications

To summarize this analysis of the three provisions for direct influence of wealth, we may notice the following:

1. In none of them did the Constitution emerge with an explicit expression of such influence
2. On representation, the southerners succeeded both in obtaining the three-fifths clause, giving representation for wealth in slaves, and in denying representation to all other forms
3. On the suffrage, the move for a freehold franchise was defeated, but no broader rule was considered, so that the property requirements in all the state constitutions were left intact
4. For office holding, property qualifications, although desired by many, fell victims of the wide disparity of wealth between North and South
5. Wilson's subtle suggestion that the states might impose such qualifications could apply only to the legislature, and even there it proved to be worthless

To comment on the analysis, some quite different things may be said. Expediency, as contrasted with principle, played a strong if not a decisive role in each of these decisions. This is most evident in the suffrage discussion; but even on representation, population was not accepted or even proposed as the sole just basis, but rather as the best available measure of wealth. So strong was the influence of expediency, especially the weather eye to the ratification struggle, that the delegates wrote a Constitution substantially less plutocratic than they would have written had they been guided only by the principles they professed.

The role of personal property is not at all prominent in any of the three debates. Ways had been found to express in the state constitutions various measures of both real and personal property, yet no specific measures were proposed in the Convention and no committee was charged to seek such rules. Toward the end of the debate on representation Wilson could say, "if numbers be not a proper rule, why is not some better rule pointed out. No one has yet ventured to attempt it" (1:605). Real property found a voice both in the freehold proposal and in the counting of slaves,[15] yet in neither case did commercial property show its strength of thought or of numbers of adherents. Had a personalty alternative to the freehold been presented, the suffrage decision might or might not have been different; but why was none proposed? To counterbalance the counting of slaves, the personalty interests could have put forward a peculiarly northern form of property (commissioned vessels, for example), but no such proposal emerged. The arguments were in terms of property; and the impression seems inescapable that the sharp distinction between personalty and realty, made by Beard and Brown, was of minor importance to the delegates.

The impression is even less escapable, however, that property in general was of great importance to them. They were acutely aware of its interrelations with government, and in particular with the role of the Convention in structuring a new government. Yet they perceived that these interrelations were very complex. The inroads of the state legislatures upon property may have been a prime reason for the movement that had led to the Convention, but the delegates were unwilling to set for the national legislature either property qualifications for office holding or suffrage requirements that differed from the state legislatures.

The Influence of Government on Wealth

The Convention preferred to deal with these complex property relations by indirection. When necessary, explicit provisions were inserted, but when

---

15. Slaves could be classed as personalty, but, aside from their importance to slave traders and their use as domestic servants, their main value was agricultural. In Virginia they were classed as realty and could be entailed like land. See Brown, *Charles Beard and the Constitution*, pp. 48, 114.

constitutional silence would serve the purpose it was used. Evidence of this has been seen in the defeat of each of the three attempts to give property a direct influence in the new government. Additional evidence appears in some of the provisions that related to the power of the new government over property.

It is not necessary to touch upon many of these provisions; only the commerce and slave trade compromise, the "obligation of contracts" clause, paper money, the public debts, and the power to create corporations will be analyzed. First the compromise.

Commerce and the Slave Trade

As has been mentioned, the delegates were quite aware of the conflicts between landed and commercial interests. As early as June 6 Madison said, "The landed interest has borne hard on the mercantile interest" (1:135). He used this distinction again on July 26 in opposing landed property as a qualification for office (above, p. 98), and Gerry (1:152), Morris (1:604), and others (1:402, 466) used it for various purposes. Yet there was no disagreement that the new government should have power to regulate commerce. This clause appeared first in the New Jersey Plan (1:243), was reported by the Committee of Detail, and was approved without debate or opposition on August 16 (2:308).

The conflicts were not over the commerce clause but rather over certain restrictions to be imposed on the legislative power: over taxes on exports, navigation acts, and the importation of slaves. Each of these had a quite narrow meaning, in spite of the general form of the restriction, and each had geographical implications. The exports of significance were tobacco, rice, and indigo—all products of the South. The navigation acts expected were preferences for American ships in the carrying of these products, which meant northern, mostly New England vessels, and less choice and higher rates for the southern exporters. And the slave trade meant importation of Africans into South Carolina and Georgia, the only states that had not already prohibited or sharply curtailed the trade. The sectional conflicts of interest are obvious.

The importance of these issues can hardly be exaggerated. George Mason, describing the compromise to Jefferson five years later, said that "the great principles of the Constn," from "such a one as he wd have set his hand & heart to," had been "changed in the last days of the Convention" through the influence of the coalition that had made this compromise (3:367). Luther

Martin, who left the Convention on September 3, expressed a similar view in his report to the Maryland legislature (3:301, 217); and Randolph, even while these late decisions were being made, warned that "if an accumulation of obnoxious ingredients should take place, that he could not give his assent to the plan" (2:453).

During the debate on representation for the slaves the southerners began to suspect that emancipation might be proposed (1:592, 605), so C. C. Pinckney demanded that the Committee of Detail "insert some security" against it (2:95). This the Committee did not explicitly do; however, it did deny to the legislature a power to tax or prohibit the importation of "such persons as the several States shall think proper to admit" (2:169, 183).

In a preliminary skirmish on part of the Committee report on August 8, King proposed that a time limit on importation be set and averred that he "never could agree to let them be imported without limitation & then be represented" (2:220). Morris also concluded a tirade against slavery by saying he "would sooner submit himself to a tax for paying for all the Negroes in the U. States. than saddle posterity with such a Constitution" (2:223). By August 21, however, when the main debate began, the men of the deep South had found a winning strategy. As Rutledge phrased it, "The true question at present is whether the Southn. States shall or shall not be parties to the Union" (2:364). With that threat of secession they would counter all arguments on importation, and, of course, if need be, on emancipation. Baldwin, Williamson, and the two Pinckneys reiterated similar views (2:364, 371–73). Wilson disagreed: "If S. C. & Georgia were themselves disposed to get rid of the importation of slaves in a short time as had been suggested, they would never refuse to Unite because the importation might be prohibited." Dickinson also "could not believe that the Southn. States would refuse to confederate on the account apprehended" (2:372). Others were not so sure. It would be "better to let the S. States import slaves," Sherman said, "than to part with them, if they made that a sine qua non" (2:374).

The votes were there to reject the Committee proposal on continuing the slave trade. C. C. Pinckney pointed out that Virginia "will gain by stopping the importations. Her slaves will rise in value, & she has more than she wants" (2:371). So four states at most might have voted for the proposal. Yet a vote would risk the secession.

Special restrictions on export taxes and on navigation acts also appeared first in the Committee of Detail. Even before the Committee was appointed C. C. Pinckney had linked "taxes on exports" with "an emancipation of slaves," insisting that the Committee "insert some security" for the southern states against both (2:95). And King linked such taxes with the three-fifths rule: "either slaves should not be represented, or exports should be taxable" (2:220). Clearly all of these subjects were interrelated, and on each of them northern and southern interests clashed.

On export taxes the Committee reported an absolute prohibition. Morris, Madison, and Wilson objected to this, but Sherman replied that "[a] power to tax exports would shipwreck the whole" (2:306–8). After lengthy debate Madison tried to "require ⅔ of each House" to tax exports, "as a lesser evil than a total prohibition." He failed, 5 to 6, defeated in his own state by Mason, Randolph, and Blair. The prohibition then passed, 7 to 4 (2:363–64).

On navigation laws, Randolph proposed in the Committee of Detail that eleven states in the Senate and ten in the House be required. Rutledge reduced this to two thirds in each house, and carried the Committee with him in its final report (2:143, 169, 183). Four southern states, with twenty-three representatives out of sixty-five, would then be able to prevent such acts.

This section of the report encountered such heavy weather that Gouverneur Morris proposed, on August 22, that the "whole subject"—the slave trade, export taxes, and navigation acts—be given to a committee: "These things may form a bargain among the Northern & Southern States." Gorham demanded to know if the intention was to require "a greater proportion of votes" to pass navigation acts. He wanted it "to be remembered that the Eastern States had no motive to Union but a commercial one. They were able to protect themselves. They were not afraid of external danger, and did not need the aid of the Southern States" (2:374). On this threatening note and without much optimism the experiment was tried; one member from each state formed a committee on the slave trade, capitation taxes, and navigation acts.[16]

Its report, providing for importations of slaves until 1800, subject to average import duty, and striking out the two-thirds requirement for navigation acts, was taken up two days later. Immediately C. C. Pinckney, a member of the committee, moved to insert 1808 instead of 1800. Only Madison, another member, futilely spoke against this, and it was approved, 7 to 4. After some desultory debate the slave trade clause was approved by an identical vote, New Jersey, Pennsylvania, Delaware, and Virginia being

16. Export taxes were not referred, as being already settled.

the minority. The import-duty phrase, amended to read "not exceeding ten dollars for each person," was then approved, but the clause on navigation acts was postponed (2:415–17).[17]

On August 29 some of the southerners tried to reinstate the two-thirds requirement for navigation acts. An acrimonious debate ensued. "The *Majority* will be governed by their interests," Mason said. "The Southern States are the *minority* in both Houses. Is it to be expected that they will deliver themselves bound hand & foot to the Eastern States[?]" (2:451). And Randolph thought that the Constitution contained "features so odious" already that he "doubted whether he should be able to agree to it. A rejection of the motion [for two thirds] would complete the deformity of the system" (2:452). On the other hand, "If the Government is to be so fettered as to be unable to relieve the Eastern States," Gorham responded, "what motive can they have to join in it, and thereby tie their own hands from measures which they could otherwise take for themselves. The Eastern States were not led to strengthen the Union by fear for their own safety." On the vote, four states—Maryland, Virginia, North Carolina, and Georgia—favored the two-thirds requirement, in effect voting to repudiate the compromise (2:453). To them, it would seem, free access to foreign shipping was more important than the agreement to continue the slave trade.[18]

By this compromise the plantation owners of the deep South were given twenty years to import African slaves instead of buying from Virginia. In exchange, the national legislature was empowered to stop the slave trade thereafter, and also in the meantime to restrict foreign shipping by a simple majority and to tax the slaves imported. The northern states, very interested in the power to enact navigation laws, gained a permanent objective while South Carolina and Georgia gained a temporary one. Virginia, wanting neither the slave trade nor navigation laws, lost on both counts, which strongly contributed to the fact that, of a total of three delegates who refused to sign the Constitution at the end, two were from Virginia.

It might seem that the southerners made a bad bargain. In the end it was, but it must be remembered that the belief was then current that the population would grow more rapidly in the South. In twenty years the

17. Not content with this victory, the southerners sought further to guarantee it. When the amending article was reached in the course of the debates (September 10), Rutledge obtained an exemption for the slave trade from amendments prior to 1808. There is, strangely enough, no record of the vote on this (2:555, 559).

18. Mason tried again on September 15 to reinstate the two thirds rule until 1808 and was defeated by an identical vote, except that North Carolina was absent (2:631).

balance might be in their favor. Buying slaves from Virginia would not increase the census count in the exporting states, but buying Africans would. So continued importation was not only an economic stopgap; it could also contribute to control of the national councils. Later, when these expectations were disappointed, the southerners would lean on the Senate, with its equal power for each state; but at Philadelphia they were clearly looking toward the House of Representatives.

There was also the point that, by playing the secession threat successfully in regard to the slave trade, the southerners foreclosed whatever moves may have been intended toward the termination of slavery itself. The *Records* display little evidence of any such intention, except the fears expressed by the southern delegates (e.g., 1:605, 2:95) themselves, but the remark of Morris quoted above (p. 103) shows that constructive thought was being given to a general emancipation. Yet it seems clear that, if the secession gambit had been declined, Virginia would not have gone with South Carolina on the slave trade as it was later to do on slavery itself. Depending on the terms worked out, it is not certain that Georgia would have, either (there was almost no opposition to ratification in that state), or even that South Carolina itself would have adhered to secession. Thus the eagerness of the commercial interests for a navigation act resulted in twenty more years of the slave trade. It also served to squander the best and last opportunity to arrive at an agreed procedure for ultimate emancipation. The cotton gin came in 1793.

Obligation of Contracts

The second of the indirect influences on property to be dealt with (above, p. 102) is the "obligation of contracts" clause of Article I, Section 10.

Considering the importance attached by many delegates to the curtailment of the economic powers of the state governments, and the effectiveness with which this clause was later used for that purpose, it is surprising to find in the *Records* no mention of the impairment of contracts until August 28. However, the Sherman Plan (3:616), which Farrand considered to be a contribution to the New Jersey Plan and which may be even earlier than that, clearly spelled out the idea: "That the legislatures of the individual states ought not to possess a right to emit bills of credit for a currency, or to make any tender laws for the payment or discharge of debts or contracts, in any manner different from the agreement of the parties. . . ." Why, then, was the protection of contracts not incorporated into the New Jersey Plan or introduced early on the floor, if the delegates were motivated as Beard has suggested?

The Convention had just made the rule against paper money an absolute, rather than a conditional, prohibition when King moved to add "a prohibition on the States to interfere in private contracts" (2:439). "This would be going too far" was the instant response, even from Gouverneur Morris. The new national courts "will be a protection" in diversity-of-citizenship cases, he continued, "and within the State itself a majority must rule, whatever may be the mischief done among themselves." Mason also thought "this is carrying the restraint too far," while Madison, Sherman, and Wilson supported King.

It would seem, however, that this convention of lawyers was not quite surefooted on this ground. Wilson said that the motion was confined to "*retrospective* interferences," whereupon Madison asked, "Is not that already done by the prohibition of ex post facto laws" (2:440), forgetting that the provision adopted the week before applied only to the national legislature. Thereupon Rutledge, following Wilson's thought, moved a substitution for King's motion, the absolute prohibition of bills of attainder and ex post facto laws to the states. This was passed by seven states against Connecticut, Maryland, and Virginia (2:440). But on the following day, having consulted Blackstone, Dickinson was able to tell the delegates that the Rutledge substitute had not touched contracts after all: "ex post facto" related to criminal cases only. "Some further provision for this purpose would be requisite." Neither he nor King nor Sherman was sufficiently interested to offer such a motion, however (2:448–49).[19]

Or did they judge it tactically more expedient to avoid debate on a separate contract motion? In any event, the "further provision" appeared two weeks later in the report of the Committee of Style, of which King was a member (2:597). It was reached at the end of the day on September 14 and was approved without debate or opposition. An effort by Gerry to lay the same prohibition on Congress was not seconded, so eager were they to adjourn (2:619).

It would seem that, having dealt with paper money and tender laws, the delegates, with the exceptions of King and Gerry, did not see much importance in the contract clause.

Paper Money

The antagonism to paper money was general, vehement, and explicit from the beginning of the Convention. In introducing the Virginia Plan, Randolph

---

19. Blackstone's view of ex post facto prevailed in *Calder v. Bull*, 3 Dallas 386 (1798), but Marshall rejected it in *Fletcher v. Peck*, 6 Cranch 87 (1810) at 138–39, a civil case.

said, according to McHenry, "Congress ought to possess a power to prevent emissions of bills of credit" (1:26). Paper, legal-tender, and installment laws were frequently deprecated in a variety of contexts by Gerry, Hamilton, Morris, and others (1:165, 288; 2:26, 299). The maverick Mercer, on the other hand, proclaimed himself "a friend to paper money" (2:309); and in between these extremes some delegates sought some restraint short of prohibition. Randolph and the Committee of Detail, for example, in formulating specific rules, included among the powers of the new government one to "emit bills" of credit, and at the same time prohibited state emissions and tender laws "without the consent of the Legislature of the United States" (2:182, 187).

When the first of these clauses came up for debate, August 16, Morris moved to strike it out, saying "The Monied interest will oppose the plan of Government, if paper emissions be not prohibited" (2:309). This stimulated the expression of a variety of views. Butler seconded the motion; Madison thought it "sufficient to prohibit the making them a *tender*"; Gorham was for striking out "without inserting any prohibition"; Mason, while declaring a "mortal hatred to a paper money," was "unwilling to tie the hands of the Legislature"; and Mercer thought it "impolitic also to excite the opposition of all those who were friends to paper money." Ellsworth "thought this a favorable moment to shut and bar the door against paper money"; Read thought the words, if not struck out, would be "as alarming as the mark of the Beast in Revelations"; and Langdon "had rather reject the whole plan" than to retain the words "emit bills." So, with New Jersey and Maryland only in the negative, they were struck out (2:308–10).

On August 28 the second clause, against state emissions and tender laws, came up. Wilson and Sherman moved to make the prohibition absolute. After a brief debate this too was done, only Virginia voting "no" and Maryland being divided (2:439). The Convention thus went far beyond Randolph's original plan to empower Congress to prevent state bills of credit: Congress was given no power to emit bills or to authorize state bills. But, strangely enough, Morris did not then or later make a motion for an express prohibition on Congress.

Public Debts

Future emissions were thus, hopefully, foreclosed; but what of the various forms of paper, national and state, that had been generated during the Revolution? These securities, greatly depreciated, were traded in commercial circles and were the objects of much political maneuvering at both state and national levels. Partly on the basis of later evidence, Beard argued elaborately that the delegates themselves were strongly motivated by their personal holdings of public securities.[20] However that might be, some of them at least, as Jensen made clear,[21] were very aware of the influence that the methods of payment of the public debt would have on the balance of power between the central and the state governments. One would expect that the nationalists would be diligent in providing for central assumption of state debts and for payment, thus drawing all creditors to the support of the proposed government. On the other hand, they knew that the influence of methods of payment was equally well understood by the enemies of centralization. Any explicit provision for assumption, or even for payment, might prove too costly in the struggle for ratification. The nationalists, therefore, would be expected to proceed by cautious indirection.

The Virginia Plan provided for the "completion" of all the "engagements" of the old Congress; this was approved without debate on June 5, Connecticut and Delaware voting "no" (1:22, 121). On July 18, however, the Convention, still unsettled by the Connecticut compromise, rejected the clause unanimously (2:47). In the Committee of Detail, Randolph tried to introduce the payment of debts as a purpose of the taxing clause (2:142), but this was omitted from the Wilson draft and from the final report (2:167, 181).

Suddenly on August 18, the subject came alive, with a series of proposals made by Rutledge, Gerry, and Sherman. The payment of the public debt and the security of creditors were referred to the Committee of Detail (2:325–26). Rutledge and King argued well the case for the assumption of the state debts. "The assumption," the former said, "would be just as the State debts were contracted in the common defense. It was necessary, as the taxes on imports, the only sure source of revenue, were to be given up to the Union. It was politic, as by disburdening the people of the State debts it would conciliate them to the plan." To this King added, "the State Creditors an active and formidable party would otherwise be opposed to a plan which transferred to the Union the best resources of the States without transferring the State debts at the same time." They proposed a committee of a member from each state to consider the matter, and this was carried; but only just: New Hampshire, New Jersey, Delaware, and Maryland voted against it, and Pennsylvania was divided (2:327–28).[22]

Three days later the committee reported: "The Legislature of the U.S. shall have power to fulfil the engagements which have been entered into by

20. *An Economic Interpretation of the Constitution of the United States*, chapter 5, criticized by Brown, *Charles Beard and the Constitution*, chapter 5.
21. Merrill Jensen, *The New Nation*, pp. 45–46, 61–62, 377, 388–89.
22. The committee consisted of Langdon, King, Sherman, Livingston, Clymer, Dickinson, McHenry, Mason, Williamson, C. C. Pinckney, and Baldwin.

Congress, and to discharge as well the debts of the U—— S: as the debts incurred by the several States during the late war, for the common defence and general welfare" (2:355–56). This gave "the power only, without adopting the obligation," Gerry quickly pointed out, thus "destroying the security now enjoyed by the public creditors of the U—— States." He urged also that the states that had done most to repay their debts "would be alarmed, if they were now to be saddled with a share of the debts of States which had done least." Sherman joined in with the remark, "It means neither more nor less than the confederation as it relates to this subject" (2:356). In further debate the following day, Ellsworth thought the whole clause unnecessary, but he was contradicted by Randolph, Madison, and Gerry. Thereupon Morris moved a substitute that answered Gerry's first objection and also carefully omitted reference to state debts: "The Legislature *shall* discharge the debts & fulfil the engagements of the U. States." This was approved by all the states (2:377). The case against the assumption of state debts was never made, so far as the *Records* show, yet that provision was thus cut out, without explanation or objection, and not again revived. It may have been concluded, in the circle around Robert Morris, that express provision for state debts would be unwise.[23] It would, as Gerry said, alarm the states that had done most to pay their own debts, which included Massachusetts and Virginia. It would be an open challenge to the policy of the states that had assumed parts of the national debt owed to their own citizens, including New York, Pennsylvania, Maryland, and South Carolina. On the other hand, without such a provision the new legislature could still take over the state debts that had been incurred in the common defense during the Revolution. The eighth Article of Confederation had provided that "[a]ll charges of war and other expenses, that shall be incurred for the common defence or general welfare, and allowed by the United States, in Congress assembled, shall be defrayed out of a common treasury. . . ." As Johnson said, "Changing the Government cannot change the obligation of the U—— S—— which devolves of course on the New Government" (2:414).

The Morris substitute, rephrased but still without the state debts, was again agreed, without a recorded vote, the next day (2:392); but on August 24 Butler, C. C. Pinckney, and Randolph obtained a reconsideration on grounds of the "different pretensions of different classes of holders" of the public debt, and of the lack of provisions for the state debts (2:400). In the ensuing discussion, the next morning, lengthy speeches were made but no

23. Congress had reached a similar decision on the express assumption of state debts when it proposed the impost in 1783. Worthington C. Ford, *Journals*, vol. 24 (ed. Gaillard Hunt), pp. 197, 257–61. The debt issue was resolved in the new Congress; see pp. 190–97 below.

one had a concrete motion for either of these purposes. Mason thought "the Creditors should be kept in the same plight" as before, and his view was echoed by Langdon and by Butler. Mason particularly wished "to leave open the door for buying up the securities" at a discount. Gerry, on the contrary, observed that "as the public had received the value of the literal amount, they ought to pay that value to somebody," although he would not object to "a revision of the debt so far as to compel restitution to the ignorant & distressed, who have been defrauded" (2:413). Neither of them made a motion. Randolph then caught the sentiments of the others, except for Gerry and Morris, in a motion to replace the "shall discharge" with "All debts contracted & engagements entered into, by or under the authority of Congress shall be as valid against the United States under this Constitution as under the Confederation." Over the opposition of Morris and Pennsylvania, ten states accepted this (2:414). The motion had the effect, not of bringing the state debts, as engagements under the authority of Article 8 of the Confederation, within the purview of the proposed government, but of making the obligation no more mandatory than before. So the Pennsylvanians opposed it both because it diluted the injunction "shall," as Morris argued, and because they preferred silence on the subject of the state debts.

Sherman's attempt again to connect the debts with the taxing clause, on the other hand, was rejected as unnecessary by ten states, only Connecticut supporting him. On the 31st, however, he obtained the appointment of a committee of eleven on postponed matters, and as a member of the committee persuaded it to report the purpose "to pay the debts and provide for the common defence & general welfare of the United States" as a part of the taxing clause (2:414, 481, 493). This time it passed without debate (2:499).

From this evidence one must conclude that provision for the public creditors was not a high-priority objective of many, if any, delegates. Vacillation and uncertainty of purpose marked their discussions and decisions regarding the debts. No one argued that the old debts should not be honored, or that specific provision for them would handicap ratification; it was only thought by some to be unnecessary. It was understood that the new power to tax would greatly improve the prospects of the security holders, but the power itself was aimed not toward that improvement but toward a "complete government" fiscally independent of the states. There were rather more expressions of antagonism toward some types of security holders than of a general sympathy with them.[24]

24. Butler referred to "the Blood-suckers who had speculated on the distresses of others," and Mason spoke of "those who purchased fraudulently of the ignorant and distressed," distinguishing them from both "original creditors" and "those who have bought Stock in open market" (2:392, 413).

At the same time, the phrases finally adopted made possible the payment of debts and obligations both national and state, as the new legislature might define them, and they did this without explicit mention of state debts and without any change in the existing obligation under the Articles of Confederation to pay them. The opponents of centralization were given little ammunition in the debt provisions.

Power to Create Corporations

Another clear illustration of the Convention dealing with property issues by indirection came in the matter of a power to grant charters to corporations. The problems encountered by Robert Morris in establishing and defending the Bank of North America from 1781 to 1787 had flashed warnings of the political passions that could be aroused by the idea of incorporation. They had also shown the advantage, to the commercial interests, of concurrent state and national powers of incorporation. So one might expect this matter to be provided for both carefully and unquestionably—but not necessarily explicitly.

None of the plans, not even Hamilton's, mentioned corporations, nor did they come up in the first two and a half months of debate. Finally the southerners introduced the subject. On August 18 both Madison and Pinckney, in their lists of additional powers to be referred to the Committee of Detail, proposed "to grant charters of incorporation" (2:325). The Committee never reported on this (and several other clauses), and these "postponed matters" were referred to the committee of eleven appointed on August 31 and mentioned above. This committee reported several times early in September, but never on incorporation.

Finally, September 14, Madison reintroduced the power to grant charters as an "enlargement" of Franklin's proposal of "a power to provide for cutting canals" (2:615). His "primary object," he said, was "an easy communication between the States" by the removal of the natural obstacles.

The motion was seconded by Randolph, and an enlightening discussion ensued. King thought the provision unnecessary and reminded the delegates of the conflicts that would be aroused over banks and monopolies. Wilson, on the contrary, thought the provision "necessary to prevent a *State* from obstructing the *general* welfare," and he denied that banks would excite the "prejudices and parties" that King apprehended. "Mercantile monopolies," he added, "are already included in the power to regulate trade." This last remark brought Mason to his feet. He was "afraid of monopolies of every sort," and he did not think they were "by any means already implied by the Constitution." A vote was then taken on Franklin's specific canal power. It was supported only by Pennsylvania, Virginia, and Georgia; Madison's more general motion was therefore dropped as clearly repudiated (2:615–16).

Many years later, as is well known, Chief Justice Marshall found the power to grant charters to be implied in the "necessary and proper" clause. That clause, however, had been before the Convention since early August and had been approved without cavil; yet neither Madison nor Wilson, two of the keenest constitutional minds in the group and both strong nationalists, thought that it included the charter power. In fact, this idea was never suggested by anyone. Had it been, the clause would have been given closer scrutiny than it ever received.

How, then, is the Convention's treatment of the power to create corporations to be interpreted? Can Madison, Pinckney, and Randolph be seen as spokesmen for the commercial interest of Philadelphia? Can the fluent Gouverneur Morris as well as the taciturn Robert have remained silent on a subject so close to their interests? Can Marshall have fabricated this part of the *McCulloch* opinion entirely from his own imagination?

Farrand's later *Records* shed some light on such questions. Jefferson recorded that Baldwin of Georgia had recounted in 1798 a conversation he had had with Wilson in 1791, while the bill to establish a national bank was being debated in the House of Representatives. According to Baldwin, he had reminded Wilson that in the Philadelphia Convention Robert Morris had "proposed to give Congress a power to establish a national bank," but that he had been opposed by Gouverneur Morris on the ground that such a power "would instantly enlist against the whole instrument, the whole of the anti-bank party in Pennsylvania" (3:376). Madison also, much later, attributed the rejection of the charter power to the dangers it would create for ratification (3:495). Madison's notes for September are much less copious than in June, so Baldwin's account may be authentic;[25] but even if this did not transpire on the floor of the Convention it may nonetheless be a reasonably accurate record of the two men's views expressed elsewhere. On that basis it would seem that Robert Morris was not a party, as might be expected, to a well-laid plan to smuggle the charter power into the Constitution hidden in the commerce or "necessary and proper" clauses.

25. Gerry, however, denied on the floor of the House in those same debates of 1791 that such a "motion" had been made in the Convention. Perhaps Morris "proposed" without making a formal motion; none is recorded in the *Journal* or in any of the notes.

The reports of King, nevertheless, suggest that he, at least, thought the power to incorporate was already provided. Why else would he call it "unnecessary"? He may have had in mind the fact that Congress had chartered the Bank of North America even though no such power was specified in the Articles of Confederation. It is doubtful that he was thinking of state incorporation as sufficient. Moreover, when the Senate was debating internal improvements in 1825 and he was the only surviving member of the Convention then in the Senate, he was asked directly whether the Convention had rejected the power to incorporate canals because it "intended to deny the power" or because it "believed the power was conferred in some other clause or grant." The editor of the *Register of Debates in Congress* reports in a footnote that King, "shaking his head, is understood to have said, 'Such a thing was not thought of' " (3:465–66). Yet it appears, on the contrary, that King, by ambiguously shaking his head, avoided making a clear statement against the idea that the power was believed to be conferred in some other clause. Such a statement would have strengthened the side he was then taking against internal improvements, so why did he not make it if it was true?

From this ambiguous, if not contradictory, evidence it is difficult to support the view that the content which Chief Justice Marshall found in "necessary and proper" was consciously put there by the Convention. It tends, instead, to support the ideas that: (1) the power to incorporate was not of prime importance to any of the delegates; (2) among those who favored it, agrarian interests were at least as important as commercial interests; (3) the anticipated costs in the ratification outweighed the gains the power might give; and (4) the advocates of the power, and their opponents as well, probably thought it was lost rather than covered by another clause.

The Implications

To summarize this survey of some of the provisions relating to the powers of the new government over property, we may say that only two of them really engaged the minds of the delegates. On paper money they were near unanimity from the beginning; all of the changes from the Virginia Plan were in the direction of strengthening the prohibition and were carried by large majorities. On the slave trade and navigation laws opinions diverged sharply, on lines not of principle but of sectional economic interest. Some, like Gouverneur Morris, expressed principled revulsion against the "nefarious practice" (2:222) yet preferred to seek a compromise rather than to test the resolution of the deep South. The New Englanders succeeded in splitting the southern states by offering the slave trade to South Carolina and Georgia in exchange for navigation acts by simple majority instead of two thirds in the legislature.

On the remaining three provisions—contracts, corporations, and debts— no deep concerns were expressed. True it is that, in the long run, each was decided to the advantage of creditor and commercial interests, but hardly after a concerted and continuous effort by such interests. The paucity of debate may indicate general consensus on these subjects, or, more likely, on the effects more explicit provisions would have on the prospects for ratification. Several conflicting moves regarding the debts ended in mention of them as a purpose of taxation, and in silence on the state debts. Gerry's late attempt to protect contracts explicitly against the national legislature was met with silence. And the power to create corporations apparently foundered in the Convention and had to be revived by the creative imagination of John Marshall.

One may conclude that the picture of the Convention as a gathering of rich men united and motivated by commercial interest is both exaggerated and distorted. No matter how accurately the researches of Beard or McDonald or others may detail the economic interests of the delegates, such researches must ultimately face up to what the delegates actually said and did in the Convention. There they displayed a great variety of motivations, among which commercial and property considerations, while clearly present, were clearly not often dominant. Even on questions of prime commercial importance they sometimes differed sharply in their views and sometimes (as on Franklin's canals) were quite indifferent. Economic matters, therefore, were not the top-priority concerns of very many of the delegates. The contrary interpretation, it may be suggested, has been a result of anachronistically attributing to the Founding Fathers the nation's prime concern with economic problems during the past century.

Economic matters, nevertheless, had an important bearing on the Convention that should not be forgotten. The resources of America (primarily land, settled and unsettled), in proportion to the population, had prevented the widespread grinding poverty so characteristic then of western Europe. Within six years the sansculottes of Paris, screaming their "memento mori," had turned a promising political revolution into an effort to deal with the impossible problems of poverty—a social revolution—from which the world has still not recovered. The economic context of America prevented that happening here. The Convention was able to stabilize a generation of traumatic change and to introduce an enduring political system before acute economic conflict arose to rearrange the agendas of the world's revolutions.

5

An Anti-Democratic Convention?

The well-known quotations from Randolph, his "Our chief danger arises from the democratic parts of our constitutions" and his "evils" found in the "turbulence and follies of democracy" (1:26, 51), coupled with Gerry's "excess of democracy" and his "danger of the levilling spirit" (1:48), to say nothing of Hamilton (1:288–89), have been accepted as expressions of a dominant attitude among the delegates. It is also accepted that the desire to restrain the states was motivated in part by the belief that the state governments were too responsive to the desires of the people. Yet it is easy to oversimplify these anti-democratic currents of thought, and thereby to miss the sophistication with which they influenced the Constitution. It was not only a matter of indirect election of presidents and senators, nor yet of review by permanent, nonelected judges, nor of the amending article. It was, in brief, a matter of delicately balancing the illusion of popular control against the reality of unresponsive power, because the people's sense of justice could not be trusted.

This chapter will take a long, hard look at the decision processes by which the convention incorporated many undemocratic features into the Constitution. It will also examine other such features that had strong advocates but were nevertheless rejected. With the decisions thus spread out, the question of motivations is raised. Were the delegates simply wealthy men protecting their property? Were they the "well born," trying to perpetuate their privileges? Or were they the wise, seeking to prevent the rule of the ignorant and the foolish?

All of these attitudes were involved, in varying proportions for different provisions; but the last was most important. The chapter will conclude that, since the popular legislatures were perceived to be unjust, the Constitution was intended to provide a system by which the making and the administering of the laws would be guided not by the popular will but by the most reasonable approximation to justice. This entailed enforceable restraints on the wills of both the rulers and the ruled, and the division of power among branches and by federal levels—the whole controlled by a written higher law.

The Founders thus understood, more clearly than their descendants, the potential conflict between popular sovereignty and the reign of law. Even if all power were in the people, as Sam Adams argued against John, since all legitimate power was limited, the people still were not sovereign.[1]

The House of Representatives

The popularly elected House of Representatives was the democratic part of the proposed government, of course, so the views regarding its structure should be particularly revealing. The general strategy of the nationalists was to use the people to overcome the state dominance of political life without giving to the people the sort of control over the new government that they sometimes had achieved over their state governments.

Wilson, the foremost advocate of popular election of representatives, argued that "all authority was derived from the people," that the govern-

1. The notion of popular sovereignty, so useful in wartime, was then in decline: "The people reigned, but in post-Revolutionary America the political elites made sure they did not rule." Daniel T. Rodgers, *Contested Truths: Keywords in American Politics since Independence* (New York, 1987), p. 86. See also Edmund S. Morgan, *Inventing the People: The Rise of Popular Sovereignty in England and America* (New York, 1988), especially chapters 3 and 11.

ment ought to reflect the "mind or sense of the people at large," and that the legislature "ought to be the most exact transcript of the whole Society" (1:132, 179). This line of reasoning was not directed toward broadening the suffrage or enlarging the legislature, however. His conclusion was that "equal numbers of people ought to have equal numbers of representatives" (1:179), that PR in both houses, and not state equality, should be the foundation of the new government (1:483). The idea of the people as the source of political authority, in other words, was being used not for democratic ends but to justify increased power for the large states.

The Size of the House

How exact a "transcript of the whole Society" was desired appears clearly in the size chosen for the first house. The Convention was determined to make the number as small as PR would permit, and then smaller still. The committee that reported the Connecticut compromise on July 5 "allowed 1 member for every 40,000 inhabitants," with each state having at least one (1:526). Filtered through two further committees, this came to a total of sixty-five members apportioned by states, so that Delaware and Rhode Island each had one and the three large states had fewer than their populations would justify. Madison tried on July 10, with the support of Mason, Read, and Gerry, to double the number, but carried only two states (1:570). In September two further attempts to get reconsideration of the clause carried five states, but the apportionment of July 10 survived all assaults. The 1 to 40,000 ratio, revived by the Committee of Detail, was made a maximum, on Madison's suggestion that the number would become "excessive" (2:221). It was changed to 30,000 only at the last possible moment after an intervention by Washington himself.

Both Madison and Mason argued that a majority of a quorum was "too small a number to make laws for America." They would be "too sparsely taken," would lack "local information," and would not possess the "confidence of the people" (1:568–69). Gerry pointed to the danger of corruption in so small a number, and Read added the danger that either Delaware or Rhode Island, with only one member, might have no voice at all "in case of accident" (1:569–70). On the other side, the objection of expense, the "increase from New States," and the difficulty of prevailing on "a sufficient number of fit men" to travel to the seat of government were used. Ellsworth said that "most" and Rutledge that "all" state legislatures were too large. "The greater the number," according to Ellsworth, "the more slowly would

the business proceed; and the less probably be decided as it ought, at last"
(1:569). In this debate Wilson, although present, had nothing to say.

It seems clear that the new-states argument could have been obviated by
reallocation, whatever the desired total, as Gerry and Read suggested at the
time and as it long has been at 435. The expense argument had been used
also in regard to the proposed inferior courts (1:125), in each case by a
delegate from Connecticut, but it may not have carried much weight.[2] The
argument from the experience of Congress was not made, but the perennial
problem with its quorum, well known to the delegates, gave force to the
argument about "fit men" being unwilling to travel to the seat of government. Nineteen of those chosen for the Convention itself had refused to
attend. It may be concluded, therefore, that an element of realism obtained
in the small size selected; yet it also seems probable that it was selected as
a positive good in itself: the smaller the number the more certain it would
be that only "fit men" would be elected as representatives. The democratic
part of the new government was thus so structured that, far from being a
"transcript" of the people, in practice only quite outstanding men could
attain seats.

That this result was intended in the Virginia Plan can be deduced from
Randolph's response to Spaight's proposal on May 31 that the second branch
be elected by the state legislatures. This would not, Randolph thought,
produce the check intended on the "fury of democracy," the state legislatures themselves being democratic. If the senators were appointed by the
first branch, on the contrary, "then the check would be compleat" (1:58).

The Term of Office

At the state level, popular control over legislation was largely a function of
frequent, direct elections. On both these points attempts were made to
reduce such control over the new legislature; they succeeded on the matter
of long terms of office, but not in eliminating direct election in the first
house.

All the states save South Carolina required annual elections for the
legislators. On June 12 Sherman and Ellsworth moved for annual election of
the first branch. Rutledge proposed two years, and Jenifer proposed three
as an inducement to the "best men" to serve. Madison seconded three

2. This was the estimate of Lansing, expressed in the New York ratifying convention (Farrand,
Records, 3:336).

years, saying that "instability is one of the great vices of our republics, to be remedied" and that "in a Government so extensive" three years would be needed "to form any knowledge of the various interests" of other states. Gerry, on the other hand, "considered annual Elections as the only defence of the people agst. tyranny" and said that the people of New England would never give them up. A vote of 7 to 4 then fixed the three-year term, Massachusetts, Connecticut, and North and South Carolina being opposed (1:214–15).

Nine days later Randolph moved to change this to two years on the ground that "the people were attached to frequency of elections." Annual elections were a "source of great mischiefs in the States," he admitted, "yet it was the want of such checks agst. the popular intemperance as were now proposed" that made them so (1:360). If adequately checked, in other words, the people could be indulged. Hamilton, however, believed that "the checks in the other branches of Governt. would be but feeble, and would need every auxiliary principle that could be interwoven." Three years, he felt, would be neither too much nor too little "dependence" on "popular sentiments" (1:362). Madison also opposed the change, emphasizing the inconvenience of so much travel by the representatives. Ellsworth preferred one year, since "the people were fond of frequent elections and might be safely indulged" in one branch (1:361). Wilson also preferred one year, as being "pleasing to the people" and "making the 1st. branch an effectual representation of the people at large" (1:361). Strong and Sherman also spoke for one year, but no vote was taken on this. The change to two years carried 7 to 3, with New York, Delaware, and Maryland holding out for three years and New Jersey divided (1:360–62). This early compromise decision was never reopened, yet only Mason had presented positive advantages of the two-year term: it would coincide with state elections in all the states, and it would avoid the geographical advantage that annual elections would give to the central states. At least ten delegates preferred the three-year term, and only five are on record for annual election.

Direct Election

Direct popular election was used by all the states for one or both houses of the legislature, and one might expect that, aside from those delegates who wanted to continue the Articles government, direct election of at least one house of the new government would be readily accepted. The Virginia Plan so provided; yet three separate attempts were made to eliminate popular election entirely. "The people do not want virtue," Gerry admitted on May 31, but "they are daily misled into the most baneful measures and opinions" by designing men. Even so, he would not object to popular election "if it were so qualified that men of honor & character" would stand for office. He was supported by Sherman and Butler, but opposed by Madison, Mason, and Wilson, and direct election was approved by six states against New Jersey and South Carolina, with Connecticut and Delaware divided (1:48–50).

Within a week, however, Pinckney secured a reconsideration and moved that the first branch be elected by the state legislatures, since "the people were less fit Judges." He was supported by Rutledge and by C. C. Pinckney, who thought the people so scattered, particularly in South Carolina, as to make direct election "totally impracticable." Gerry now thought the people needed a role in one branch "to inspire them with the necessary confidence" and suggested that they nominate twice the number "out of whom the State Legislatures shd. make the appointment." On the other side, Madison, Mason, and Wilson were joined by Dickinson and Pierce, both of whom argued that state legislatures should choose one house and the people the other. The vote on Pinckney's motion showed eight states for popular election and Connecticut, New Jersey, and South Carolina against (1:132–38).[3]

The South Carolina delegates were still unwilling to accept defeat. On June 21 C. C. Pinckney, seconded by Luther Martin, tried again with a proposal that state legislatures be permitted to choose the method of election. Rutledge suggested election by the legislatures "would be more refined" than popular election, as witness the Convention itself: the people would not have elected "such proper characters." This time Hamilton joined in the fray. The South Carolina proposal "would essentially vitiate the plan," he said. "It would increase that State influence which could not be too watchfully guarded against." Mason urged the retention of popular election as "the only security for the rights of the people." Wilson considered it "not only as the corner Stone, but as the foundation of the fabric." And again direct election survived, but with only six states: Jenifer and Martin divided Maryland, and Delaware changed sides (1:358–60). Yet the impression comes through from these debates that it survived because it was needed to secure ratification and to reduce the influence of the state legislatures—not

3. The arrival of Johnson, who sided with Sherman, shifted Connecticut one way, and the presence of all five Delaware delegates shifted that state the other way. The arrival of Jenifer of Maryland made eleven states.

because of its inherent rightness or value but in spite of its disadvantages. Mason alone appears to have valued the "democratic principle" as a positive good, as a "dictate of humanity" and not a matter of expediency (1:49).

Rotation and Recall

The Virginia Plan provided two other elements of popular control of the first branch, rotation in office and recall of representatives (1:20). These were customary for members of Congress under the Articles, but not for the first house of the state legislatures. The Plan seems in this to lean toward more thoroughgoing democratic responsibility. However, the second branch could negative any bill passed by the first, and neither rotation nor recall was provided for it. It is possible that they were applied to the first house to retard the accumulation of experience among its members, while appearing to increase voter control. The point was to facilitate control over the popularly elected branch—not by the people but by the second branch. In any event both provisions seemed of so little value that they were stricken out on motion of Pinckney on June 12, without opposition and without recorded discussion, and never heard of again (1:217).

This change, opening the door to reelection, strengthened the first house vis-à-vis the second. Was it, then, a modification of the Virginia Plan in the direction of democracy? Pinckney had been from the beginning most eager to do away with direct election of the representatives. Already defeated twice on this, he had not abandoned hope. Clearly he was not trying to strengthen popular control but rather to weaken it, looking for ways to make the people's representatives less dependent upon the people. Had anyone wished to change the Virginia Plan in the direction of democracy in regard to this aspect of the balance between the two houses, his method would not have been the elimination of rotation and recall in the lower house but rather the extension of these provisions to the Senate as well. At no time, however, was such a proposal made.

The Senate

The first house being thus, by its small size and the elimination of annual election and the recall of members, rendered compatible with the undemocratic views of the delegates, why was a second house necessary? Was it conceived as primarily an additional restraint upon the legislative will of the people's representatives?

Why Bicameralism?

It was impossible for the Convention to debate the relative merits of bicameral and unicameral systems as abstractions. Experience with upper houses in the colonial legislatures and with Parliament might have been expected to lead to widespread unicameralism after independence. The distinctions of estates upon which the old practice rested supposedly had no basis in American society. Nevertheless eleven states established bicameral legislatures. Pennsylvania and Georgia (as well as Vermont) were unicameral, and Congress, of course. In Pennsylvania this feature was a bone of contention between its defenders, the Constitutionalist party, and the Republicans, who dominated the state's delegation in the Convention. But it was the connection with the conflict over PR that distorted the debates. Those who spoke against the bicameral feature of the Virginia Plan, Lansing (1:336) and Sherman (1:341), were intent upon defending state equality, while those who spoke for it, Mason (1:339) and Wilson (1:343), favored PR. The issue of one versus two houses was always linked to the other, more basic issue.

Obviously, as Martin said, Congress could be organized into two houses with state equality; and, conversely, PR was compatible with one. Why, then, did the nationalists think it necessary to push for two houses? To guard against impulsive legislation? To restrain further the direct representatives of the people even when not impulsive?

On a query from Butler on May 31 Randolph gave the "general object" of the second branch as a check on the "turbulence and follies of democracy" (1:51). On the same day, however, Spaight of North Carolina argued that the second branch should be elected, not simply nominated as the Virginia Plan provided, by the state legislatures—a proposal aimed at making the Senate an instrument of the state governments, "to shew the sovereignty of the State in one branch of the Legislature," as Pierce phrased it (1:59). From the beginning, then, the Convention reflected two divergent lines of thought: the second branch as protection against democracy, and as protection for the states against the new central government itself.

Spaight withdrew his motion but it was again advanced by Dickinson on June 7. "The preservation of the States in a certain degree of agency is indispensible," he said. "If the State Governments were excluded from all agency in the national one, and all power drawn from the people at large, the consequence would be that the national Govt. would move in the same direction as the State Govts. now do, and would run into all the same mischiefs" (1:152–53). After a whole day's debate, election by the legislatures passed by a vote of 10 to 0 (1:150–56). The alternative proposed by Wilson, election by the people in special districts, was presented as a logical extension of the large-state idea of PR. It was opposed on that ground by the small states; it also aroused doubts about the use of such districts, as well as the opposition of the anti-democrats. Read's proposal, appointment by the executive, drew no support. The vote, therefore, reflected dissatisfaction with the alternatives and general exhaustion with the subject, but it showed the strength of the opponents of PR when combined with those who, while wanting PR, also wanted to protect the states.

The question of two houses was raised again by Lansing on June 20. According to Mason, "an attachment to more than one branch in the Legislature" was one of the few settled convictions of the American people.[4] This, coupled with the fact that it was not directly elected, made them unwilling to enlarge the powers of Congress (1:339). Since the Convention planned a great enlargement of the legislative powers, it followed, if Mason was right, that the conversion of Congress into a directly elected, two-house legislature was a sine qua non for ratification. The second house, far from being defended as a restraint upon the people's representatives, was thus derived from the desires of the people themselves.

Mason may well have been right about a general public preference for two houses. If so, this preference, in an age of minimal government, was probably based on a suspicion that a single house would be more active and dangerous and that the restraint of a second house would help to protect the governed against their governors. This sort of motivation was quite opposite to the desires of the nationalists for a strong, active central government, so it is more likely that the purposes stated on May 31 were controlling and that popular satisfaction was an incidental bonus.

Another question, however, should be raised. Did the Virginians make a mistake, from their own point of view, when they opened the door to bicameralism? The proposal was immediately seized upon by their opponents as a method to preserve a larger role for the states in the new system. So successful were they in this that the second branch, in the end, stood as a state bastion against the great desideratum of the large-state men, PR.

4. Yates, King, and Hamilton all report Mason as referring to two branches; only Madison gives "more than one" (1:346, 349, 351).

Clearly, if they had been able to carry PR in both houses, as they still hoped to do on July 16, bicameralism would not have been a mistake; but how realistic was that hope, even in May? The small-state men regarded the establishment of PR in one house as a major concession on their part, a view the large-state men were unable either to foresee or to accept. They were, therefore, unprepared to propose a reciprocal concession. They were asking the small states, then in control of Congress, to concede the legislative branch to the large states. They could have offered, in exchange, to concede the executive branch to the other states through some method of election giving the states equal weight. Their unwillingness to reciprocate cost them their control of the Convention.

How would they have fared had they started with a proposal for PR in a unicameral Congress? Wilson could still have used all his arguments about the people, rather than the states, being the legitimate bases of authority. The second house could then, if necessary, be proposed as a concession to the small states, perhaps limited to specific powers rather than being coordinate with the first house. It may be surmised that this approach, without a really reciprocal concession, would also have failed. Yet it seems that the prospect must have been better in May that PR could be achieved in a single house than in both houses of a bicameral legislature. The Virginians, in opting for the latter, chose the more difficult objective. They needed a popularly elected house to justify PR; they needed a second house to restrain the people's representatives. Perhaps such restraint was more important to them than PR, but it is more probable that they myopically miscalculated the resistance of the small states.

The Method of Election

When the method of electing senators was again debated on June 25, Wilson proposed indirect popular election, but was not seconded. In response Ellsworth made the anti-democratic point that the legislatures would be more likely than the people to endow the second branch with "Wisdom." It became increasingly clear that the role of the Senate as a defender of the states was the main consideration with most delegates. Mason "wondered that there should be any disagreement about the necessity of allowing the State Govts." a power of self-defense (1:407). Ellsworth, Johnson, Pinckney, and Williamson spoke in similar vein, as others had done since the end of May.[5] Legislative election was retained by 9 to 2, the negative votes of

5. Some spoke of the state governments and others of the states, but it is doubtful that a real

Pennsylvania and Virginia displaying the connection of the method of election with the issue of PR (1:405–8).

As long as the latter issue remained unsettled the extreme nationalists refused to concede the Senate to the states. In an elaborate argument on June 26 Madison disclosed some additional motivations. The "ends to be served" by the second branch were, he thought, three: "to protect the people agst. their rulers," to "interpose agst. impetuous counsels," and to protect the minority against the majority. The particular minority he had in mind were those who were "placed above the feelings of indigence," who would in time be outnumbered by those who "secretly sigh" for a more equal distribution of property. "No agrarian attempts have yet been made in this Country, but symptoms of a leveling spirit, as we have understood, have sufficiently appeared in a certain quarter to give notice of the future danger" (1:422–23). Similarly, Mason believed that "[o]ne important object in constituting the Senate was to secure the rights of property" (1:428).

Gouverneur Morris, returning on July 2 after a month's absence, was even more blunt. The object of the second branch, he said, was "to check the precipitation, changeableness, and excesses of the first branch . . . excesses agst. personal liberty[,] private property & personal safety." It must, therefore, have a personal interest opposed to the popular branch. "It must have great personal property, it must have the aristocratic spirit; it must love to lord it thro' pride . . ." (1:512). These views, it will be noted, were not concerned only with the occasional "impetuous counsels" attributed to the popular branch, but with the protection of property against the poor, who were expected to become a majority—against majority rule, in other words, no matter how sober and deliberate.

Morris, like James Harrington, sought a balance of the rich against the poor in the two houses. He thought, like Hamilton, that the senators should have life terms and, like Read, that they should be appointed by the executive to avoid both popular and state influence upon them. Yet these views drew no support. No votes were taken on a life term, on executive appointment, or on the Morris plan of excluding the rich from the lower house and the poor from the Senate.

The Term of Office

If it was intended to restrain a popular house, a second chamber had to be differentiated from it in some definite way. Every state using such a chamber

---

distinction was meant. The voices of Mason and the Pinckneys further show that this was not exclusively a small-state position.

had differentiated it by making it smaller. The use of different election districts, property qualifications, and age and residence requirements had also been tried. Four states had given their senates longer terms of office than the usual year: Delaware, three years; New York and Virginia, four years; and Maryland, five.[6] By combining a system of indirect election and a high property qualification with this extreme term, Maryland had achieved the most complete differentiation, and thus became the model for those in the Convention who desired to use the Senate in this way. Delaware, New York, and Virginia had also provided for the election of one third or one fourth of their senators each year, an attractive form of "rotation" that retarded the impact of changes in public opinion. Read of Delaware, who still preferred "during good behavior," proposed nine years, with "one third going out triennially." Madison supported him with two further suggestions: that the age requirement be quite high and that "a perpetual disqualification to be re-elected" should be added. Wilson and Hamilton also supported Read, but on the vote only Pennsylvania, Delaware, and Virginia wanted the nine-year term. On June 25 the Convention had divided evenly, five states to five (with Maryland divided), on identical votes on six years and then on five years; but after the nine-year term was rejected on the following day, six years was accepted, 7 to 4 (1:408–26).

The strong nationalists, arguing for stability and wishing to push beyond the extreme of the Maryland model (1:218–19), succeeded when Massachusetts, led by Gorham, changed sides. Wanting to make the Senate resistant to the influences of the separate state governments, even though elected by the legislatures, they succeeded also in this, beyond their expectations.

The Method of Voting

In the Continental Congress and in the Convention the vote of a state was lost whenever its delegates divided evenly on a question. This was reasonable enough if a state were supposed always to have a unified view or interest, but the incidence of even divisions in the Convention itself belied that supposition. Appropriate among sovereign nations, this decision rule was less so in a legislative body of one nation.

On July 14, still defending his committee report of the Connecticut compromise, Elbridge Gerry made the conciliatory suggestion "that the States should vote per capita. which he said would prevent the delays &

6. South Carolina also gave two-year terms to both houses.

inconveniences that had been experienced in Congs. and would give a national aspect & Spirit to the management of business" (2:5).

On the 23d Gouverneur Morris made the formal motion, supported by King and Ellsworth, and opposed by Martin and Carroll of Maryland. This alignment showed that the delegates were very clear that, as Martin objected, individual voting was "departing from the idea of the States being represented in the 2d. branch." Yet the motion was carried 9 to 1, with only some six lines of discussion, and the decision was not later reopened. Senators were thus emancipated from a need to agree upon a state position in voting and were free as individuals to vote their own judgments.

Early in the tenure debate C. C. Pinckney of South Carolina proposed four years: "A longer term wd. fix them at the seat of Govt. They wd. acquire an interest there, perhaps transfer their property & lose sight of the States they represent" (1:409). Martin of Maryland expressed, some five months later, a similar view of the impact of the long term (3:194). These men foresaw that the Senate would not be an effective instrument to protect the states against the central government, and they saw why.[7] Chosen for six years, with no threat of recall, the senators would immerse themselves in the activities and powers of the central government. They would become, psychologically, a part of that government and gradually forget their role as spokesmen for the separate states. And the nationalists achieved this, not by paying the senators with national funds, but by the simple expedients of the long term of office and per capita voting.

The Results

From these lengthy debates on the second branch a number of points may be concluded. The Senate as it emerged from the Convention differed from the Virginia Plan proposal, but not in the direction of democracy. It was shaped, in part, by the conflicting desires of the large-state men to use the people to justify proportional power for their states while restraining the influence the people might exert on the new system. The Virginians could have proposed a Congress based on population without providing that it be directly elected; but, given a popular preference for bicameralism, as shown in the state constitutions, and given the plan for a form of final popular ratification, the justification of PR seemed easier if a popularly elected house

7. Others may have shared this view. The same four states—New York, New Jersey, South Carolina, and Georgia—voted to the end against five years, six years, and nine years. Significantly, no votes were taken on shorter terms.

was provided. But if the "meeting of ambassadors" that had been the old Congress was to be converted into a powerful legislature, it would have to be restrained in some way—by its method of election, by a veto on its actions, by a second chamber, or by some combination of these and other methods. This restraint was desired both against Randolph's "fury" (1:58) or "follies" (1:51) of democracy and against Madison's anticipated assaults on property.

The Senate was thus proposed as a part of the nationalists' plan for a strong government with PR. But the proposal, once made, was seized upon by the defenders of the states and established in a form that seemed to preserve state equality. This form, however, was not incompatible with the undemocratic purposes of the original plan. In fact, it carried them still further: state equality was a less democratic concept than was PR. This equality made the small states eager participants in the building of central power and in the ratification of the resulting Constitution. As a means of defense of the states against this central power, however, it was to prove illusory.

The Executive

It is well known that the early state constitutions avoided the creation of strong executives, motivated in part by bad experiences with colonial governors and also by a general revulsion against concentrated power— particularly any form of it that might evolve toward kingship. Wary of this latter attitude and divided among themselves, the Virginians inserted a blank for the number of executives in their Plan.

When, on June 1, Wilson moved that the executive "consist of a single person" a long silence ensued, as had occurred two days before (above, p. 52). Franklin begged the delegates to express their views, which they did with much diversity. Randolph strongly advocated an executive of three persons, one from each section of the country, saying that a single executive was "the foetus of monarchy" and would be unacceptable to the people (1:65–66, 88, 92).

All of the delegates had been, only a dozen years before, loyal subjects of a monarch. Monarchy was much on their minds, from June to September, since the history of extensive republics, both ancient and modern, showed their tendency to revert to that form. "There is a natural inclination in mankind to Kingly Government," Franklin observed, expressing in his first major speech his apprehension that "the Government of these States, may in future times, end in a Monarchy" (1:83). "It was pretty certain," Williamson thought in July, "that we should at some time or other have a King; but he wished no precaution to be omitted that might postpone the event as long as possible" (2:101).

On the other hand, Dickinson and others expressed great admiration for the British system (1:92, 136, 150, 289, 398) and thought it desirable, although impossible, to establish a similar mixed and balanced government here. It was impossible not only because there was no titled aristocracy but because of the deep revulsion against King George after so many colonial appeals to him for help in the long struggle with Parliament. "There were not ⅟₁₀₀₀ part of our fellow citizens," Gerry declared, "who were not agst. every approach toward Monarchy" (1:425).

Hamilton, however, disagreed. He not only "acknowledged himself not to think favorably of Republican Government"; he also pointed to what he called the "progress of the public mind." He saw "evils operating in the States which must soon cure the people of their fondness for democracies. . . . The people will in time be unshackled from their prejudices . . ." (1:424, 288, 291).

Hamilton was alone in expressing this view, but was he also, as is usually thought, alone in holding it? Perhaps in jest, Mercer (according to McHenry) showed his Maryland colleague a list of those who, he said, "were for a king" (2:192). The list (according to Martin, who took it seriously) contained "more than twenty" names (3:321). "There was a considerable number, who did not openly avow it, who were . . . acting upon those principles, covertly endeavouring to carry into effect what they well knew openly and avowedly could not be accomplished" (3:179).

Quite apart, however, from Martin's judgment of their motivations, the nationalists did create an executive office of almost incredible power. Leaving behind Sherman's early desire that the executive be "nothing more than an institution for carrying the will of the Legislature into effect" (1:65), they employed the prestigious doctrine of separation of powers to justify an executive almost completely independent of the legislature. He would be armed with a veto and the powers of appointment of the whole executive and judicial branches, of the conduct of foreign relations, and of commander of all land and naval forces. This was a concentration of power not only far beyond that held by any state governor but well beyond that proposed in any of the plans submitted to the Convention, except that of Hamilton.

A Design for Monarchy?

Early in June, Butler, Franklin, and Mason had each warned that executive power has a tendency to grow. "The Executive," Franklin predicted, "will be always increasing here, as elsewhere, till it ends in a monarchy" (1:103; cf. 100, 113). And Rutledge objected that "[t]he people will think we are leaning too much toward Monarchy" (1:119); yet the Convention, in the end, was not deterred. In its executive article it had, it seemed, as Randolph said in September, "made a bold stroke for Monarchy" (2:513). Was Martin right, and had this been the covert intention all along?[8]

Martin believed, or at least professed to believe, that an unholy alliance of cryptomonarchists and large-state men had broken the federal system of equal states, had given the new government "great and undefined powers as to its legislative and executive," and thus "paved the way for their favorite object, the destruction of the State governments, and the introduction of monarchy" (3:179–80).

Such interpretations, unconvincing in the ratification contest, were later reinforced by the policies and practices of Washington's and Adams's administrations, which repeatedly aroused suspicions by their parallels to Court Whig methods in England.[9]

There are, of course, alternative interpretations. The Convention may, in effect, have followed John Adams, not in his desire to approximate the government to an admired English monarchy, but in his desire for a mixed and balanced system of the one, the few, and the many.[10] If so, the

8. See Louise B. Dunbar, *A Study of "Monarchical" Tendencies in the United States from 1776 to 1801* (Urbana, 1922), and *The Documentary History of the Ratification of the Constitution*, Merrill Jensen et al., eds. (Madison, 1976–), 13:168–72.

9. The Republican press continually accused the Federalists of monarchical motives. By 1798 the Virginia legislature, in launching its Resolutions against the Alien and Sedition Acts, warned against "the artificers of monarchy." Its "Address to the People," in saying that "a lover of monarchy . . . may confound monarchy and republicanism by the art of definition," exactly described the tactic John Adams had employed for many years. And Jefferson, after his triumph, thought it "very important" that ordinary citizens "should see and fear the monarchist," i.e., the Federalist leaders, whose "hearts [are] devoted to monarchy." See the "Address" in Elliot, *Debates*, 4:531; Adams, *Defence of the Constitutions of Government of the United States of America* (1787–88), vol. 1, chapters 3 and 9, on "monarchical republics," including England, and letters to Samuel Adams and Roger Sherman, in his *Works*, vol. 4 and vol. 6, pp. 405–36; and Jefferson to John Dickinson, July 23, 1801, in his *Works*, ed. Paul L. Ford (New York, 1905), vol. 9, pp. 281–82.

10. A recent student of Adams's thought has emphasized that, in the first two volumes of the *Defence*, he was most concerned to use the balance against the threat of aristocracy, but that in the third volume (finished after he had seen and approved the new Constitution) he shifted

president, instead of being a "foetus of monarchy," was part of the project of preserving republican government by preventing it from becoming democratic—or, to use the recent euphemism, by making democracy "decent."[11] Without the president's wisdom to guide them, and his veto to restrain them, the direct representatives of the people might well destroy republican government by stimulating a reaction to their injustices.

So the Convention, in its executive article, aimed neither at an open door for monarchy nor at democracy however decent. It aimed at a highly undemocratic, yet permanent, republic. Only a very sparse representation of the people was provided, and it was to be restrained, in the exercise of its legislative will, not only by a second chamber not directly elected and not proportioned to population but also by an executive who could block any legislation opposed by more than one third of either chamber.

The Powers

Wilson's motion for the single executive, remade by Pinckney and supported by Gerry, Butler, and Rutledge, was carried by seven states against New York, Delaware, and Maryland on June 4. Williamson again urged the Randolph executive on July 24, but this vote of June 4 was never rescinded.

In order to avoid a conflict with his colleagues Randolph and Mason over the plural executive, Madison had suggested that "as certain powers were in their nature Executive . . . a definition of their extent would assist the

---

his concerns to stress its use against democracy. Howe, *Changing Political Thought of John Adams*, pp. 167–75.

11. This adjective became a favorite of Martin Diamond in his many publications defending the Constitution as a democratic document against the Progressive historians' anti-democratic thesis. Yet in an unusually frank article in 1976 Diamond admitted that the Founders "did not expect that the mass of mankind could ever rise to such levels of mind and character as would warrant the untrammeled rule of the majority. They did not believe that such a transformation of human nature could be effected by any means. . . . On the contrary, they took for granted as a fact of human nature the impossibility of finding wisdom and virtue in sufficient quantities as to warrant, confidingly, the basing of a democracy upon them. . . . The American Founders regarded an unrestrained democracy to be an invitation to disaster." They had used instead the "new science of politics," procedural and institutional restraints that "would work out decent political solutions." In this same article Diamond contrasted the "new science" with the ancient Greek idea "that every resource of the political art should be employed to draw out and up the potential of the exceptional few," which he rightly called an aristocratic idea; but he then went on, without noticing the parallel, to claim for "American democracy," against the egalitarians, an "aspiration to be that political society which best defers to the deserving." "The American Idea of Equality: The View from the Founding," *Review of Politics* 38 (July 1976): 313–31.

judgment in determining how far they might be safely entrusted to a single officer." He proposed that the executive "carry into effect the national laws," appoint to offices not otherwise filled, and execute other powers delegated by the legislature. He succeeded with the first two, but the third was rejected (1:67). And thus matters stood until August 6 when the Committee of Detail, in its report, brought forth a list of specific powers and, more important, the ambiguous sentence, "The Executive power of the United States shall be vested in a single person" (2:185). Did this simply embody the early decision against a plurality, or did it convey also a grant of substantive power? No one raised that question, and these words, modified by the Committee of Style to read "The executive power shall be vested in a president . . ." emerged from the Convention.[12]

The Method of Election

Far more difficult than the unity or the powers of the executive, however, proved to be the problems of selection and tenure. Governors were chosen by legislatures except in New York and New England, which used popular election; and thus, if delegates applied their local customs to the new national office, legislative election started with the support of eight states to three, since New Hampshire and Rhode Island (and Vermont) were not in attendance. Moreover, in stating his preference for election by the people, Wilson threw a flood of light on the delegates' attitudes by saying that he feared this idea "might appear chimerical" (1:68). The ordinary voter, it was widely believed, could not know or choose wisely among national leaders, so Wilson, when he reduced his ideas to a motion, called for indirect popular election, the voters choosing electors (1:80). The alternative, legislative election, was also open to objections: it would lead to cabal, foreign influence, and the dependence of the executive on the legislature—in

12. In treating the powers of the president in nine numbers of *The Federalist* (Nos. 69–77), Hamilton dealt only with the specified powers, defending them as necessary and minimal, and denying that any others were conveyed (No. 77; Cooke ed., p. 519). When it came to justifying Washington's Neutrality Proclamation of 1793, however, Hamilton was not so inhibited. He noted the difference in the ways in which Articles I and II begin: the words "herein granted," limiting the legislative power, were omitted in the executive article. "The enumeration ought therefore to be considered, as intended merely to specify the principle articles implied in the definition of executive power; leaving the rest to flow from the general grant of that power . . . subject only to the *exceptions* and *qualifications*, which are expressed in the instrument." *The Works of Alexander Hamilton*, ed. John C. Hamilton (New York, 1851), 7:80–81 (the "Pacificus" essays).

violation of Montesquieu's separation-of-powers doctrine, to which many, indoors and out, subscribed.[13] To minimize this dependence it seemed necessary to give the executive a long term and make him ineligible for reelection, which had obvious disadvantages.

Choice by the legislature for a seven-year (or longer) term with no reelection formed one logically consistent package of decisions; this was opposed by another package, election by electors for a shorter term with eligibility for reelection.[14] Delegates shifted between these two solutions, and several other alternatives were proposed, but the first package seemed the more acceptable and was reported by the Committee of Detail. When reached in debate on August 24, however, Rutledge moved an amendment to provide for a joint ballot of the two houses.[15] This insertion of the one word "joint" entirely changed the meaning of legislative election, as Sherman quickly pointed out, "depriving the *States* represented in the *Senate* of the negative intended them in that house."[16] But Rutledge was supported by Gorham, Langdon, Madison, and Wilson, and his motion carried, 7 to 4. This brought on a series of amending motions, two of which divided the states evenly and two others 5 to 6, leading to a postponement "till tomorrow" (2:401–4).

The Brearley Committee

The subject was not taken up on the morrow nor again until it came into the hands of the committee on postponed parts proposed by Sherman and appointed by ballot on August 31 (2:481). This committee, on which all the states were represented, was very strong, imaginative, and energetic, making a series of reports beginning on September 1.

13. This doctrine was explicitly stated in the constitutions of New Hampshire, Massachusetts, Maryland, Virginia, North Carolina, and Georgia (and Vermont). See M.J.C. Vile, *Constitutionalism and the Separation of Powers*, pp. 119–75.

14. These logical packages were noticed by Charles Warren, *The Making of the Constitution* (Cambridge, Mass., 1928), pp. 364–65, and more thoroughly analyzed by Calvin C. Jillson, "The Executive in Republican Government: The Case of the American Founding," *Presidential Studies Quarterly* 9 (Fall 1979): 386–402. Details of the debates on the presidency in general are summarized in William B. Michaelsen, *Creating the American Presidency, 1775–1789* (Lanham, Md., 1987).

15. All the states using legislative election of governors also used a joint ballot except Georgia, which had a one-house legislature. Even the unicameral Pennsylvania Assembly joined with the state's Executive Council.

16. Sherman was probably correct that the omission of the word "joint" was intended as he said. In a Randolph draft for the Committee of Detail the word "joint" is crossed out and "each Ho. havg a Negative on the other" inserted by Rutledge (2:145 and 4:46).

The composition of the committee is surprising when viewed with regard to the conflicts over executive selection. So far was it from reflecting the decision of August 24 for legislative election by a joint ballot that it seemed instead to reflect the general dissatisfaction with that decision. Of the eleven members only Sherman and Williamson had spoken in favor of legislative election, and that had been back on July 17. On the other hand, of the seven members of the Convention who had expressed themselves favorably toward direct popular election, six were on this committee: Morris (2:29), King (2:55), Madison (2:56), Williamson (2:113), Dickinson (2:114), and Carroll (2:402). Of these six, four had supported popularly chosen electors as a means for solving the problems of direct election, and Butler had preferred electors to legislative election if they were chosen by the state legislatures (2:56, 404, 112). The other three members of the committee were Gilman (who had said nothing and thus was less committed than his colleague Langdon to legislative election), Brearley (who was chosen chairman, and who was most interested in preserving small-state influence [2:402–3]), and Baldwin (a native of Connecticut and graduate of Yale, who also had said nothing on the subject). In terms of states, the most consistent votes for legislative election had come from New Hampshire, Massachusetts, North Carolina, South Carolina, and Georgia, yet each of these states, in selecting its committee member, passed over its outspoken advocates of legislative election. As with the committee that drew up the Connecticut compromise (above, p. 63), the composition of the Brearley committee suggests that the decision to abandon legislative election had already been made.

How could this come about in spite of the strength that method had displayed only one week earlier? There are no notes or memoirs from inside the committee, and Madison's notes are increasingly sparse toward the end of the Convention, so we are on speculative ground in attempting to answer the question. The committee did have the advantage of two new ideas that will be discussed below: unassembled electors and the distinction of a nominating step from the electing step. But there is also some evidence of weakness in the support for legislative election to be gleaned from an examination of votes taken on August 24.

The Rutledge motion for a joint ballot was a bid by the nationalists to eliminate state influence in the choice of executives. It therefore aroused the opposition of both the state federalists and the state-sovereignty men. The New Jersey delegates immediately moved to insert "each State having one vote" and mustered five states, only one short of a majority. Morris then moved election "by Electors chosen by the people of the several States" and also got five states; but in this group were Pennsylvania and Virginia, which had not supported the New Jersey motion. The support for legislative election by joint ballot was therefore not solid, for these states saw the method of electors as giving their large populations even more advantage than the joint ballot, since the latter would still be influenced by the equal state representation in the Senate (2:403–4). Thus seven states had voted against aspects of the new form of legislative election, including three of the seven that had voted to insert "joint" (above, p. 135). An eighth state, New Hampshire, had voted against these motions and for the joint ballot, even though Langdon recognized that it was "unfavorable to N. Hampshire as a small state" (2:402). Both he and Gilman must have been later won over, however, since New Hampshire fairly consistently supported the committee report.

Both methods of election (by the legislature or by separate electors) could be compatible with either state equality or the proportional aim of the nationalists, depending, in the former method, on how the vote was to be taken, and in the latter on how the electors were allocated. The choice between them, therefore, could be based on other considerations. Among these other considerations three carried the most weight—the fear of influence and cabal, the problem of the independence of the executive, and the difficulties of assembling a competent college of electors. As long as electors were expected to assemble in one body to make their choice both methods seemed equally open to cabal, but there was no satisfactory way to make an executive independent of a legislative body that elected him. This great disadvantage was balanced by the disadvantage of assembling electors. When it was realized that electors need not assemble nationally, the method of separate state meeting of electors seemed to solve at once the three problems of independence, of cabal, and of travel. At the same time it opened up for separate decisions on their merits the questions of length of term and reeligibility for office.

Nomination Distinguished from Election

From the point of view of the nationalists this neat solution entailed the obnoxious reintroduction of a role for the separate states. The coalition that had formed against them was so strong, however, that they could not prevent this.[17] They were only able, presumably with the help of the state federalists,

17. As uncovered by factor analysis by Professor Jillson, the six states were New Hampshire, Massachusetts, Connecticut, New Jersey, Delaware, and Georgia, with Connecticut at the center of the cluster. Jillson, "The Executive in Republican Government," p. 397.

to achieve a creative synthesis of state and national elements in the total executive-selection process. This was based on a realization that nomination was different from election and that one could be national and the other federal. By giving each state a number of electors equal to its senators and representatives, requiring them to vote for two candidates, one from outside the state, and then requiring a majority to elect a president (with no runoff ballot), the committee made possible a national election; but in so doing it made more probable (after Washington) multiple nominations instead, nominations determined by the large states. To balance this national aspect of the plan, the final choice was made federal, given to the states, voting equally in the Senate.

Mason fairly accurately expressed the nationalist reaction to the committee report when he guessed that in practice election would take place in the Senate "nineteen times in twenty" (2:500). Sherman explained frankly that the large states would choose the candidates and the small states would finally elect. Most of the criticism of the report focused on the growth of power in the Senate. When Sherman deftly turned this aside by shifting the election to the House of Representatives, voting by states, he carried ten states, and the major decisions were finished (2:527).

Now, how democratic was this final solution? If almost all of the advocates of popular election were on the Brearley committee and, in fact, were a majority of the committee, why did they not report some variant of popular election? There were six variants then in use in the North, counting Vermont.

The committee plan permitted any state to choose its electors by direct popular vote, but even if the electors produced a majority this was at best only indirect democracy. For the electoral college to work as an electing device a method of prior nomination was needed that would avoid the scattering of votes. For example, the House, the Senate, and the president might each have made a nomination. Or the state governors might have nominated candidates from other states. Alternatively, election by plurality might have been advocated—it was working in New York.[18] Or the electors might have reballoted between the top two. The possibilities are endless, but the committee knew that the Convention was not searching for ways to make popular election work. When votes were taken on direct election on July 17 and August 24, only Pennsylvania, and then Pennsylvania and

18. Hamilton was absent during the July and August debates on the executive and did not return until after the Brearley committee had reported its plan. But in his plan he had proposed the use of electors (1:292; 3:617–18).

Delaware, supported it (2:32, 402). Nor was the Convention searching for ways to make the electoral college work as anything more than a nominating device. The nationalist motions designed to improve the chances of the electors electing were easily defeated, solely that of Madison to count only voting electors in determining a majority being supported by more than two states (2:514–15). Moreover, in the Senate in 1824 Rufus King (who had served on the Brearley committee), in attacking nominations by the Congressional caucus, laid it down that the Convention had intended that no method "of any sort" be used "by which a concentration of the votes for the President may be effected, previously to the choice of Electors in the several States." The whole system of election, in his view, was a "matter of compromise and compact between the States, without which no Constitution or Union could have been formed." And the essence of the compromise was the concession of the nomination (and the possibility of election) by the state federalists and state-sovereignty coalition to the large states, in exchange for which "the election of the Pr . . . . . except in the first stage of the process, is assigned to the States acting in their federal equal capacity" (3:462).[19]

Presidents were, in sum, to be elected by the states, not by the people. If the scheme did not work out as anticipated (by both its friends and its opponents) it is largely because party nominating methods converted the intended nominating step, the electors, into an election. That step, ironically the more democratic of the two, now seems undemocratic because the electoral majority may not go to the candidate who polls the highest popular vote. Yet this criticism serves to show how far the whole process has moved away from the perspectives of the Founders. To them, the selection of the president, this new and powerful central executive, was second in importance only to the selection of the legislative branch itself. The smaller states, strengthened by their earlier victory, were no more willing to see a proportional system select the president than they had been to see PR in both houses of Congress. The Brearley committee achieved a complex balance of state and national elements—but in no sense a democratic balance—which Gouverneur Morris could later call "perhaps the most valuable provision in favor of the small States, which can be found in the Constitution" (3:405).

19. See also the account in Richard P. McCormick, *The Presidential Game: The Origins of American Presidential Politics* (New York, 1982), chapters 1 and 2; *Annals of Congress*, 18 Congress, 1 Session, cols. 355–62; *Life and Correspondence of Rufus King*, ed. C. R. King (New York, 1900), 6:557.

The Council of Revision and the Veto

Another strongly anti-democratic proposal did not fare so well. This was the council of revision, a sort of third house in the legislative process. As an item of the constitutional "chaff" from the Convention, this proposal has not had much scholarly attention; but the importance attached to it by Madison, Mason, Wilson, and Morris makes it a useful indicator of Convention opinion.[20]

The Virginia Plan provided that "the Executive and a convenient number of the National Judiciary" should exercise a "rejection" of laws unless overriden by an unspecified vote "of the members of each branch" of the national legislature (1:21).[21] This provision involved issues of the meaning and implementation of the separation-of-powers doctrine, and it also aroused apprehensions derived from the use of the veto by the Stuart kings and from colonial experience with laws disallowed by the Privy Council.

In the first debate on this, June 4, Wilson wanted an "absolute negative" instead: "Without such a Self-defence the Legislature can at any moment sink it [the executive] into non-existence." He believed that the power "would seldom be used. The Legislature would know that such a power existed, and would refrain from such laws, as it would be sure to defeat. Its silent operation would therefore preserve harmony and prevent mischief." In ordinary times a qualified veto, "requiring a large proportion of each House to overrule" the executive, "might do"; but there might be "tempestuous moments in which animosities may run high between the Executive and Legislative branches, and in which the former ought to be able to defend itself" (1:98, 100).

Wilson's view, however, was vigorously opposed; even Franklin, who spoke infrequently, twice took the floor against it. Butler and Mason thought it smacked of monarchy. Drawing, like Franklin, on the Country ideology, Mason anticipated that the executive "may refuse its assent to necessary measures till new appointments shall be referred to him; and having by degrees engrossed all these into his own hands, the American Executive, like the British, will by bribery & influence, save himself the trouble & odium of exerting his negative afterwards. . . . Do gentlemen mean to pave the way to hereditary Monarchy?" (1:101). Only Hamilton and King voted

20. Jane Butzner, ed., *Constitutional Chaff: Rejected Suggestions of the Constitutional Convention of 1787* (New York, 1941).

21. New York's constitution of 1777 contained a similar joint executive-judicial veto.

with Wilson for the absolute veto (1:103). The idea was included in the Hamilton plan on June 18 and proposed informally by Read on August 7 and by Morris on the 15th, but it clearly had little support (1:292; 2:200, 299).

At the opposite extreme another Delaware delegate, Bedford, opposed all forms of the negative. It would be sufficient, he thought, to mark out "the boundaries to the Legislative Authority" in the Constitution. "The Representatives of the People were the best judges of what was for their interest, and ought to be under no external controul whatever" (1:100–101). All reports of his speech agree that Bedford believed the two houses of the legislature would be sufficient checks on each other. He made no motion, however, perhaps sensing that he, too, had little support.

The real issue was the formal association of the judiciary in an executive veto. As long as the executive was to be chosen by the legislature, some delegates doubted that he could stand alone against the legislature's wishes. Madison, according to Pierce, "proved" from history that "the only way to make a Government answer all the end of its institution was to collect the wisdom of its several parts in aid of each other whenever it was necessary. Hence the propriety of incorporating the Judicial with the Executive in the revision of the Laws" (1:110). "We must," he said, according to King, "introduce the Checks, which will destroy the measures of an interested majority . . . for the safety of a minority" (1:108). Gerry, on the contrary, saw "no necessity for so great a controul over the legislature as the best men in the Community would be comprised in the two branches of it." Moreover, he believed, it was quite foreign to the nature of judicial office to "make them judges of the policy of public measures" (1:97–98). Gerry and King carried eight states for their motion eliminating judicial participation in the veto (1:104).

Undaunted, Wilson and Madison moved, two days later, to reinsert the judiciary. In a revealing speech Madison indicated that their purpose was not purely defensive. A republican executive, unlike a monarch, "would not possess those great emoluments from his station, nor that permanent stake in the public interest which wd. place him out of the reach of foreign corruption: He would stand in need therefore of being controuled as well as supported." The judges would "diminish the danger" and also supply positive advantages. Madison professed to expect "much good" from the "perspicuity, the conciseness, and the systematic character wch. the Code of laws wd. receive from the Judiciary talents" (1:138–39).[22] Gerry responded

---

22. Madison's purposes may also have included a desire to preclude the judicial review of Congressional acts. Writing to Monroe in 1817 he remembered "the attempts in the Convention

that the executive alone would be more impartial than when "covered by the sanction & seduced by the sophistry of the Judges" (1:139). No one followed Madison into "foreign corruption"; the proposal was again defeated, three states to eight (1:140).

On July 21, when the veto came up again, a few more voices were heard in support of Wilson's new attempt to add the judiciary to the "Revisionary power." Ellsworth "approved heartily" and Mason "had always been a friend to this provision." Morris "concurred in thinking the public liberty in greater danger from Legislative usurpations than from any other source." Mason argued that, "Notwithstanding the precautions taken in the Constitution of the Legislature, it would so much resemble that of the individual States, that it must be expected frequently to pass unjust and pernicious laws. This restraining power was therefore essentially necessary." Recognizing that the judges could defend their constitutional rights through judicial review, Wilson believed the review process would not reach far enough. "Laws may be unjust, may be unwise, may be dangerous, may be destructive; and yet not be so unconstitutional as to justify the Judges in refusing to give them effect." Madison also hoped to use this form of restraint as an "additional check agst. a pursuit of those unwise & unjust measures which constituted so great a portion of our calamities" (2:73–78).

Against them, Gerry, Gorham, Strong, Martin, and Rutledge reaffirmed the need to avoid a "dangerous innovation," to avoid "an improper coalition" of executive and judiciary, to keep the making distinct from the expounding of laws, so that the judges would "carry into the exposition of the laws no prepossessions with regard to them" (2:73–80). The Wilson proposal again went down to defeat, three states to four; but such a vote could hardly be conclusive. [23]

Madison and Wilson tried again on August 15 when the veto was debated as reported from the Committee of Detail. To avoid the separation-of-powers argument they proposed separate submission of all bills to the executive and to the "Supreme Judiciary," with a majority of three fourths in each house required to override "if both should object," and of two thirds if either should object. Mercer "heartily approved," but Pinckney and Gerry opposed, so, with little debate, the motion failed 3 to 8 (2:298). [24]

---

to vest in the Judiciary Dept. a qualified negative on Legislative *bills*" that, had they succeeded, "would have precluded the question of a Judiciary annulment of Legislative *Acts*" (3:424).

23. Connecticut and Virginia continued to support it; New York, which had voted "ay" in June, had departed; New Jersey was absent; New Hampshire had not yet arrived; Pennsylvania and Georgia, which had voted "no," were now divided; and Maryland changed to "ay."

24. The three this time were Delaware, Maryland, and Virginia. Thus Virginia consistently supported the participation of the judiciary in policy making on June 6, July 21, and August 15.

Even then, Morris "regretted that something like the proposed check could not be agreed to." He "enlarged on the tendency of the legislative Authority to usurp on the Executive" and wanted more than two thirds to override the veto. In this he was supported by Carroll of Maryland, by Wilson, and by Williamson, who moved "¾" in place of "⅔ of each house." This carried, 6 to 4, with Pennsylvania divided (2:301).

This fraction was named by Randolph on September 10 among his "objections to the system" (2:563), and two days later Williamson himself moved the restoration of "⅔," having become convinced that three fourths "puts too much in the power of the President." He was supported by Sherman, Gerry, Mason, and Pinckney and opposed by Morris, Hamilton, and Madison. The latter were still eager "to check legislative injustice and incroachments," and thought that state experience had shown that "⅔ is not sufficient to answer the purpose" (2:585–87). The vote again was 6 to 4, with New Hampshire divided, for the smaller fraction.[25]

These persistent efforts to increase the restraints on the legislative branch, even after its powers had been specified, displayed clearly the strong fears of democracy felt by leading members. Their versatility in this was as remarkable as their tenacity. There was no precedent for an absolute veto in republican government. Its connection with monarchy deterred most but not all of them. No state constitution provided a separate judicial veto, and none required three fourths to override.

The Convention, in the end, rejected these proposals and accepted the least extreme form of the veto—but not because the sentiments expressed by Bedford were widely shared. Even in opposing the revisionary council concept on July 21, after the Connecticut compromise had radically differentiated the two houses, Gorham said that "all agree that a check on the Legislature is necessary" (2:79), that the two houses would still not adequately check each other. The delegates worked repeatedly on the problem, but seemed unable to devise a more "sufficient" answer than the two-thirds override of an executive veto. Yet this least extreme form still made possible the frustration of the legislative majority.

Legislators' Eligibility for Executive Offices

Throughout the eighteenth century the Country Whigs in England had complained that ministerial management of Parliament, by the appointment

---

25. This vote is interesting as an indicator of the instability of opinion in the Convention. Only two states, Delaware and Virginia, favored three fourths on both August 15 and September 12; and only New Jersey and Georgia favored two thirds on both dates.

of its members to offices and sinecures, was a subversion of the traditional constitutional balance of the three branches of the mixed government. Following them, the American revolutionaries came to see this as a prime source of their great conflict with the mother country.

So it should occasion no surprise that the Virginia Plan had provided that both representatives and senators should be ineligible for "any office established by a particular State, or under the authority of the United States . . . , during the term of service, and for the space of _____ " thereafter (1:20–21). These provisions indicate that the Virginians were very aware of the need to protect the independence of the legislature against the type of executive influence that had developed in England, a view no doubt widely shared.[26] Nevertheless a contrary view had great strength in the Convention. The ineligibility provision was assaulted repeatedly, from various angles, and in the end attenuated.

The provision against state offices seemed most vulnerable and was assailed on June 12, but it withstood this initial assault. The clause thus remained, but the narrow margin (5 to 4, with Massachusetts and Maryland divided) guaranteed that another trial would be made (1:217).

On June 22 Gorham attacked the whole idea of ineligibility as "unnecessary and injurious" (1:375). Butler opposed him, citing the British example: "This was the source of the corruption that ruined their Govt." Mason elaborated on the example: "corruption pervades every town and village in the kingdom," and concluded, "I consider this clause as the corner-stone on which our liberties depend—and if we strike it out we are erecting a fabric for our destruction" (1:376, 381). For King, however, it was "a mere cobweb": "we refine too much by going to *utopian* lengths." Wilson, without using the name, reminded the delegates that Washington had been a member of Congress when chosen as commander of the Revolutionary armies.

It remained, however, for Gorham and Hamilton to show the real colors of their school of thought. "The corruption of the English Government," Gorham averred, "cannot be applied to America. This evil exists there in

26. Gerry reported later that the Massachusetts legislature had instructed its delegates not "to agree in any case to give to the members of Congress a capacity to hold offices under the Government," that it had repealed that instruction to conform to the Act of Congress, but that "the Sense of the State however was still the same" (2:285). Plural office holding had been such a problem in Massachusetts that the constitution of 1780 used four paragraphs of Article VI to curtail it. See Ellen E. Brennan, *Plural Office-Holding in Massachusetts, 1760–1780* (Chapel Hill, 1945).

the venality of their boroughs: but even this corruption has its advantage, as it gives stability to their government" (1:381). Hamilton agreed with Gorham that it was impossible to say what the effect of ineligibility would have been in England. "We have been taught to reprobate the danger of influence in the British government, without duly reflecting how far it was necessary to support a good government." He then cited David Hume, "one of the ablest politicians," who had "pronounced all that influence on the side of the crown, which went under the name of corruption, an essential part of the weight which maintained the equilibrium of the Constitution."[27] Corruption was not really an evil. It was advantageous, according to this Mandevillean logic, even essential. Nevertheless the attempt again failed, but by an even narrower margin: 4 to 4, with New York, Pennsylvania, and Delaware divided (1:376–81).

Madison then (June 23) tried a new tactic: limit the ineligibility "only" to offices newly created or newly enhanced. "If we expect to call forth useful characters," he said, "we must hold out allurements." He was supported in this by King and Wilson, but opposed by Butler, Rutledge, Mason, Gerry, and Sherman. His motion carried only Connecticut and New Jersey and divided Massachusetts (1:386–92).

Spaight was more successful. His new tactic called for a separate question on the year of ineligibility after the term for which a representative was elected. This part was defended by Mason, Gerry, and Rutledge, but it was eliminated, 6 to 4, with Pennsylvania divided (1:390, 394).

On June 26 Butler and Williamson succeeded in removing the ineligibility of senators for state offices (1:428–29). But no one moved to eliminate the extra year as had been done for the representatives, so with these two changes the Virginia Plan provisions went to the Committee of Detail and were included in its report of August 6 (2:180).

When this section came up for debate, August 14, the attacks began again with improved subtlety and increased acrimony. Pinckney thought ineligibility was "degrading" to the members, as well as "inconvenient" and "impolitic." He wanted members eligible for offices without salary or other emoluments—an idea that stimulated Mason to propose to strike out the whole section "as a more effectual expedient for encouraging that exotic corruption which might not otherwise thrive so well in the American soil." This debate took place during Mercer's brief visit to the Convention, and he

27. See Hume's "Of the Independency of Parliament," in his *Essays, Literary, Moral and Political* (London, 1870), p. 30.

twice supported eligibility with the argument that government can only be maintained by force or influence. "The Executive has not *force*[;] deprive him of influence" by the ineligibility of members, "and he becomes a mere phantom of authority." Williamson, on the other hand, echoed Mason's sarcasm. "We have now got a House of Lords which is to originate money-bills. To avoid another *inconveniency*, we are to have a whole Legislature at liberty to cut out offices for one another." Pinckney and Wilson stressed the need to attract able men from the states (where legislators were not ineligible) to the national legislature, while Gerry countered with the statement that "[i]f our best Citizens are actuated by such mercenary views, we had better choose a single despot at once" (2:283–89). Pinckney's proposition divided the Convention evenly, and by general agreement the section was postponed (2:289–90).

The subject thus passed to the Brearley committee on postponed matters (above, p. 135), which reported a version that balanced legislative ineligibility to executive office with executive ineligibility to legislative membership, and also silently eliminated the extra year for senators (2:483).

At his first opportunity, on September 3, Pinckney made his August 14 motion again, but this time he carried only Pennsylvania and North Carolina. This vote seemed to show that the fear of corruption was more prevalent than ever; but, on the contrary, views had moved toward parts of the Madison proposal of June 23. King first tried to limit ineligibility to offices newly "created," failing on an even vote. Williamson (who had voted the other way in June) then added the second element of Madison's proposal: "created or the emoluments whereof shall have been increased." Both men omitted Madison's "only," thus leaving the prohibition against concurrent office holding. This addition divided Georgia and therefore carried, 5 to 4 (2:489–92). The Brearley committee version, thus amended, went into the Constitution, as Article I, Section 6.

The debate leading to this result saw Sherman, Gerry, Randolph, and Mason still opposed to eligibility and Morris, Gorham, Wilson, and Pinckney still favoring it. When Sherman argued that it would "give too much influence to the Executive," Morris responded that, on the contrary, it "wd: lessen the influence of the Executive." The "relations and friends" of members would be appointed and the executive thus retain "the service and votes" of the members, whereas "the appointment of the members deprives him of such an advantage." Wilson agreed with this analysis and added that "the exclusion of members" would diminish "the general energy of the Government" (2:490–91).

If the votes of September 3 are compared with those of June 23 on Madison's similar motion, it can be seen that only two states voted consistently: Maryland and South Carolina voted "no" in June and again in September. Georgia did the same, except that it divided on the final vote on Williamson's motion. New Hampshire was absent in June, and New York and Delaware were absent on September 3. Of the remaining six states that changed sides, all had lost or gained a delegate or two. Yet only in one case did the departure or arrival of a delegate account for the change: the departure of Strong enabled Gorham and King to cast the Massachusetts vote for the amendment. In the other five cases one or more delegates shifted position—in Connecticut and New Jersey from "yes" to "no" and in Pennsylvania, Virginia, and North Carolina from "no" to "yes." How can these seemingly inconsistent shifts be explained?

No clear answer to this question appears in the records. The whole idea of ineligibility was related to concepts of the separation of powers and thus also to the methods of electing the executive. In June election by the legislature was established, whereas on September 3 it may have been known that the Brearley committee was about to recommend the method of electors, which it did the following day. On the other hand, if this was not known, and if the joint-ballot rule adopted on August 24 (above, p. 135) was the general expectation, the larger states might have an interest in weakening the ineligibility in anticipation of controlling the choice of executives. In fact, it was the larger states that carried the Williamson motion. If, however, this extremely close vote had been based on that expectation, it would surely have been reconsidered after the method of presidential election was so drastically altered. Moreover, the large states had not voted that way when Gorham tried on June 22 to strike out ineligibility. They had just rejected the New Jersey Plan and still hoped to win PR in both houses, yet neither Virginia nor Pennsylvania supported him.

Ineligibility was also related, even more basically, to fears of concentrated power. After all, the corruption of Parliament by the patronage of the Crown had numbered among the causes of the Revolution itself. Yet the attitude of the Convention toward this potential danger shows clearly its distance from the sentiments of the 1770s. While some of the delegates, such as Gerry, Mason, and Randolph, retained the Country antagonism to all forms of influence, others, such as Gorham, Hamilton, and Morris, expressed the Court view of the great advantages of eligibility. The Convention was almost evenly divided on the issue in general,[28] but in the end only the concurrent

28. Votes on various aspects of ineligibility were evenly divided three times (in June, in

executive office holding, applied to national offices, and Madison's new and enhanced offices remained of the Virginia Plan restrictions. In the end, too, it was precisely the men who had fought hardest for those restrictions who refused to sign the Constitution.

The Judiciary

Excluded from the conditional political veto on legislation (above, pp. 140–42), the judges were given an absolute legal veto. The Virginia Plan provided both "supreme" and "inferior" tribunals (1:21), as well as the revisionary power and the legislative negative on state laws. These courts were intended as restraints upon the legislative and the executive branches of the new system, and, of course, as its judicial branch, making it independent of the state courts. But the "supremacy" clause and the prohibitions on the states were expected to operate through the courts, so the structure and powers of the judiciary must be seen as established, more than incidentally, to restrain the states as well.

The need for a supreme national court was generally accepted, being included in all the plans; the "inferior tribunals," however, were controversial. The state courts, already in existence, could hear cases initially, with proper appeals to the supreme court; besides, "the people will not bear such innovations"—so argued Rutledge, Sherman, Butler, and Martin (1:124–25, 341). On the other hand, conceiving state judges to be dependent upon the legislatures, and the states to have interests contrary to the national interest as expressed by the new legislature, Madison spoke of "improper Verdicts" obtained in state courts by "biassed directions" to the jury and of the "local prejudices of an undirected jury" (1:124). The inferior tribunals, nevertheless, were struck out of the Virginia Plan, 5 to 4; but, by a transfer of their establishment from the Constitution to the discretion of the national legislature, the nationalists revived them. Their opponents tried again to eliminate them on July 18, but they were unable to carry a single state delegation. Randolph told them bluntly, "the Courts of the States cannot be trusted with the administration of the National Laws" (2:46).

August, and in September), and six different states were divided: Massachusetts, New York, Pennsylvania, Delaware, and Maryland in June and Georgia in August and September (1:217, 377, 399; 2:289, 492).

Judicial Review

There is no doubt that the Convention expected these courts to reject unconstitutional laws, both state and national.[29] The power of judicial review was only beginning to be exercised at the state level, and was hardly understood by the public, but this convention of lawyers was well aware of it. Repeatedly, beginning with Gerry and King on June 4 (1:97, 109), it was mentioned in connection with two subjects, the proposed legislative negative on state laws and the executive veto of national laws.[30] It may have exerted decisive influence on the abandonment of the negative and on the refusal of the Convention to associate the judges with the executive in the veto power, giving them "a double negative" as Martin expressed it (2:76). Madison struggled long yet unsuccessfully for the latter, as for the former. While the Convention thus shaped its decisions on the assumption of judicial review, only two delegates spoke in opposition to it. On August 15 Mercer "disapproved of the Doctrine that the Judges as expositors of the Constitution should have authority to declare a law void." Dickinson "was strongly impressed" with Mercer's point and "thought no such power ought to exist" (2:298–99). But no response was made to Mercer.

Why, in view of the difference of opinion thus expressed, and the great importance of the matter, was the review power not explicitly included in the lengthy section on the jurisdiction of the courts? Gouverneur Morris, who penned the final draft for the Committee of Style, recalled in 1814 that he had used clear language, "excepting, nevertheless, a part of what relates to the judiciary," where "it became necessary to select phrases, which expressing my own notions would not alarm others."[31] A comparison of the phrases regarding the judiciary approved and sent to the Committee of Style, however, with those emerging from the Committee, shows that the few changes made were not substantive; so why, after a quarter of a century, did Morris single out the judiciary article as the only one intentionally made ambiguous or equivocal? One may speculate that this article had impressed itself upon his mind not through his work in the Committee of Style (after all, it took only a week) but through the way in which the Convention itself

29. The individual views of the delegates were examined in detail by Charles A. Beard in *The Supreme Court and the Constitution* (New York, 1912). His analysis was criticized by (among others) Edwin S. Corwin in the *American Political Science Review* for May 1913.

30. By Sherman (2:27, 28), Morris (2:28, 92, 299), Wilson (2:73), Martin (2:76), Mason (2:78), Madison (2:28, 93, 440), Randolph (2:144); and in opposition to it by Mercer (2:298) and Dickinson (2:299).

31. Morris to Timothy Pickering, December 22, 1814 (Farrand's *Records*, 3:420).

had dealt with judicial review. The whole process of structuring and empowering the judiciary was conditioned by a consciousness that the courts would exercise the review power and by an equally vivid consciousness that this could not be openly said in the document. The recent use of judicial review in Rhode Island and in North Carolina had provoked vigorous public protest,[32] and Madison found an oblique way to remind the delegates of this (2:28). No denial was ever made of the review power when it was used in debate, and no motion was ever made to make it explicit.

Nothing said in the Convention pointed clearly to the form of judicial review later developed by Chief Justice Marshall. The conception held was closer to that of Coke in *Dr. Bonham's Case* that statutes in violation of fundamental principles of "common right and reason" (e.g., denying jury trials) are void in themselves and may be disregarded by the courts. The contrary view of Blackstone, reflected in Mercer's remarks, was influential in America but was currently losing ground because written constitutions, as statements of fundamental principles, gave the courts clearer criteria to compare with the statutes than English courts had ever had. These constitutions limited the legislatures in some ways, but "legislative supremacy" remained and the courts usually deferred to the legislatures in doubtful cases.

The Convention established the judiciary as a coordinate branch, and Marshall seized upon this to terminate all deference in doubtful cases and to assert not only an equality of the three branches but a unique role for his Court as the final interpreter of the law. For him the Constitution was not a restatement or elaboration of fundamental principles but a positive enactment, the supreme law, subject to the same rules of interpretation that were applied to statutes. He thus converted judicial review from a rarely used "delicate and awful" power, as Justice Iredell called it (in *Calder v. Bull*, 3 Dall. 386 [1798])—a judicial substitute for revolution to protect fundamental principles—into a normal process of law enforcement.[33]

32. *Trevett v. Weeden* (Rhode Island Superior Court of Judicature, September 1786) and *Bayard v. Singleton* (North Carolina Superior Court, May 1787). These and other early precedents are discussed, with lengthy quotations, in Charles G. Haines, *The American Doctrine of Judicial Supremacy*, 2d ed. (New York, 1959), pp. 88–121.

33. For a penetrating history of the evolution of review concepts see Sylvia Snowiss, "From Fundamental Law to the Supreme Law of the Land: A Reinterpretation of the Origin of Judicial Review," in *Studies in American Political Development*, ed. Karen Orren and Stephen Skowronek, vol. 2, pp. 1–67 (New Haven, 1987); see also her *Judicial Review and the Law of the Constitution* (New Haven, 1990). For a different reading of Marshall see Robert L. Clinton, *"Marbury v. Madison" and Judicial Review* (Lawrence, Kans., 1989). For the transition from review based on unwritten concepts of justice to a basis in the people's will as found in written

Thus, those who were avid, like Madison, for the legislative negative on state laws, and who feared that the new national legislature itself might respond to public opinion in the manner of the state legislatures, had forged a secret weapon for both purposes. All forms of human law, and perhaps natural law as well, had been named within the jurisdiction of the national courts, appointments to which would be successively filtered through the executive and the Senate at two removes from the people, and would be for life—the only offices for which this tenure was thought feasible.[34]

In spite of all this, however, it remains doubtful that the Convention understood, or intended, that the Supreme Court would become the final arbiter of all disputes between the central government and the states.[35] The delegates, with the exceptions noted, were complacent with regard to cases in which the courts might reject state laws or the laws of Congress as being repugnant to the Constitution. No votes were cast against the "supremacy" clause when Martin introduced it on July 17 nor later against its revised forms (2:29, 389, 417). Nor was any vote cast against the jurisdiction of the courts as those provisions made their way through the Convention. But is it conceivable that this level of agreement would have obtained with regard to a case in which Congress clearly exceeded its powers, in the opinion of one or more states, and the Supreme Court did *not* reject the law?[36]

To see the distinction clearly, let us recall that the colonies had submitted peaceably to Privy Council review of their laws and judicial decisions, but had risen in revolt when the legislative power of Parliament exceeded what they held to be its limits. So, under the Constitution, a vast difference would exist between judicial review and restraint of the legislative power within the bounds of the Constitution, on the one hand, and judicial aid and

---

constitutions see Leslie F. Goldstein, "Popular Sovereignty, the Origins of Judicial Review, and the Revival of Unwritten Law," *Journal of Politics* 48 (February 1986): 51–71. For a brilliant examination of the difficulties in recent theories of judicial review see Mark Tushnet, *Red, White, and Blue: A Critical Analysis of Constitutional Law* (Cambridge, Mass., 1988).

34. On the anti-democratic motivations and results of this, see the chapter on the judiciary in J. Allen Smith's *Spirit of American Government* (New York, 1907). For a more balanced discussion see Albert P. Melone and George Mace, *Judicial Review and American Democracy* (Ames, Iowa, 1988).

35. For the counterargument see John R. Schmidhauser, *The Supreme Court as Final Arbiter in Federal-State Relations, 1789–1957* (Chapel Hill, 1958).

36. Such was, of course, the case in *McCulloch v. Maryland* (4 Wheat. 316, 1819), and it is interesting that Marshall thought it necessary to insert into his opinion some amazing obiter dicta. This opinion was ably attacked by Judge Spencer Roane in the *Richmond Enquirer* and by John Taylor in *Construction Construed, and Constitutions Vindicated* (Richmond, 1820). For Roane, see *The John P. Branch Historical Papers of Randolph-Macon College* 2 (June 1905): 51–121.

support for the extension of that power outside those bounds, on the other. The Convention never really confronted this problem. For the nationalists it was not a problem but rather a part of the plan. For the state federalists and the state-sovereignty men, however, it amounted to a major failure of foresight.[37]

It may be, however, that those among the delegates, if there were any, who realized that such a problem might arise were not able to see their way through to a solution. Many partial solutions are obvious—such as suspending the act of Congress until reenacted after the next election (as the Pennsylvania constitution provided) or, for a judicial solution, state judges joining the justices of the Supreme Court in a special tribunal. But for men who were trying, as the state federalists were, to balance the general government with the states, there is no obvious way to provide an arbiter between them without tilting the balance toward that final authority. It is essentially the problem of protecting a minority, one of the most complex and difficult of all political problems. Still, it is difficult to imagine a man like Dickinson, who was skeptical of the whole idea of judicial review, consciously and silently turning the matter over to the courts.

The Assault on the Jury System

The review power, however, was not the only weapon in the judicial arsenal, nor the only one in camouflage. Having little confidence in the people's representatives sitting in legislative bodies, the nationalists had as little or less in the people themselves sitting on juries. So three provisions were inserted to undermine the jury system, all of which were later eliminated by the Sixth and Seventh amendments.[38]

37. Robert Yates, if he was the author of the "Brutus" papers, most clearly anticipated this line of development a few months later, but he left the Convention without calling attention to the problem. See especially Brutus No. 12, *New York Journal*, February 7 and 14, 1788, reprinted in *The Complete Anti-Federalist*, ed. Herbert J. Storing (Chicago, 1981), 2:422–28. Storing also discusses the authorship on p. 358.

38. Lord Chief Justice Mansfield had curtailed the powers of English juries and introduced other changes. William Holdsworth, *A History of English Law* (16 vols., London, 1938), 10:672–96, 12:465–560. Forrest McDonald noted that Hamilton, Wilson, and Gouverneur and Robert Morris were fully aware of Mansfield's changes "and were hopeful, even determined, that a similar transformation could be made to happen in America." McDonald, *Novus Ordo Seclorum*, p. 115. Jefferson, on the contrary, was a critic of Mansfield. Julius S. Waterman, "Thomas Jefferson and Blackstone's *Commentaries*," in *Essays in the History of Early American Law*, ed. David H. Flaherty (Chapel Hill, 1969), pp. 467–72, and Jefferson to John Brown Cutting, October 2, 1788, in his *Papers*, 13:649.

In *The American Revolution in the Law* (Princeton, 1990), Shannon C. Stimson cogently

First, jury trials in criminal cases were expressly required (Article III, Section 2). But where? "Such Trial shall be held in the State where the said Crimes shall have been committed," not "in the vicinage," as was immemorial custom. This would give great flexibility in the location of trials—perhaps a dangerous flexibility—but no voice was raised in the Convention to restrict this flexibility for the protection of accused persons.

Second, the express provision of juries in criminal cases suggested the presumption that they were not required in civil cases. Here voices were raised, but very late. The jury clause first appeared in the Committee of Detail and was reported August 6. On September 12 Williamson and Gerry tried to have the Committee of Style bring in a provision for juries in civil cases. Gorham objected that "it is not possible to discriminate equity cases from those in which juries are proper." Mason agreed: "the jury cases cannot be specified"; but nevertheless "a general principle laid down on this and some other points would be sufficient." The civil-jury proposal was then connected with the general motion for a "Committee to prepare a Bill of Rights" and was defeated 10 to 0 (2:587–88). Again three days later Pinckney and Gerry tried a direct provision: "And a trial by jury shall be preserved as usual in civil cases." They were answered, again by Gorham, with the specious argument, equally true of criminal cases, that the states differed in their usages of juries. King joined him, and C. C. Pinckney thought that such a clause "would be pregnant with embarrassments." The motion lost, 11 to 0 (2:628). The suspicion is unavoidable that something more lay behind this near unanimity. Civil juries were guaranteed by the Seventh Amendment in a single sentence.

Third, appeals were allowed on jury findings of fact. Like the "supremacy" clause, this provision appeared first in the New Jersey Plan and was subtly altered. Paterson proposed that cases be heard first in the state courts "subject nevertheless, for the correction of all errors, both in law & fact in rendering judgement, to an appeal to the Judiciary of the U. States" (1:243). Defeated along with the rest of the Plan on June 19, this idea lay dormant for ten weeks until it was given sudden vitality on August 27, a Monday when Massachusetts, New Jersey, and North Carolina happened to be absent. Morris asked whether or not the appellate jurisdiction "extended to matters of fact as well as law—and to cases of Common law as well as Civil law." Wilson, for the Committee of Detail, replied: "The Committee he

---

analyzes the history of the jury in colonial America, both as a type of democratic limitation on government and as a precursor of a similar role of judicial review.

believed meant facts as well as law & Common as well as Civil law. The jurisdiction of the federal Court of Appeals had he said been so construed."[39] Dickinson thereupon moved to insert "both as to law & fact" (2:431). It is interesting, and probably significant, that no motion was made in this apparently well-planned effort at clarification to insert the other dichotomy of Morris. Appeals of both facts and law are characteristic of the civil but not of the common law, so the one insertion might be taken to open the door also to the civil law. Like judicial review, this matter was judged best left unexpressed. In any event, Dickinson's motion was accepted without discussion and without opposition. Gone were the limiting phrases "for the correction of all errors" and "in rendering judgment." Appeals on other grounds were possible, even on findings of facts by juries in both criminal and civil cases. Madison had asked, on June 19, "Of what avail wd. an appellate tribunal be, after an acquittal?" (1:317). Here was an answer: the government might appeal from a finding of "not guilty." Here too was a power, as Martin pointed out the following March, "very different from what our court of appeals, or any court of appeals in the United States or in England enjoys" (3:287).

This covert assault on the jury system, which was to prove so costly of public confidence in the ratification struggle, would not have been attempted without strong motivations. The state interests that rose up to turn back PR in the Senate and the legislative negative on state laws were not aroused to defend the individual against the centralized power they were creating. On the contrary, most of the state-oriented delegates shared with the nationalists a belief that they must erect a Chinese wall against the "excesses of democracy" that seemed to be subverting republican government and threatening the rights of property. The jury system of the common law might severely handicap the unwonted application of the new government directly to individuals and the unwanted collection of the new national taxes. The attempt to obviate that handicap, along with the cavalier rejection of Mason's bid for a bill of rights, stand as measures of the lengths to which they were willing to go to restrain democracy.

The antagonism toward juries was continued in the drafting of the Judiciary Act in the Senate in 1789. Senator William Maclay of Pennsylvania

---

39. One might ask what significance should be attached to the order of words chosen by Morris and exactly repeated by Wilson, as Madison records them. In "as well as" questions, the doubtful member usually comes first, which is clearly the case regarding "facts." This leads to a presumption that the common law was the doubtful member of the second pair, since there is no apparent reason for a stylist like Morris to avoid the parallel construction.

recorded an episode on July 10 in which "the lawyers showed plainly the cloven foot of their intentions. . . . Now we see what gentlemen would be at. It is to try facts on civil-law principles, without the aid of a jury, and this, I promise you, never will be submitted to." Maclay's entries on the judiciary debate help to clarify the events in the Convention.[40]

The Amending Article

Perhaps no other part of the Constitution has been more universally regarded as undemocratic than has the amending article. It is easy to compute the tiny fraction of the population, properly distributed so as to constitute a bare majority in the smallest states, that could legally defeat any amendment. Writing some thirty-five years after the Civil War amendments, during which time no amendment had been made, J. Allen Smith found the fraction to be one forty-fourth, and concluded, "As a matter of fact it is impossible to secure amendments to the Constitution, unless the sentiment in favor of change amounts almost to a revolution."[41] He went on to suggest that the Framers had deliberately made the process difficult in order to "dethrone the numerical majority" and to perpetuate the influence of a minority.

It can, of course, also be shown that a properly distributed minority could carry an amendment. But such computations tell us little about the Framers' intent. A more recent student, Martin Diamond, found that they intended to "ensure that passage of an amendment would require a *nationally* distributed majority, though one that legally could consist of a bare numerical majority."[42]

It would not be appropriate to review the controversial literature on

40. *The Journal of William Maclay* (New York, 1927), pp. 101–2. The legislative history of the Judiciary Act of 1789 contains many ambiguities, but the version sent to the House on July 17 included several clauses requiring findings of fact by juries. Two of these clauses, by their locations as the final sentence of a section, look like amendments added in Senate debate. *Legislative Histories*, ed. Charlene B. Bickford and Helen E. Veit, vol. 5 (Baltimore, 1986), pp. 1200, 1202, 1203, 1208 (sections 9, 12, 16, and 29), in the *Documentary History of the First Federal Congress*, ed. Charlene B. Bickford et al. (Baltimore, 1972–).

41. *The Spirit of American Government*, p. 46. For an analytical history of interpretations of Article V from the Convention to the present, see John R. Vile, *The Constitutional Amending Process in American Political Thought* (New York, 1992).

42. "Democracy and *The Federalist*: A Reconsideration of the Framers' Intent," *American Political Science Review* 53 (March 1959): 57.

Article V, but it is obvious that the spectrum of interpretation is wide. It may be more profitable to look at the Convention history of the article, which supplies a few answers and also raises some interesting questions.

Convention Discussion

From the beginning of the Convention the absence and known hostility of Rhode Island put the delegates on notice that the amending procedure of the Articles of Confederation could not be used to make the desired changes. On the other hand, the extreme difficulty of the unanimity rule might be used to perpetuate the new system once it was established. And the ratification rule could be, and was, physically separated from and different from the rule for subsequent amendments. Yet it could not but have occurred to the delegates that, if they wrote a unanimity rule to protect their own handiwork, another convention might some day throw out the whole (as they were doing with the Articles), whereas an operable amending procedure might leave most of the structure intact. What was needed, then, if their motives were such, was a rule that could be used, but only with considerable difficulty, a sort of safety valve to prevent more serious explosions. But were their motives such?

The Virginia Plan contained an amending article expressing two ideas: that amendments should be provided "whensoever it shall seem necessary," and "that the assent of the National Legislature ought not to be required thereto" (1:22). This was debated briefly on June 5, when Gerry defended it, saying: "The novelty & difficulty of the experiment requires periodical revision. The prospect of such a revision would also give intermediate stability to the Govt." (1:122). Pinckney and others doubted the need for an amending provision and the policy of excluding the legislature. Mason defended both ideas: the plan "will certainly be defective," and amendments "will be necessary, and it will be better to provide for them, in an easy, regular and Constitutional way than to trust to chance and violence"; and should the legislature abuse its power, it would refuse an amendment designed to curb such abuses (1:202–3). The exclusion of the legislature was postponed and the main clause approved unanimously. Again, on July 23, it was passed unanimously, apparently without debate (2:87).

In the Committee of Detail Randolph and Rutledge began the conversion of this statement of principle into concrete provisions. They proposed a national convention called by the legislature on application by two thirds of the state legislatures (2:148). This was reported on August 6 and reached for debate on the 30th. The only remark recorded was the suggestion of Morris that the legislature "be left at liberty to call a Convention, whenever they please." The article was then passed, again unanimously (2:468).

On September 10, however, Gerry moved to reconsider the matter, objecting that such a convention might "subvert the State-Constitutions altogether." Hamilton, on the other hand, wanted "an easy mode . . . for supplying defects which will probably appear in the new System." He proposed that the national legislature be empowered to call a convention by a two-thirds vote in each house. Only New Jersey voted against the reconsideration, which began immediately with a motion from Sherman allowing the legislature to propose amendments, "but no amendments shall be binding until consented to by the several States." Wilson moved to amend Sherman's motion by inserting "two thirds of" before "several States." No debate is recorded on this, but it failed by a vote of 5 to 6, being supported by New Hampshire, Pennsylvania, Delaware, Maryland, and Virginia. Wilson then moved to insert "three fourths of," which carried unanimously. Thereupon Madison and Hamilton introduced a substitute motion that eliminated the national convention completely, leaving proposal to the legislature and ratification to the legislatures or conventions in three fourths of the states. Rutledge insisted upon an exemption for the slave trade until 1808, and this new version was approved by nine states, New Hampshire being divided and Delaware voting "no" (2:557–59).

When the version of this reported by the Committee of Style was reached, on September 15, the most extensive of the debates on the subject took place, although it was only sketchily recorded by Madison. Morris and Gerry succeeded in reinstating proposal of amendments by a national convention. Sherman, speaking for a minority of small states, feared "that three fourths of the States might be brought to do things fatal to particular States, as abolishing them altogether or depriving them of their equality in the Senate." He moved to strike out the words "of three fourths," which would require ratification by all states; this carried Massachusetts, Connecticut, and New Jersey, and divided New Hampshire. Gerry tried to strike out ratification by conventions in three fourths of the states; he carried only Connecticut. Sherman then moved to add a proviso "that no State shall without its consent be affected in its internal police, or deprived of its equal suffrage in the Senate." Madison made a surly response to this: "Begin with these special provisos, and every State will insist on them . . ." and it was defeated 8 to 3—Connecticut, New Jersey, and Delaware supporting. Now thoroughly aroused, Sherman proposed to strike out Article V altogether.

He was seconded by Brearley, and carried Connecticut and New Jersey and divided Delaware. Sherman's fears seemed abundantly justified: the nationalists who were ready to protect the slave trade against amendments (without recorded vote or debate) were unwilling to extend similar protection to the states. However, "circulating murmurs of the small States," as Madison called them, "dictated" that Gouverneur Morris remake a part of Sherman's motion "that no State, without its consent shall be deprived of its equal suffrage in the Senate." This time it "was agreed to without debate, no one opposing it, or on the question, saying no" (2:629–31). In this polarized atmosphere discussion of the article ended.[43]

The Implications

Were these debates evidence of a concerted conspiracy to deprive the sovereign people of their sovereignty? Or to guarantee the proposed system against change? Or even to minimize the influence of the people on the process of change?

To deal with these questions in reverse order, some negative evidence must be noticed. No proposal was made for ratification of amendments by popular referendum, either on a national or on a state basis. No proposal was aimed at guaranteeing the support of a popular majority for amendments. Nor was it suggested that ratification by states containing a majority of the national population should be sufficient. No catalog of the state constitutional provisions for amendments was made (so far as our records show) in search of alternatives, although about half of them gave the voters a direct or indirect voice in the process.[44] On the other hand, the provision for conventions, both national and state, opened additional doors for popular influence. At the state level they were traditionally directly elected and were more popular than the state senates. The efforts of Madison and Hamilton to eliminate them at the national level, and of Gerry at the state level, were ultimately overwhelmingly defeated.

43. Why did Sherman drop the remainder of his motion? Recalling his defeat on "internal Police" back in July (2:25–26), he may have thought (a) the Senate would protect the states, because (b) the internal autonomy of the states was so well established. The Galloway Plan in 1774 and the Franklin Plan of 1775 had provided this. In 1776, in preparing for independence and a confederation, nine states had reserved internal authority; and the Dickinson draft of the Articles, responding to these reservations, contained two provisions protecting "internal police." These reservations are collected and analyzed in Crosskey and Jeffrey, *Politics and the Constitution*, 3:93–97, 525–26.

44. Those of New Hampshire, Massachusetts, Pennsylvania, Maryland, South Carolina, and Georgia (and also Vermont).

If the delegates can be taken at their words, far from opposing change, they thought their handiwork would in practice be found defective and in need of amendment. Moreover, delegates as far apart as Hamilton and Mason used the word "easy" to describe a desirable method. Why, then, did they not make amendments easy? Perhaps they did—in comparison with the unanimity rule of the Articles. They provided two methods for proposal and two for ratification—easier, of course, than either method singly. But the limiting influence in this direction was not the delegates' fear of the people; it was the small states' fear of the large. The purely national method reported by the Committee of Detail on August 6 contained no distinction between proposal and ratification and no special protection against a popular majority in a national convention both proposing and ratifying. Once Gerry pointed out the danger to the states, however, state ratification was an obvious line of defense, and Sherman immediately moved the unanimity rule. The nationalists did not try to defend the reported method nor to argue any national form of procedure. On the other hand, ratification by a simple majority of the states would be dangerous to the large states. Instead, Wilson proposed ratification by two thirds of the states, then by three fourths. If he had been seeking to make amendments difficult he would have tried three fourths before two thirds. The small-state men, of course, were seeking to do just that, but in terms of states, not of people. Neither for proposing nor for ratifying did any of them suggest a special majority within a state.

But can the delegates, in this matter, be taken at their word? After all, amendments were made difficult, whatever the motive. Protection for the states led them to propose a Constitution that a majority of the people could not control unless they happened to be properly distributed to control three fourths of the states. It is not credible that they were unaware of this result. Why were no voices raised, like Wilson's before the Connecticut compromise, eloquently arguing for the people, not the states, as the foundation of the system? If the prevailing conception had been of one sovereign "people of the United States," as Marshall was later to say, one might expect debate to center on appropriate methods for distinguishing the people's legislative will from their constitutional will. But no such debate took place. Instead, attention centered on the dangers to the separate states and the conditions under which they would agree to be bound by the other states. In this manner the matter of popular sovereignty, whether to implement it or to restrain it, at the national or at the state level, was simply passed over in silence.

This focus on the states makes it clear that the defeat of the nationalists on the Connecticut compromise was not confined to the Senate or to the structure of the government.[45] Here at the end of the Convention their opponents were relentlessly building the equality of states into the foundations of the system whence it could reassert itself on all future amendments. The idea of a single national body politic whose people were the source of supreme power, and therefore of the supreme law, was not even a debatable position.

Yet the state-sovereignty men also had been defeated. When only three states supported Sherman's motion to replace "¾" with the old unanimity rule (above, p. 157), he did not propose a larger fraction. So why did none of the state federalists propose, as they had done with regard to representation (1:526, 550), that amendments be ratified by a majority of the states containing a majority of the people? Or that a national popular referendum be used in some manner? Was it necessary to give the small-state men both the fraction of three fourths and the guaranty of equality in the Senate? The thought is irresistible that, if the guaranty had been obtained before the vote on Wilson's fraction of two thirds (September 10), at least one additional state would have voted "ay" and two thirds would have carried. Why, then, did no one propose this fraction on September 15?

It is, perhaps, ungenerous to raise such questions about tired men at the end of their long march. Some conclusions nonetheless appear.

1. With the exceptions of Sherman, Mason, and Gerry, the delegates seem to have considered the amending process not to be of major import; this article, not the shortest, occasioned the least debate of any.
2. Nevertheless, the basic conception of the amending article as well as its wording were entirely changed, beginning on September 10, from a national convention system working on proposals from the states to a system of proposal at the national level followed by ratification at the state level.
3. The states and not the people were the focus of attention; no argument was made either that amendments should have the support of a majority of the people or, on the other hand, that a simple majority should not be sufficient.

45. Both the content and the atmosphere of the debate on September 15, and not Madison's churlish remark alone (above, p. 157), are related to the acrimonious debates of June and July on the bases of representation.

4. The nationalists had so far abandoned their original intention to make the new government independent of the states that they did not think it worth while even to propose an alternative to state ratification.

5. The delegates had no more, and probably less, desire to make their system responsive to the people's will in the amending process than in ordinary legislation, so this basic restriction of popular sovereignty may have been in their eyes a positive good.

6. Their idea of "easy" amendments was aimed primarily at the avoidance of situations such as those under the Articles when one or two states blocked amendments.

7. The defenders of the states, in insisting upon state ratification, were not defending state sovereignty, since, without debate, every state voted for ratification by three fourths, which meant that any of the states, up to one fourth of the total, might be bound against its will. Even Sherman, who had second thoughts after that unanimous decision, was concerned to protect the states' "internal police" and their equality in the Senate—not their sovereignty.

In more general terms it may be concluded that the consideration of amending procedures was one of the least adequate of the Convention debates. The subject had been before the delegates explicitly since May, but serious debate did not occur until the last week of the Convention. No committee was charged with canvassing the alternatives. No use was made, so far as we know, of the experience with various state procedures. No computations were made of the degrees of difficulty or other incidence involved in the alternatives that were discussed. No evidence appears in the records that the delegates evaluated the alternatives in terms of their implications for the locus of sovereignty; the word was never used.

In view of this relatively inadequate debate it may be unwise to lean heavily on Article V in interpreting the Convention. J. Allen Smith started with a conception of one national sovereign people, but that was not the conception in the Convention. The amending procedure, therefore, was not, in the minds of the delegates, an ultimate exercise in restraining popular sovereignty. It was, instead, a new embodiment of the prevailing view that the United States was both one nation and several nations. Madison was clear about this in *Federalist* Number 39. Were the Constitution wholly national, he wrote,

> the supreme and ultimate authority would reside in the *majority* of the people of the Union; and this authority would be competent at

all times, like that of a majority of every national society, to alter or abolish its established government. Were it wholly federal, on the other hand, the concurrence of each State in the Union would be essential to every alteration that would be binding on all. The mode provided by the plan of the convention is not founded on either of these principles. In requiring more than a majority, and particularly in computing the proportion by *States*, not by *citizens*, it departs from the *national* and advances towards the *federal* character; in rendering the concurrence of less than the whole number of States sufficient, it loses again the *federal* and partakes of the *national* character.

He might also have stressed that formal proposal of amendments is a national procedure, while ratification is a state procedure. Even Calhoun, enamored as he was of state sovereignty, recognized that "the right of a State originally to complete self-government . . . has been modified by the Constitution, as already stated, so that three fourths of the States may now grant power. . . . It is then clear that it was not intended that the States should be more united than the will of one fourth of them, or, rather, one more than a fourth, would permit."[46]

Calhoun's view of this fraction as a measure of the degree of unity intended by the Convention may have been roughly correct. He cites in support of his view the failure of Wilson's motion for ratification by two thirds, but he did not mention that five states supported the motion. Another difficulty lies in the fact that, on September 15, three states preferred unanimous consent for amendments. It may be inferred that the degree of unity intended was not a matter of unanimous agreement nor of settled conviction.

It is also correct that the degree of unity has not remained constant since 1787. If popular sovereignty is now generally thought of only in national terms, then Article V is anachronistic, and rightly subject to the strictures of Smith on its effects—if not on the motives of its authors. It is not reasonable that a sovereign people should be able to control its own fundamental law only by conforming to restrictions intended for other purposes. On the other hand, if popular sovereignty is still a valid concept

---

46. "Letter to General Hamilton on the subject of State Interposition," August 28, 1832, in *The Works of John C. Calhoun*, ed. Richard K. Crallé, vol. 6 (New York, 1879), pp. 177–78. For a recent analysis of Calhoun's views of the amending article, see John R. Vile, *The Constitutional Amending Process*, pp. 79–93.

at the state level, then the United States is still both one nation and several nations, and the theoretical foundations of Article V—the state-federalist approach—remain valid. From this it does not follow that the article embodies the best possible implementation of that approach, or, in particular, that the fraction three fourths now approximates the degree of unity that has been attained.

The Mode of Ratification

The methods of ratification worked out for future amendments could have been written in for the ratification of the Constitution itself. The existence of the Articles of Confederation, however, and delegates' fears of the state legislatures, made some differences necessary.

As an assembly called and instructed by the Confederation Congress, the Convention felt bound to report its handiwork to that body. From the beginning the Virginia Plan had provided for the "approbation of Congress," and this provision stood until the end of August, when Dickinson raised the question whether "Congress can concur in contravening the system under which they acted" (2:469). Without debate the provision was struck out (2:478), those who might doubt the power of Congress to approve being joined by those who doubted its willingness. On September 10, however, Gerry obtained a reconsideration. Yet his reinstatement motion was unanimously rejected after Wilson cataloged the enemies of the plan and asked, "Can it be safe to make the assent of Congress necessary[?]" (2:562–63). The delegates apparently agreed with King that it would be safer and "more respectful to Congress to submit the plan generally" rather than "in such a form as expressly and necessarily to require their approbation or disapprobation" (2:561).

There were other, more basic issues. Did ratification require agreement by the separate states, or could a single national convention be assembled? Could Congress be persuaded to call a ratifying convention? Some of the states had responded to the call by the Annapolis Convention even before Congress had done so; but the absence of Rhode Island and the partial attendance of New York and New Hampshire, to say nothing of the quorum problems of Congress, showed the precariousness of such assemblies. A greater difficulty, however, blocked that path: the certainty of instructed delegations. Already the State of Delaware had forbidden its delegates to surrender the equality of states; so it could be foreseen that, with the full text of the Constitution to work with, the state legislatures, if they were willing to send delegates at all, would require or forbid them to do certain probably irreconcilable things. The handiwork of the long summer would thus come unstuck, and the ratification would probably fail. Pinckney succinctly stated the prevailing view: "Nothing but confusion & contrarity could spring from the experiment. The States will never agree in their plans—And the Deputies to a second Convention coming together under the discordant impressions of their Constituents, will never agree" (2:632).[47]

Much as the nationalists (but not the state federalists or the state-sovereignty men) may have wished for a purely national mode of ratification, they could think of none that did not entail the risks of instructions.[48] There was, of course, an obvious way out. Had there been a genuine democrat among them he might have suggested a simple submission to the voters—Massachusetts and New Hampshire had established constitutions in that way—as one national constituency, with a safety clause exempting any state that chose not to vote or whose people voted "no." A referendum would have had the advantage, from the Convention's point of view, of avoiding the attachment of any conditions or proposed amendments. They were, however, unwilling to trust the voters. There was no way to escape the state legislatures.

Working then for state ratifications, the Convention encountered more difficulties. Could the old Confederation be set aside without the consent of all the states? Some delegates were prepared, early on, to go for a partial Union (1:123 Wilson), while others, near the end, still felt scruples against so direct a violation of the Articles (2:475 Sherman, 2:561 Gerry). Once over that scruple, the question seemed to be, How many states should be required? To his credit, Madison managed, drawing on Sherman (1:550), to base his answer upon principles: "require the concurrence of a majority of

47. The idea of a single ratifying convention was so tightly connected with the idea of amendments after public discussion that it was supported by only Franklin, Mason, and Randolph, who were dissatisfied with the document at the end. Morris might be added; back in July, in the wake of defeat by the Connecticut compromise, he had moved for "one general Convention . . . to consider, *amend* & establish" the plan (2:93). Morris wanted, as he made clear on August 31, a convention "that will have the firmness to provide a vigorous Government, which we are afraid to do" (2:479).

48. To minimize those risks by avoiding a new convention (at great individual sacrifices), the Convention might have formulated procedural rules for dealing with irreconcilable instructions and then adjourned until the following May to seek authority (from Congress or from the states) to consider amendments and then to ratify. This was not suggested.

both the States and people," which might be seven states, whereas requiring nine states, without regard to their populations, might lead to ratification by less than a majority of the people. He was supported by Wilson and Clymer, but no vote was taken on his motion—if he made one (2:469, 475, 477).[49]

Instead, a simpler numbers game was tried. Wilson wanted to start with "seven," but motions were made for "thirteen," then "ten," and then "nine," which carried, 8 to 3. That magic number, which had been used for important decisions under the Articles, was reconsidered on September 10, when Hamilton and Gerry proposed that each state legislature be given the option to decide if it wanted to give its state convention the option to go with nine states or not. This dubious effort to escape from the Articles' unanimity clause was attacked by Wilson, Clymer, King, and Rutledge, and it carried only Connecticut (2:560–63). But no one, in this new discussion, cared enough about majority rule to try again Madison's idea of seven states with a majority of the people, which could have been added as a supplement to the magic nine.[50]

Another crucial issue was the manner in which the states should act. The Articles provided for the legislatures to act on amendments, but the Virginia Plan called for "an assembly or assemblies . . . recommended by the several Legislatures" and to be "expressly chosen by the people" (1:22).[51] Good reasons were adduced for this deviation: King pointed out that "[a] Convention being a single house, the adoption may more easily be carried thro' it" than through "several branches," and furthermore, the legislatures, "being to lose power, will be most likely to raise objections" (1:123). Moreover, legislative ratification would stand on the same footing as any other legislative act, open to conflict with later laws and even to repeal by a later legislature (1:122, 2:88, 89). Madison and Wilson wanted ratification in "the most unexceptionable form, and by the supreme authority of the people themselves" (1:123, 127). By this they meant not plebiscites but popularly

49. Madison was wrong in saying that his proposal, in the form that is recorded, would require the concurrence of a majority of the people, since the states ratifying might do so by narrow majorities. His slip illustrates, however, the fact that the minds of the strong nationalists were still operating in a universe of states as separate bodies politic, whose people would all be bound by the state's majority.

50. The contingency Madison foresaw actually came to pass. The first seven states to ratify contained about fifty-seven percent of the population (using Brearley's figures for whites, 1:573), and the contest would have been over in April. Yet it should be said that the failure to press the idea of a popular majority in ratification illustrates again the Convention's awareness that serious political issues may not yield to simple majorities.

51. This rather strange wording may have been chosen to accommodate a national ratifying convention.

elected conventions in the separate states. Thus ratification meant nine or more separate ratifications. And the repeated use of the singular word "people" as the ultimate source of power did not denote a single national people as distinguished from the peoples of the separate states, nor did it imply any democratic conception of the ongoing political process. The people were used abstractly, much as Locke had used them. Responding to objections that the Maryland constitution required other methods for changes, Madison said, "The people were in fact, the fountain of all power, and by resorting to them, all difficulties were got over. They could alter constitutions as they pleased" (2:476).

It may be concluded that the Convention, unwilling to risk a decision by the people themselves, either as one constituency or as thirteen, chose to risk instead the debates and proposals for amendments that might come from state conventions. By rejecting all conditional ratifications the leaders hoped that, in the new Congress, they would be able to reject also any undesirable amendments, and that the new system would remain intact. At the end Mason felt that "[i]t was improper to say to the people, take this or nothing" (2:362). But in its provisions for ratification the Convention said just that.

Why an Anti-Democratic Bias?

It has been almost customary to attribute these various restrictions on popular control of power to the delegates' desire to protect property, and to see their motivations as selfish—the legacy of Beard. A single-minded interest in matters of property, however, did not characterize the Convention, if the argument that I present in chapter 4 is valid. To the extent that the delegates were men of wealth they had, of course, an interest, even a selfish interest, in the defense of property rights; but property had not only private but social and civic functions as well. To confine their motivations to the selfish aspects of property is too restricted a reading of this assembly of very complex and sophisticated men.

As noted in chapter 2 (p. 26), their thought world contained conceptions of the relationships of property to political power derived from the Country ideology and deeply rooted in English history. Private property, especially landed property, gave its owners, they believed, a "permanent fixed interest" in the republic and the independence of thought, resources, and action to stand against any egregious concentration of governmental power that might arise.

The Revolution had not eliminated corruption in government circles as some had hoped it would,[52] so the old Country suspicion of politicians continued, focused frequently on the actions of the people's representatives in the state legislatures when they attacked property by passing various kinds of debtors laws. The search for new refinements in institutional structures began: Madison's famous "republican remedy for the diseases most incident to republican government."[53]

There being no ideological democrats in the Convention, there was no abstract debate distinguishing democracy from republicanism. The delegates assumed that only a republic could be accepted, and the debate dealt, not with democracy, but with democratic influences, how best to incorporate or exclude, improve or diminish them.

At the very beginning of the Convention, in the speech with which Randolph "opened the main business," he stated clearly the problem and his attitude toward it: "It is a maxim which I hold incontrovertible, that the powers of government exercised by the people swallows up the other branches. None of the constitutions have provided sufficient checks against the democracy. The feeble Senate of Virginia is a phantom. Maryland has a more powerful senate. . . . The check established in the constitution[s] of New York and Massachusetts is yet a stronger barrier against democracy, but they all seem insufficient" (1:26–27). His view was widely shared, Gerry, for example, saying that the people had "the wildest ideas of Government in the world. They were for abolishing the Senate in Massachusetts and giving all the other powers of Government to the other branch of the Legislature" (1:123).

Many of the delegates, students of classical history, no doubt remembered that the plebeians of Rome had supported Caesar, not Brutus. There were enough examples in the Greek city states of popular demagogues becoming tyrants to enable Polybius to construct a cycle of types of government in which democracy deteriorated into mob rule and then into despotism.[54] In modern times Florence and other Italian city republics had become monarchies, and the Dutch republic had surrendered power to a stadtholder.

52. E. James Ferguson and Elizabeth M. Nuxoll, "Investigation of Governmental Corruption during the American Revolution," *Congressional Studies* 8, no. 2 (1981): 13–35.
53. *Federalist*, No. 10, last paragraph.
54. Polybius, *The Histories*, Bk. VI, secs. 1–9; conveniently reprinted in Francis W. Coker, *Readings in Political Philosophy* (New York, 1938), pp. 114–21.

The delegates had not forgotten that, in a crisis of their own Revolution, the powers of a dictatorship for Washington and a small committee had been ardently proposed in Congress.[55] Dictatorship had been an old Roman institution, always of short duration; but the Roman republic also had succumbed to a princeps and then to an emperor.

The proposals of dictatorship during the Revolution were connected with the military circumstances and were elitist rather than popular. They came from the nationalists and were blocked by localist adherents of the Country ideology. After the war, however, the concentrations of political power came to be located in the state legislatures, and particularly in the lower houses. The threat to republican government thus shifted from the man on horse-back to legislative tyranny. The nationalists, therefore, assumed the blocking role, eager to forestall the growth of popular power before it polarized the separate states (as threatened by the dissension in the piedmonts of North Carolina, South Carolina, and Virginia and in the western counties of Pennsylvania and Massachusetts) and found more ideological and competent leadership than that of Daniel Shays.

The nationalists also believed that the growth of popular power was a threat to the Union. The compelling confirmation of this view lay in the reluctance of the legislatures to meet the requisitions of Congress even during the war; but they saw this reluctance as evidence of a more general popular debility: the incapacity of ordinary, inexperienced, and minimally educated men to take the broad and long-range view in public affairs. This endemic narrowness of horizon and shortness of foresight produced a reactive politics, coping with problems after they arose instead of anticipating and preventing them. It also produced value structures ranking local needs ahead of national needs and thus undermining unity in the pursuit of parochial goals—New York's import duties, for example.

It is not necessary, therefore, to believe that the delegates' distrust of democracy was concerned solely with actual or anticipated attacks on property. True enough, both the fragmentation of the Union and legislative

55. The fairly widespread maneuvers in 1780 are summarized in Jensen, *The New Nation*, pp. 43–53; see also Burnett, *Letters of Members*, 5:xiii–xviii. Washington is usually thought to have been adverse to such schemes, but on May 14, 1780, he sent identical letters to Congressmen James Duane and Joseph Jones saying that the "authority" of a "*small*" committee of Congress at his headquarters "should be Plenipotentiary to draw out men and supplies of every kind and give their sanction to any operations which the Commander in chief may not think himself at liberty to undertake without it, as well beyond, as within the limits of these States" [in Quebec?]. *The Writings of George Washington*, ed. John C. Fitzpatrick (Washington, 1937), 18:356–58.

tyranny had implications for property; but political motivations as well as those of property drove the nationalists to erect barriers against the people.

At the same time, the localists and the state federalists, fearing a strong central government in the hands of the nationalists, found some of the same barriers useful for their purposes. The result was a government with restraints on literally all parts and participants, including the people themselves.

On a more fundamental level, however, the Convention sensed the incompatibility of popular sovereignty with the rule of law.

A tyrant's decrees can take the form of law, but such arbitrary government hardly qualifies as a rule of law. It is precisely against such capricious power, in rulers and in citizens, that men have tried to erect the barriers of established, enforceable laws. If a legislative power is admitted, then the law is subject to change; yet the law needs some stability if it is to be a known, established barrier to tyranny.

Medieval jurisprudence—Hebrew, Christian, and Islamic—had seen the unchanging mind and will of God as the ultimate source of justice and of law. After Hobbes and Hume, however, this tradition, undermined by the theory of sovereignty, lost its grip on the establishment in England and was replaced (as was seen in chapter 2) by a jurisprudence of Parliamentary supremacy and unlimited sovereignty. The medieval definition of law as "an ordinance of reason" was largely supplanted by notions of law as the will of the legislature. Even so, in both England and America, strong feelings persisted that law should be just. The result, for the Revolutionary generation in America, was a clear demonstration that the legislative will of a distant and unrepresentative government was incompatible with the British constitution as they understood it. Hence the influence in America of the Country ideology, with its rejection of unlimited power.

Hence also, more recently, the opinion of the leading nationalists that the state legislatures, even if neither distant nor unrepresentative, were also capable of violating the basic principles of justice. If the law were simply the will of an ephemeral majority, it would not only be changeable but totally ineffective against majority tyranny. Like the will of an autocrat, the will of the people's representatives had proven to be an unreliable guide in the search for justice. With these demonstrations, separated in space and time, the educated elite of the Convention did not need the more drastic experience of the French in 1793 to learn the dangers of an unrestrained popular will. From their viewpoint the application of reason to the problems of social and political order was more promising than the assertion of will—both empirically and theoretically. They were also clear that men were not equally rational and that, as Sherman said in May, "The people should have as little to do as may be about the Government. They want information and are constantly liable to be misled" (1:48). Empirically, this might lead to an emphasis, such as Harrington's or Madison's, on the role and value of a Senate.[56] Theoretically, it might cut more deeply to excise the influence of majority will from important parts of the government, from control of the judicial process and of the Constitution itself.

Two general types of restraints on democracy came easily to mind. One was elitist: property qualifications, indirect elections, long terms of office, large districts, reeligibility, and Madison's idea of filtering. The other was the conception of fundamental law as a limitation on government. Elitism leans toward Blackstone and unlimited power: the people are restrained, but not the government. Fundamental law derives from notions of justice and from Opposition Whig ideas; it restrains both the people and their agents. The Convention made use of both types.

Hannah Arendt, contrasting the French and American revolutions, perceptively observed that the French leaders, under the influence of Rousseau's notion of a "general will," saw the people as the source of all power and the origin of all laws as well, whereas, she said, the Americans "were never even tempted to derive law and power from the same origin. The seat of power to them was the people, but the source of law was to become the Constitution, a written document, an endurable objective thing, which, to be sure, one could approach from many different angles . . . but which nevertheless was never a subjective state of mind, like the will."[57]

Arendt was wrong in crediting the Americans with such perspicacity. It was the inadequacy and injustice of law derived from the people's will through the state legislatures that stimulated the Convention to seek, not another source of law, but an institutional structure that, hopefully, would confine the creation of law within the bounds of wisdom and justice. The Constitution was not the source of law but a framework of limitations on the making of law by those to whom the people delegated the legislative power. Thus both power and law flow, theoretically, from the people, but through two different channels: power inheres in office and goes directly by virtue of election, but law flows slowly and indirectly—filtered by committees, chambers, vetoes, and courts.

---

56. *The Political Works of James Harrington*, ed. J.G.A. Pocock (Cambridge, 1977), pp. 170–78, 257–66; Madison, *Papers*, 8:350–51; and also Farrand, *Records*, 1:218–19, 222.
57. *On Revolution*, pp. 155–56.

But Arendt was right in seeing the Constitution as an enduring "objective thing," and not as a changeable embodiment of the popular will. The people were useful, as Locke had used them, as an abstract origin and justification for political authority, and in that sense they might be termed "sovereign." Once the government was established, however, the people and their representatives must be restricted to the lower levels of law and controlled by the Constitution—a higher level largely impervious to the popular will— if it was to be a government of laws and not of men.

In sum, the Founding Fathers proposed restraints on majority will for many reasons, both economic and political. They feared the future influence of the propertyless (already adumbrated in the state legislatures), as a threat to their own wealth, but also as a threat to the wisdom of republican decision making. They wished to protect republicanism against economic polarization within each state. They wished to protect the Union against short-sighted localism. And they wished to protect a structure of dependable law against the fickle winds of popular opinion.

They retained the antique belief, inherited in the Country tradition, that law was not solely a matter of legislative will but even more a matter of justice. From the days of Bracton, as we saw in chapter 2, the king was under the law. Later, the King-in-Parliament was the source of law but also (for those who rejected the innovations of Hobbes) under the laws of justice. The Revolution had displaced the old rulers, but the new rulers, the people and their agents, still needed to be under the law. Confident that justice was an intricate, long-range principle beyond the reach of popular foresight, they designed a dynamic system—primarily for a reign of law and therefore only conditionally for a reign of the people.

The General Result

The political motivations of the delegates, to preserve the Union and to restrain democracy by strengthening the central government, gave the nationalists an opportunity to set the agenda of the Convention with the Virginia Plan. Their thrust for a new system, a near replication of England's relation to the colonies, with general powers and a blanket veto over the states, was at first accepted by the Convention. Their uncompromising attitude and their summary rejection of the New Jersey Plan, however, alerted the other delegates to the danger that they might vitiate their own work by proposing a departure from established political customs too radical for the people to accept. Moreover, the nationalists' denigration of the states seemed too extreme, both unnecessary and unrealistic. For the state federalists the dual nature of American political society, as both one nation and several nations, required the recognition, the preservation, and the utilization of the states in the new system. Some older delegates especially, such as Dickinson, Gerry, Johnson, Mason, Rutledge, and Sherman, who had been active in the conflicts of the 1760s and 1770s, remembered the dangers of central power against which the Revolution had been fought. Under these influences the Convention moved back from its early extremism, defeated the nationalists in the Connecticut compromise, and preserved an important role for the states.

This accomplished, and the supposed dangers from the large states obviated, the state federalists and several exponents of the New Jersey Plan joined with the nationalists in building the central power. But it was not to take the Court Whig form. General powers were replaced by enumerated powers; the branches of government were more clearly separated; most offices were given fixed terms; and both the central and the state governments were limited by numerous restraints. Yet the powers enumerated were very broad; the word "expressly" was carefully avoided, leaving room for implied powers; no restraints were laid on reelections or on standing armies; and no bill of rights was included.

Madison's Congressional veto of state legislation was rejected, but so also was Sherman's special protection for the "internal police" of the states. Internal sovereignty was thus excluded, and the only supremacy mentioned was vested in written national law. The foundations were laid for an unprecedented role for the judicial branch in the preservation of a rule of law, both against the other branches and against the people themselves.

6

The Convention Congress

Because of its manner of assembly and its role in the constitutional settlement after the departure of James II, the Parliament of 1689 is frequently called the Convention Parliament. It declared (contrary to fact) that James had abdicated, placed William and Mary on the throne, enacted the Bill of Rights, and thus established the ultimate supremacy of Parliament in the mixed and balanced government of England.

With equal or even more justice the Congress of 1789–91, the first under the new Constitution, can be called the Convention Congress. By its enactments and its precedents it gave living structure to the new system. It created the executive departments, organized the Supreme Court and inferior courts, chose a site for the national capital, resolved the old problems of debts and taxes, and wrote the first ten amendments to the Constitution. In these amendments it played the role of the second Convention that the Antifederalists had desired, but its manner of working was very different from that of the Convention of 1787.

Before it could meet, of course, the Constitution had to be ratified and elections held, but those processes need not be examined in detail.[1]

After a cursory look at the ratification, this chapter will examine the attitudes and objectives of the nationalists as displayed in Congress in the debates on amendments and on other issues, frequently contrasting them with the interpretations by which they had achieved the ratification of the Constitution. We shall see that their overwhelming majority enabled them to establish for the Senate a role very different from the institutional voice of the states that the Convention, led by the state federalists, had tried to institute. They thus converted the coordinate distribution of powers that the ratification debates had described (and that had probably been required for success) into a hierarchical relationship, leaving the states with no structural protection in the new system.

We shall then examine the passage of three important bills, one in each session, as examples of the patterns of reasoning and conflict and of the trend toward the expansion of central control, particularly in the president, in cavalier disregard for the minority's views. As this trend progressed cohesive voting blocs appeared, divided along lines influenced less by the Federalist-Antifederalist split over ratification than by the perennial differences between North and South. We shall see that most of the nationalists quickly forgot the limitations and protections they had professed to find in the Constitution during the ratification struggle and found instead the touchstones of purpose, implication, and construction—in the Preamble, the "necessary and proper" clause, the opening of Article II, and the "supremacy" clause—which opened vistas of unsuspected power.

Thus is raised the question whether or not the system can be controlled. The chapter will conclude that the intricate structure created by the Framers preserves a rule of law—even against the majority's will—yet does respond, at least at times, to changes in public opinion.

Ratification

The nationalists, after doing their best to destroy federalism in the Convention, cleverly assumed the name Federalists and called their opponents

---

1. Jensen et al., *Documentary History of the Ratification*. In contrast to earlier neglect, the past thirty years have seen much scholarly work on the ratification debates of the Antifederalists, starting with Jackson T. Main, *The Antifederalists: Critics of the Constitution, 1781–1788* (Chapel Hill, 1961), and culminating with Storing, *The Complete Anti-Federalist*. The precarious New York convention has been examined by Linda G. DePauw, *The Eleventh Pillar* (Ithaca, 1966), and Stephen L. Schechter, ed., *The Reluctant Pillar* (Troy, N.Y., 1985); the election data are in Merrill Jensen et al., eds., *Documentary History of the First Federal Elections, 1788–1790* (Madison, 1976–).

Antifederalists—misnomers, but now too firmly embedded in the literature to be corrected. They started with the advantage that even their opponents believed that some changes in the Articles were necessary. Aided substantially by the prestige of Washington and their control of the urban centers, they literally out-generaled the Antifederalists. The latter were generally older men whose political thinking had been shaped by the Country ideology in the struggles of the 1760s and 1770s. They saw the Constitution as an amazing and a dangerous revival of the kind of central power that England had claimed, threatening to the autonomy of the separate states and too far removed from popular control. The new executive with appointing power, the very exclusive Senate, unlimited taxing power, the possible standing army, and the complete absence of annual elections and rotation in office—these and other features powerfully reminded them of parallel elements in English government and politics that had aroused the Country ideologues and, until checked by the Revolution, had threatened to destroy the liberty of the colonies.[2]

After a strong start (with unanimous ratifications in three small states, a two-to-one victory in Pennsylvania, and three-to-one triumph in Connecticut), the nationalists encountered mounting difficulties. In the Massachusetts convention in February their all-or-nothing strategy finally collapsed. Facing a major defeat, they had to enter into a gentlemen's agreement to propose amendments through the first Congress.

The Antifederalist strategy of coordinating the state conventions to secure changes through a second national convention also collapsed.[3] In February the Antifederalists of New Hampshire acceded to an adjournment of their convention until June, when the conventions of New York and Virginia would meet. In June, however, failing to coordinate with New York, a few men shifted sides and New Hampshire ratified, becoming the crucial ninth state.[4]

The Antifederalists in the New York and Virginia conventions gradually

2. Wood, *Creation of the American Republic*, pp. 513–32, gives a concise and perceptive summary of the conflict; but see Gary J. Schmitt and Robert H. Webking, "Revolutionaries, Antifederalists, and Federalists: Comments on Gordon Wood's Understanding of the American Founding," *Political Science Reviewer* 9 (Fall 1979): 195–229. For a scholarly but uneven survey, see Gillespie and Lienesch, *Ratifying the Constitution*.

3. See Linda G. DePauw, "The Anti-Climax of Antifederalism: The Abortive Second Convention Movement, 1788–1789," *Prologue* 2 (Fall 1970): 98–114.

4. Little primary material on the New Hampshire convention has survived. The Antifederalists had a three-to-two majority, and they seem to have voted rejection, even with recommended amendments, by 54 to 51. Langdon, who was presiding, then arranged a vote for adjournment until June. Neither roll call is extant. Samuel Tenney to Nicholas Gilman, March 12, 1788, Gratz Collection, Pennsylvania Historical Society, Philadelphia; Peter Curtenius to George Clinton, March 2, 1788, George Clinton Papers, New York Public Library; John Langdon to George Washington, February 28, 1788, Washington Papers, Library of Congress.

realized that previous amendments were no longer possible, that the new government would be organized, and that the best chance to change the Constitution was from within by using the amending process of Article V. Enough opponents then changed sides in New York and possibly in Virginia to give the nationalists narrow victories in both states.

The nationalists were also generally victorious in campaigning for control of the state legislatures, which would appoint senators, and for election to the new House of Representatives. Only Virginia sent Antifederalists to the Senate, and a mere ten were elected to the House.[5] The electorate, it seems, finding itself committed to the new experiment, preferred to commit its management to its friends rather than to its enemies.

Amendments

The material on which the work of the Congress was most exactly a continuation of that of the Convention was, of course, the proposal of constitutional amendments. In spite of the gentlemen's agreement for amendments by which the crucial ratification in Massachusetts had been obtained, the Congress showed great reluctance to face the issues involved. It was left to Madison, almost single-handedly, to drive the chariot of amendments between the obstacles thrown up on the one side by the Federalists, who wanted no amendments, and on the other by the Antifederalists, who wanted far more and who could foresee that his abbreviated list (unless itself drastically amended) would foreclose the possibility of other amendments for the immediate future.

Madison had shown no interest in amendments until attacked by Jefferson in his famous "I will now add what I do not like" letter of December 20, 1787, from Paris, responding to the new draft Constitution. Even then, in reply to Jefferson's repeated goading, he remained skeptical: "I have never thought the omission [of a bill of rights] a material defect, nor been anxious to supply it even by *subsequent* amendment, for any other reason than that it is anxiously desired by others. I have favored it because I supposed it might be of use, and, if properly executed, could not be of disservice" (October 17, 1788). The realities of Virginia politics, however, changed

5. Two each from Massachusetts and New York, and three each from Virginia and South Carolina. Jensen, *First Federal Elections,* 1:749–51, 3:197, 2:254, and 1:149. In 1790 North Carolina sent one more.

Madison's tactics if not his opinions. Patrick Henry blocked his chances for a seat in the Senate, and placed Madison's candidacy for the House in such jeopardy that he felt constrained to promise his constituents that he would support amendments.

Thus committed, Madison undertook to push through Congress, not the Virginia convention's list of amendments, not a list that had the support of most state conventions, but a sanitized list that he judged (1) could be carried through the Federalist Congress, (2) would be ratified, and (3) would not weaken the new central power. These parameters permitted the inclusion, from the eighty-odd different proposals by eight state conventions, of twenty-two items of civil rights (which were ratified) and of eleven statements of principle and other proposals (which were not).[6] Not included, however, were restrictions on the national taxing power, on standing armies, on the power of Congress over times and places of elections, on the exercise of powers not expressly delegated, or others desired by several states. In thus rejecting proposals that would have reduced various types of central power Madison may have gauged fairly accurately the temper of his Federalist colleagues. They almost uniformly rejected additional amendments introduced by others—for example, a requirement of a two-thirds vote in each house for a standing army, the insertion of the word "expressly" to limit delegated power, and Gerry's motion to consider all the amendments proposed by the ratifying conventions.

Even with the mass of state proposals pushed aside, it still took months (from May 4 to September 25) to push any amendments through Congress.[7] Almost nothing is known of the debate in the Senate, since Senator Maclay of Pennsylvania, whose journal provides our best view behind its closed doors, was out sick at the time.[8] The Virginia senators, Lee and Grayson, both Antifederalists, led the struggle there against even heavier odds. As a body protecting state power, the Senate eliminated Madison's original

6. According to the convenient tabulation of Edward Dumbauld, *The Bill of Rights and What It Means Today* (Norman, Okla., 1957), pp. 160–65. Nineteen of the twenty-two items had been proposed by Virginia and from two to seven other states. See also Paul Finkelman, "James Madison and the Bill of Rights: A Reluctant Paternity," *Supreme Court Review, 1990* (Chicago, 1991): 301–47.

7. Dumbauld, *The Bill of Rights*, pp. 33–49, concisely describes the course of the amendments through Congress. He also reprints, pp. 206–22, the texts at the various stages. More complete is Helen E. Veit, Kenneth R. Bowling, and Charlene B. Bickford, eds., *Creating the Bill of Rights: The Documentary Record from the First Congress* (Baltimore, 1991).

8. *The Journal of William Maclay*. Maclay did record that, on arrival from the House, the amendments "were treated contemptuously by Izard, Langdon and Mr. [Robert] Morris," who tried to postpone them until the next session (p. 131).

proposal protecting freedom of religion, speech, press, and trial by jury against state actions, which the House had accepted.

The first two resulting amendments, on the size of the House and on the control of Congress over its own salaries, failed of ratification, and the whole list failed in Massachusetts, where the movement began. The remaining ten, the "Bill of Rights" of which Americans have become so proud, represented a minimum demanded by political expediency, not a maximum indicating concern for human rights under strong government. The concept of inalienability was not expressed, and no attempt was made, as in the case of equal representation of states in the Senate, to place the bill of rights beyond the reach of future amendments. Natural rights were thus converted into civil rights. Their protection by moral forces was exchanged for the greater precision of judicial interpretation. The rights expressly included probably profited by this conversion, but those not mentioned gained little from the Ninth Amendment, which was designed to protect them. Popular involvement in defending rights in terms of moral indignation, as during the 1760s and 1770s, gave place to the complacency of legal process.[9]

Yet there might have been no bill of rights at all if Madison had not driven the chariot as well as he did. He surely would not have taken the reins had he not been goaded by Jefferson and by Henry; and he might have failed in the effort had some Federalists, at least, not felt the danger of violating the Massachusetts agreement (p. 175) worked out with the help of John Hancock and Sam Adams. So it can be said that, in the bill of rights as well as in the ratification of the Constitution, the men of '87 were rescued from their errors by the men of '76.

The Nationalists in Control

Their victory in the elections for Congress meant a continuation of the nationalists' struggle for central power. Having failed to achieve in the Convention the degree of centralization they desired, they were not content

9. William E. Nelson gives a much more consensual and complacent reading to the origins of the first ten amendments; see his "Reason and Compromise." Hadley Arkes takes seriously the Federalist argument against a bill of rights, and he attributes the modern divorce of law from ethics to the substitution of positive formulas in place of the principles of justice. See his *Beyond the Constitution* (Princeton, 1990), especially chapter 4. Bruce Ackerman discusses the entrenchment of constitutional rights against future amendment, as the former West Germany did. See his *We the People*, vol. 1, *Foundations* (Cambridge, Mass., 1991), pp. 14–16, 320–21.

to implement the Constitution as they had interpreted it during the ratification struggle.[10] Realizing the strength of their majorities in both House and Senate, they began instead to bend the Constitution into a shape more consistent with their original desires.

This process did not align Federalists against Antifederalists, who were too few in Congress to matter much,[11] but rather the centralizers against those who feared central power. This realignment was a gradual polarization toward the later Hamiltonian and Jeffersonian parties as individual members, mostly from the South, realized the implications of the ideas and plans of the nationalists. It began long before the appointment of Hamilton as Secretary of the Treasury, but his position gave it a strong stimulus and superior coordination.

A key element in this gradual division and realignment among the Constitution's supporters lay in the gradually unfolding differences between the powers of the new government as argued and implemented after ratification and those powers as described by the Federalists during the ratification struggle. Many who believed that additional enumerated powers were needed, and who were elected as Federalists, arrived in New York wholly unprepared for the expanding interpretations they began to hear from others.

The general aims of the centralizers were three: to expand the power and resources of the national government, to tilt the balance in favor of the executive branch, and to withdraw power and support from the states. As sources of power the elastic clause, the Preamble, and even the Declaration of Independence were drawn upon. The debts of the Revolution were manipulated, and the sale of the western lands delayed in order to establish a maximum of central taxation and to divert even the state creditors to the support of the central government.

The First Session had hardly begun when voices of caution were raised against excessive taxation. Scott of Pennsylvania thought the special duty on salt would be so odious to the people that it "will have a tendency to shake the foundation of your system. . . . Will it not be wise, therefore, to let the administration of your power slide gently along, inoffensive to so great a body? Let them become reconciled to your views, before you stretch out

10. For example, they repudiated Senate consent to removals as expounded in *Federalist* No. 77 (p. 515 in the Cooke edition); see *Annals of Congress*, 1:474. The *Annals* will be cited hereafter in parentheses in the text. See also Wood, *Creation of the American Republic*, p. 562.

11. But see the contrary view of John H. Aldrich and Ruth W. Grant, "The Antifederalists, the First Congress, and the First Parties," *Journal of Politics*, 55 (May 1993): 295–326.

the hand of oppression" (1:166). Reminding the members that the Constitution had been "adopted by a small majority in some States," White of Virginia argued that "wisdom and prudence will, therefore, teach us not to exercise powers under it which opinion may judge oppressive" (172). And Madison, while supporting the salt duty, asked if the people would submit to an excise instead: "If they would, I trust it is not in the contemplation of gentlemen to propose it" (170).

Such pleas for moderation did not stop the salt duty, however, nor did they deflect the nationalists from their aims. Repeatedly they were accused of bringing about a consolidated government (e.g., 1418, 1493, 1691–92), and repeatedly their proposals were condemned as confirmations of the dire predictions of the Antifederalists that the new government would be a tyranny (509, 570, 1418).

Soon the opposition found itself arguing, not only against what it took to be the impolitic exercise of the clearly granted powers of Congress, but also against the use of powers not clearly granted. The members on both sides were very conscious that they were implementing a new constitution and that their actions would become precedents. This led the nationalists toward the early—even unnecessary—exercise of powers lest any be lost through disuse. It led their opponents to fight proposals, not in proportion to their immediate import, but to their long-range implications. Already in the First Session the accusation of unconstitutionality began to be voiced (509, 539–40, 569, 614, etc.).

In these debates logic was frequently bent to political purposes. At first it was contended that, where the Constitution was silent, Congress could fill in the gaps as it saw fit (505). Smith of South Carolina, however, urged that "[i]f the Legislature can supply defects, they may virtually repeal the constitution" (528; cf. White of Virginia, 537). Madison soon withdrew from that position, yet he believed that, in regard to "doubtful" parts of the Constitution, "an exposition of the constitution may come with as much propriety from the Legislature, as any other department of the Government" (479–482). In the same debate his colleague Richard Bland Lee declared, "This Government is invested with powers for enumerated purposes only, and cannot exercise any others whatever," yet he proceeded to quote the "necessary and proper" clause to support the exercise of an implied power (544–45). Even stranger logic was used by Boudinot of New Jersey, who asserted that he should "certainly attend to the terms of the constitution" and indeed never wished to see them "departed from or construed, if the Government can possibly be carried into effect in any other manner"; yet in the same paragraph he denied that there had been or could be "any solid reason adduced to prove that this House has not power to modify the principles of the constitution. . . . I believe, sir, we were not sent here to carry into effect every principle of the constitution" (547).

Many of these accusations were related to the "necessary and proper" clause. Early in May, Gerry of Massachusetts interpreted the clause as being restricted by the preceding clauses: "To this clause there seems to be no limitation, so far as it applies to the extension of the powers vested by the constitution; but even this clause gives no legislative authority to Congress to carry into effect any power not expressly vested by the constitution" (277). Similarly, White of Virginia held that "[t]his is a Government constituted for particular purposes only; and the powers granted to carry it into effect are specifically enumerated. . . . We can neither enlarge nor modify them" (535).

The nationalists, however, viewed the matter differently. For those ends entrusted to the national government, they argued, the people must have intended to convey all necessary means, some expressly and others by implication. When Tucker of South Carolina tried to insert the word "expressly" into the Tenth Amendment, Madison objected: ". . . because it was impossible to confine a Government to the exercise of express powers; there must necessarily be admitted powers by implication, unless the constitution descended to recount every minutia" (790). Sherman went further, observing that "corporate bodies are supposed to possess all powers incident to a corporate capacity, without being absolutely expressed" (790). When, subsequently, the nationalists began to use the Preamble to define the ends of the government broadly, this doctrine that all necessary means were conveyed began to approximate the doctrine that the people had conveyed not particular powers but general powers limited only by express prohibitions such as those in Article I, Section 9. The famous distinction between the state and the national government (coined by James Wilson in the ratification struggle) by which, in the former, "every thing which is not reserved, is given, but in the latter the reverse proposition prevails, and every thing which is not given, is reserved"[12]—which was the accepted Federalist interpretation during ratification—was thus gradually subverted.

The burden of struggle against this trend was carried largely by congressmen from the South. In June 1789, Smith of South Carolina denied that

12. *Selected Political Essays of James Wilson*, ed. Randolph G. Adams (New York, 1930), p. 154.

Congress could exercise any power "not within the enumerated powers
delegated to Congress" (488), and Jackson of Georgia saw the Constitution
"delegating only enumerated powers" (505). But the nationalists' appetite
for power grew as their bills were passed, and the accusations of unconstitutionality were more frequent toward the end of the First Congress. In
February 1791, near the close of the Third Session, Madison—having
departed from the nationalist camp—reminded the members that the
Antifederalist demand for a bill of rights had been countered with the
argument that "the powers not given were retained; and that those given
were not to be extended by remote implications. . . . The explanations in
the State Conventions all turned on the same fundamental principle, and on
the principle that the terms necessary and proper gave no additional powers
to those enumerated" (2:1901). And Stone of Maryland drew the conclusion:
"The end of all Government is the public good; and if the means are left to
legislation, all written compacts were nugatory." The "sober discretion of
the Legislature," which the nationalists held to be paramount, was, he
pointed out, "the very thing intended to be curbed and restrained by our
Constitution" (2:1932).

In the course of this mounting conflict the viewpoint of the state federalists was clearly expressed. "I understand our system as differing in form and
spirit from all other Governments in the world," proclaimed White of
Virginia. "It is in part national, and in part federal; and though it is more
extensive in its powers than most other Governments, yet the Congress is
not to be compared to National Legislatures . . ." (1:535). To the latter
general powers were granted, but not to Congress. He went on to say that
"[i]f this principle had not been successfully maintained" in the Virginia
convention "the constitution would never have been ratified." He then
quoted from the Virginia ratification, which said "that the powers granted
under the Constitution being derived from the people of the United States
[may] be resumed by them whensoever the same shall be perverted to their
injury or oppression, and that every power, not granted thereby, remains
with them and at their will. . . ."[13]

Against the Bank bill in the Third Session, Madison presented a most
thorough catalog of such "contemporary expositions" of the Constitution,
drawing on published debates in the conventions of Pennsylvania, Virginia,
and North Carolina and on "explanatory declarations and amendments

13. Elliot's *Debates*, 3:656. White's quotation was omitted by the editors of the *Annals of
Congress*.

accompanying the ratifications of the several states." The Massachusetts convention, for example, proposed as its first amendment "That it be explicitly declared that all Powers not expressly delegated by the aforesaid Constitution are reserved to the several States to be by them exercised."[14] Similar provisions were adopted by every state convention thereafter, New Hampshire adding "particularly" delegated and New York "clearly," but Virginia omitting the "expressly."[15] Madison then read, as even more authoritative, the Ninth and Tenth Amendments proposed by Congress, which had already been ratified "by nearly three-fourths of the States" (*Annals*, 2:1901). Elbridge Gerry also believed that the "Constitutional balance between the Union and States" should be preserved. "I view the Constitutions of the United States and individual States as forming a great political machine, in which the small wheels are as essential as the large; and if the former are deranged, the system must be destroyed" (2:1325).

A separate state-federalist position, however, could not be maintained. The initiative being seized by the nationalists to overthrow the balance between the states and nation achieved by the Philadelphia Convention, it was natural for those who wished to preserve that balance to join forces with those who might prefer to tilt it in favor of the states.

This gradual process of polarization can be shown more clearly by the use of three examples, one from each session: the removal power in the First, the assumption of state debts in the Second, and the creation of the Bank of the United States in the Third. Before looking at these examples, however, it may be desirable to take a closer look at the Senate.

The Ambiguity of the Senate

During the Convention several divergent, even contradictory, conceptions of the role of the Senate were entertained. The proposal of a second chamber expressed distrust of a single legislative body that, in order to justify PR, would have to be popularly elected. A second scrutiny of legislation was thus a basic element. The smaller size and the longer term of office suggested that this scrutiny should be more mature, experienced and wise. The choice of the name, derived from Rome, indicated that a somewhat

14. *Documentary History of the Constitution of the United States of America* (Washington: Department of State, 1894), 2:94.
15. Ibid., pp. 142, 191, 270, 311, 381.

aristocratic body was intended. Related, but not identical, was the idea that the second chamber should represent property, in order to protect the wealthy against the more numerous poor, but also because property as well as people was entitled to representation in its own right. When the idea of a special advisory council for the president was abandoned, the small Senate was given several nonlegislative functions as an executive council; and when the trial of impeachments was removed from the Court the Senate became a judicial body as well. So great, in fact, did the mass of Senatorial powers become that strong objection was expressed against giving it also a role in the elections of presidents.

From very early in the Convention, however, the view was advanced that the second chamber should represent the separate states as political entities, as distinguished from the people of the separate states, who were represented in the first chamber. All the way from the Stamp Act Congress to the Convention, all central meetings of delegates had been meetings of colony and then state representatives, never representatives of the people; so it was hardly to be expected that this pattern of thought would be entirely abandoned. It lay, of course, at the heart of the New Jersey Plan, and it was used by the state federalists as an essential ingredient in the Connecticut compromise. Representation of states as such thus became an essential part of the new Constitution, without which there was little chance that it would be ratified. The Senate was created as the continuing voice and influence of the states within the central government, linking and balancing the two levels of government.

This did not mean that those delegates who had opposed the Connecticut compromise then abandoned their conceptions of the Senate as a body representing maturity, stability, aristocracy, and property. Reflecting these differing conceptions, fundamental ambiguity was built into the second chamber, not only in its legislative, executive, and judicial roles, but more basically in the matter of whom or what it should represent. By the equality and the manner of election Senators clearly were intended to represent political entities, their separate states. But by their long and staggered terms of office and by the age requirement they also clearly were intended to represent stability and maturity.

In their choice of the members, the state legislatures had an opportunity to establish the First Senate as a guardian of state interests as against central power, and thus to implement the idea that America was a unique new polity, both a union (of people) and a federation (of states). They did not, however, feel threatened. Believing the new government to be one of enumerated powers, and anticipating the improvements to flow from the lists of amendments and interpretations that had issued from the ratifying conventions, the legislatures—except in Virginia—chose as senators supporters rather than critics of the new system.

Since we do not have the debates of the First Senate we cannot be sure how the individual senators reconciled their dual roles as defenders of their states' interests and as important members of the central government. The nationalists' programs did not directly attack the states, and the inevitable differences of interest in the assumption of state debts were reconciled. The members were, no doubt, more alert to the interests of their own states than to the erosion of state power in general that the assumption accomplished. It is probable also that the term of office—longer than any nonjudicial tenure in any state—tilted senators toward their national role in two ways: individuals who were primarily state oriented would be reluctant to spend six years away, while those who were more willing became enmeshed in the exercise of central power. Per capita voting facilitated this.

In any event the almost solidly Federalist composition of the First Senate made for a general bias against strengthening the role of the states in the new system. The continuity of membership and the gradual accumulation of precedents made the Senate, in spite of its mode of election, a predominantly national body rather than a champion of the role of the states.[16]

Now for the examples.

The Removal Power

The Constitution had mentioned "executive Departments" but it had not created them, so on May 19 Boudinot of New Jersey moved the establishment of a "Department of Finance" (1:384). He added that, when this was done, "we may then go to the consideration of the War Department, and the Department of Foreign Affairs. . . ." Thus was started a long and important debate that effectively decided the direction in which the executive branch would develop.

For those eager to strengthen the presidency, however, Boudinot's sequence was wrong. A question would arise as to the responsibility of the

16. For an insightful account of the nationalizing of the Senate see William H. Riker, "The Senate and American Federalism," *American Political Science Review* 49 (June 1955): 452–69.

secretary of finance to the president or to the House, which was traditionally and constitutionally entrusted with money matters. If this question were decided in favor of the House, the decision might lead to a form of general ministerial responsibility to Congress, leaving the president as head of state (to use modern parlance) but not head of government. To forestall that possibility Madison (still a centralizer at that time) deftly turned aside Boudinot's proposal, with the help of Benson of New York, and gave priority to a Department of Foreign Affairs. It would be easier to justify complete presidential control over this department, and a precedent would then be set that could be applied to the other departments.[17]

In his motion Madison included the seemingly innocent provision that the secretary for foreign affairs "be removable by the President." The motion was divided and the main idea of the department quickly accepted, but the removal provision was objected to by Smith of South Carolina and others. After two days of debate, however, presidential removal was accepted by the committee of the whole for all three departments (385–412). Yet the contest was not over; a month later five more days were required to beat back the opponents of presidential removal.

It is not necessary to follow the details of this long debate.[18] It brought into discussion the powers of both the legislative and the executive. The issues were argued also on policy grounds, but the main conflict was over constitutional interpretation. Here was an ambiguous area of the Constitution, seen by the nationalists as an opportunity to do four things: to enlarge, on the one hand, the power of the president; to diminish, on the other hand, that of the Senate; to set a precedent of legislative interpretation of the Constitution; and to exercise a power not expressly granted.

The debate had hardly begun when Vining of Delaware leaned on the opening words of Article II to advance for the first time the doctrine that "all executive power" not "otherwise qualified" was vested in the president (388). Madison then thought it necessary to confer the removal power by

17. This strategy was noticed at the time by Madison's opponents and criticized by Jackson of Georgia (550).

18. The most complete analysis is in James Hart, *The American Presidency in Action, 1789* (New York, 1948), pp. 152–248. Four general positions were defended: (1) removal is a purely executive function conveyed as a part of "the Executive power" by Article II; (2) removal is parallel to appointment and must similarly require the advice and consent of the Senate; (3) removal can be determined by Congress when it creates an office; and (4) removal requires conviction upon impeachment. John A. Rohr, in his *President and the Public Administration* (Washington, D.C., 1989), also gives an able analysis of these debates and the present implications.

legislative grant (387, 389); but by June 16, under the influence of Vining and Benson, he also embraced the theory that the opening words of Article II were a general grant and conferred the removal power. He even copied Vining's use of the word "all" (480–81).[19]

The advocates of Madison's removal clause argued that the separation of powers required that the Senate intrude into executive functions no further than expressly provided by the Constitution; that the executive power was conferred on the president with specified exceptions for treaties and appointments but not for removals. Besides, the power was necessary to give him control and responsibility, and to give energy to the government. They defended the explicit clause as a clarification of power already granted to the president by the Constitution, and yet they objected, inconsistently, that striking it out would leave the power with the Senate and the president (561).

Early in the debate Livermore of New Hampshire remarked that the clause seemed "altogether to be aimed at the Senate" (498). His surmise was confirmed two days later when Scott of Pennsylvania lashed out at the Senate as "the representatives of the state sovereignties . . . that species of beings which, if any thing stands in the way of the just execution of the Federal Government, they are the creatures" (554).[20]

Among the opponents of the removal clause, of course, the Senate had able defenders. Like the attackers they came from both large and small states. Page of Virginia called it a "safe and salutary" branch intended "to preserve the sovereignty and independence of the State Governments. . . . The principles laid down in the constitution clearly evince that the Senate ought not only to have a voice in the framing of laws, but ought also to see to their execution" (540; also Stone of Maryland, 589–91).

The effort to diminish the Senate was paralleled by the exaltation of the president. This tendency had been manifested in the earlier debate over titles (331–37). The Senate, and particularly its presiding officer, John Adams, by their persistence in pushing for an exalted title for Washington had aroused suspicion that their hidden agenda included monarchy. This suspicion was expressed most vigorously by Page, who asserted that the removal clause "contains in it the seeds of royal prerogative" and would tend

19. Hart suggests that Madison's change of mind was stimulated by Sherman's interpretation of the power of Congress to create offices, by which Congress was free to place the removal power anywhere it chose. Sherman's view threatened Madison's objective of a strong presidency, particularly in relation to the Treasury Department.

20. See also the attack on the Senate by Vining of Delaware, 593–95.

to confirm the Antifederalist fears "that the new Government would run instantly headlong into a monarchy" (509, 570). As in the titles debate, this antagonism toward "heaped-up powers" of the president was mostly a southern attitude, shared by Parker and Page of Virginia, Burke and Tucker of South Carolina, and Jackson of Georgia (332, 333, 335, 572, 604, 683). "To what a height do gentlemen exalt that character in their own minds!" exclaimed Stone of Maryland. "If gentlemen will exalt a character above themselves, call him what you will, he will be possessed of monarchy," and only the obsequious will be willing to serve at his will and pleasure (590–91). Moreover, according to Page the doctrine that energy is needed in government is "the true doctrine of tyrants" (572, 603).

Madison's view that no implied exceptions to the grant of executive power should be admitted was turned against him by his colleague White. Both the legislative and the executive had only enumerated powers, White contended; if the executive had all powers not expressly excepted, the same rule of interpretation would give the legislature all powers not expressly excepted and make a mockery of the list in Article I, Section 8. The president would then have "the powers of the most absolute Monarch," and the government would be "as absolute and extensive as any despotism" (485–534).

The two Virginians shared a high estimate of the importance of this issue. The decision would become a "permanent exposition" of the Constitution, as Madison said, and on it "will depend the genius and character of the whole Government" (514). For Madison, the object was to "retain that equilibrium which the constitution intended," but for White the issue was a bit different: "whether we may grant to others, or assume to ourselves, powers which the constitution has not given, either in express terms or by necessary implication" (533). He acknowledged that the power would be conferred on "a man whom all the world admires," but he insisted that only "natural and necessary construction" of the Constitution was permissible: "constructions of every other kind are beyond the limits of the constitution" (536, 539). Having joined the Senate in the appointment process, he believed, the Framers naturally and necessarily implied that the Senate would join in removals. To imply that the Senate, because it did not initiate appointments, could be excluded from removals was parallel to an implication that the Senate, because it did not initiate revenue bills, could be excluded from the repeal of revenue laws (533, 538).

However cogent such arguments might seem to the opposition, they did not deflect the majority from its interpretation, yet they did lead to the removal of the obnoxious clause from the bill. Benson of New York proposed a compromise using the phrase "whenever the said principal officer shall be removed from office by the President . . . ," which avoided any claim by Congress to a power to grant or deny the removal power yet at the same time achieved a legislative interpretation (601).[21] This was approved, and the words "to be removable by the President" were then deleted. The modification, while hardly changing the substance of the bill, made the two roll call votes on Benson's changes somewhat ambiguous. Some who had fought most tenaciously to keep Madison's original words, like Ames of Massachusetts, Lee of Virginia, and Madison himself, voted for their deletion along with their most vigorous opponents like White of Virginia, Sherman of Connecticut, and Smith of South Carolina (603, 608).

Before the third vote, on the final reading, Sumter of South Carolina condemned the bill as "so subversive of the constitution, and in its consequences so destructive to the liberties of the people" that he had to express publicly his "detestation of the principle it contains" (614). It passed, 29 to 22, with New England opposing it 9 to 5, the middle states favoring it 14 to 2, and the South divided 10 for and 11 against.

The bill came up in the Senate on the same day that the Parisian sansculottes stormed the Bastille. It might be expected that senators would wish to secure a hand in removals as well as appointments. Back in June, however, Maclay had predicted that the "court party" would favor presidential removals, since "many people are aiming with all their force to establish a splendid court with all the pomp of majesty." On the second day of debate he reported "more caballing and meeting of members in knots this day than I ever observed before," and on the third day he "began to suspect that the court party had prevailed"—as indeed they did, by the casting vote of John Adams.[22]

In this debate Grayson of Virginia remarked that "[t]he matter predicted by Mr. Henry is now coming to pass: consolidation is the object of the new Government, and the first attempt will be to destroy the Senate, as they are the representatives of the State Legislatures" (Maclay, 113). Grayson was both right and wrong in this remark. By this vote it was demonstrated that

21. Rohr, *President and the Public Administration*, pp. 26–31, examines this compromise in detail in convincing derogation of *Myers vs. U.S.*, 272 U.S. 52 (1926).

22. *The Journal of William Maclay*, pp. 80, 111–14. Maclay was probably correct in listing Butler against the removal power and Ellsworth in favor, but both are omitted in the *Documentary History of the First Federal Congress*, ed. Linda Grant DePauw (Baltimore, 1972), 1:86.

a sufficient number of senators could be persuaded to support nationalist measures even against the interest of the Senate itself. Becoming thus, at the beginning of its career, an instrument of the centralizers of power, the Senate never assumed the role that Grayson described and that the Convention had created. It did not need to be destroyed: it was captured instead.

Assumption of State Debts

In the assumption of the debts of the states the Congress moved from the interpretation of the silence of the Constitution to the active exercise of power not expressly granted.

The men of the Revolutionary generation were intensely aware of the relationships of economic and political power. "Both the nationalists and the federalists believed that national payment of the war debt would mean the supremacy of the central government over the states; that state payment would mean the retention of ultimate power in the hands of the states."[23] Since 1781, therefore, the methods of debt payment had been sharply fought issues of political power.[24] The taxing power of the new Constitution was an ultimate victory for the nationalists. Their strong central government was achieved; yet they remained dissatisfied—arousing suspicions of their motives.

The Articles of Confederation had provided, in Article 8, that "[a]ll charges of war and all other expenses, that shall be incurred for the common defence or general welfare, and allowed by the United States in Congress assembled, shall be defrayed out of a common treasury. . . ." This Article clearly contemplated state expenses during the Revolution, but it also clearly stipulated that they must be for the common defense or general welfare and that they must be "allowed" by Congress—which many were but some were not.

Assumption had been proposed in the Constitutional Convention, and a committee had reported a clause empowering Congress to pay the debts "incurred by the several States during the late war, for the common defence

---

23. Jensen, *The New Nation*, p. 400.
24. These struggles are well analyzed by Jensen, *The New Nation*, pp. 72–76, 407–21; E. James Ferguson, *The Power of the Purse*, pp. xiv–xvi, 124, 142–45, and passim; Henderson, *Party Politics*, pp. 325–32; and Joseph L. Davis, *Sectionalism in American Politics, 1774–1787* (Madison, 1977), pp. 34–49.

and general welfare." This was thought of as an inducement to ratification, but it was dropped without debate, perhaps because the small states did not relish helping to pay the debts of others (New Hampshire, New Jersey, Delaware, and Maryland had voted against committee consideration). Brought up again by Randolph, it was again dropped without debate.[25] The final constitutional provision said only that all debts and engagements "entered into, before the adoption of this Constitution shall be as valid against the United States under this Constitution, as under the Confederation" (Article VI). The Convention had tried to write a completely neutral statement neither advancing nor retarding the claims of the state creditors.

The state debts were an especially thorny issue. Massachusetts and South Carolina had much larger debts than the other states, and a large item in each (the Penobscot expedition of Massachusetts and the frigate *South Carolina*) was widely thought to have been an expenditure locally motivated and not primarily in the common defense (*Annals*, 2:1380, 1484). This imbalance was aggravated by the fairly general impression that some states had made much greater efforts than others to pay their debts. Some states had also assumed and in part paid some of the federal debts to their own citizens. Moreover, it was feared that an assumption would impede and perhaps finally foreclose the long-anticipated general settlement of accounts between the nation and the separate states (2:1489–91, 1496, 1509, 1526, 1493). The "landless" states still saw a connection between the debts incurred in the Revolution and the unoccupied lands that had been won by their common efforts. Assumption therefore involved the perennial subject of land sales versus taxes as sources of revenue. The unknown yet surely very great magnitude of the state debts made this issue more pertinent.[26]

Hamilton largely succeeded in discounting the land issue by recommending that the creditors be offered repayment of one third of their principal in western land.[27] Yet his rationale for the assumption, which he included in his Report on Public Credit, itself stimulated controversy. In an effort to

---

25. Farrand, *Records*, 2:327–28, 377, 355–56, 400.

26. Maryland, Virginia, North Carolina, and Georgia were far more, and rightly, concerned about a final settlement than about assumption. In the end, all debts assumed came to $18.2 million, while the settlement credited the South with $51.6 million of war-related expenditures—Virginia alone with over $19 million. E. James Ferguson, *The Power of the Purse*, pp. 321, 324.

The assumption issue in Congress is well summarized in ibid., 306–25, and in Rudolph M. Bell, *Party and Faction in American Politics: The House of Representatives, 1789–1801* (Westport, Conn., 1973), pp. 116–27.

27. See, however, *Annals*, 2:1422.

show the greater ease and convenience of discharging a single consolidated debt he painted an alarming picture of competing and conflicting state and national tax systems.[28] His arguments were obviously as valid against state taxes for any purpose as for the purpose of paying debts. They thus seemed to confirm the old Antifederalist fear that the taxing clause would be used to destroy the states by depriving them of all revenue.

On the first day of debate on the assumption the question of its constitutionality was raised. "It does not appear to me," said Stone of Maryland, "that the debts of the particular States are the debts of the United States. . . . Can Congress, by their own authority, saddle the Union with a debt of this magnitude, independent of the particular powers they derive from the Constitution and then justify the collection of taxes under the general powers of the Constitution?" (2:1314). Five months later the question was still unsettled. "The Constitution was formed for the restoration of public credit," Jackson of Georgia maintained, "and if the State debts were a part of the debt of the Union, provision would have been made for them." The Convention did not make such provision; "neither, sir, have we a power, under that Constitution, to provide for the payment of them" (1689).

To circumvent the constitutional question Sherman and Gerry put forward the view that "the debts of the States," in fact, were "the debts of the United States; for the States had contracted the debts, as agents of the Union" (1348). "By the Confederation," Sherman explained, "Congress were authorized to raise money; but not being able to effect this, in an immediate and direct manner, they did it mediately, through the intervention of the State Governments; so that, in fact, these debts are to be looked upon as the absolute debts of the Union" (1318).

This agency argument, however, was rejected by others. "I consider the States as agents of the people," said White of Virginia. "When they formed a Confederacy, Congress was appointed the agent of the particular States. . . . [C]onsequently, the debt is due by the State, and not by Congress" (1355; Gerry's reply, 1361). That the state debts were not the debts of the United States was also maintained by Moore of Virginia (1348), Stone (1327), and Jackson (1689). In their view, Congress was empowered to tax to pay the debts of the Union but had been given no power to assume other debts.

---

28. *The Works of Alexander Hamilton*, pp. 13–14. For a grass-roots attack on Hamilton's proposals, even in Massachusetts, see Ruth Bogin, "'Measures So Glareingly Unjust': A Response to Hamilton's Funding Plan by William Manning," *William and Mary Quarterly* 46 (April 1989): 315–31.

This difference of view persisted throughout the debates. Two months later, Madison (now opposing centralization) still found it necessary to say that "[t]he debts of the particular States cannot, in any point of view, be considered as actual debts of the United States; and the United States are not bound, by any past requisition, or any resolution now existing, to assume them" (1535). If "such a proposition" had been made in the old Congress, he went on, "it never would have found a second; and for this reason, that the debts of the particular States were never considered as the debts of the United States" (1539).[29] Yet Sherman's and Gerry's argument that the state debts had been incurred by them as agents, and were therefore already Union debts, was the basic answer of the assumptionists to the question of constitutional power.

In conjunction with the problem of the absence of any expressed provision regarding state debts a broader constitutional problem was also raised by Stone of Maryland—that of the balance between the states and the nation. "But if we add to the strength, and extend the energy of the General Government, by the adoption of measures which the Constitution nowhere contemplates, you will destroy the balance of power which the Constitution distributed between the Government of the United States and the State Governments" (1328). White of Virginia agreed: the influence of the states would be reduced, "while, at the same time, the General Government would be elevated on their ruin. This would be unjust and impolitic; the freedom and happiness of America depended as essentially on the State Governments as the General Government, perhaps more so" (1344). The assumptionists were very eager to fund the debts and establish the credit of the central government, but they showed no interest in the credit of the state governments. "I conceive, sir," said Page of Virginia, "the present Government was intended to give stability and credit to the individual State governments, as well as to the Federal Government; that it is our duty to attend as much to the one as the other" (1354).

The assumptionists countered this line of thought in several ways. Sherman and Gerry denied that assumption would strengthen the central government; "If it had that tendency I should oppose it," the latter said (1317, 1325). His colleague Ames, on the contrary, held that assumption

29. Had Madison's memory failed him? Assumption had been proposed in Congress on March 6, 1783, as part of the second 5 percent impost proposal, but had been rejected for the final proposal. Madison had been a member of the committee. *Journals of the Continental Congress* (Washington: Government Printing Office, 1922), 24:173, 257–61; Jensen, *The New Nation*, p. 74.

was "not a neutral measure"; its great political merit was precisely that it would strengthen the central government. "Is the principle of union too strong? Do not all good men desire to make it perfect?" (1613). This view was more generally held (1421, 1482). Smith of South Carolina held it and also thought that the states "would derive strength from the strength of the Union" (1357).

The great increase of indebtedness by assumption was expected, paradoxically, to strengthen the central government in two ways. By detaching the state creditors from their states and attaching them to the new government, a strong and capable group of citizens would be voluntarily enlisted in support of national measures and their anticipated resistance to national taxes would be forestalled (1352, 1502). And by engrossing almost all of the debts the central government would have a correspondingly greater claim to engross almost all of the sources of revenue (1316–17, 1379). Early in the debate, Stone of Maryland put it pithily: "I think, sir, wherever the property is, there will be the power. And if the General Government has the payment of all the debts, it must, of course, have all the revenue; if it possesses the whole revenue, it is equal, in other words, to the whole power; the different States will then have little to do" (1312).

Both sides generally accepted the connection of the debts with the taxing power. To the nationalists the unlimited taxing power of the new Constitution was a justification for the assumption, and the assumption would be a justification for the exercise of the power. When the Constitution was adopted, recalled Smith of South Carolina, "it was, I believe, the general idea . . . that when the General Government got possession of all the revenue they would provide for all the debts of the Union" (1357). Bland of Virginia, who had been an Antifederalist, and who was the only member from the state who supported assumption, averred that "from the first" he had expected "that the adoption of the Constitution would necessarily absorb all the efficient revenue of the United States" (1418). So he expressed surprise that anyone was "so squeamish at this time of day" about direct taxes. He and others argued that it would be unfair to leave the states saddled with their debts after their revenues were taken by the central government (1317, 1320–21, 1362, 1403, 1495, 1615).

On the other side it was denied that all resources had been surrendered (1499). In the ratification struggle the advocates of the Constitution had defended the taxing clause by saying it would be used only in cases of extreme necessity. The assumption, if carried, would require excises and direct taxes, thus fulfilling the predictions of the enemies of the Constitution and belying the interpretation of its friends. Without assumption "the states will have direct taxes in their own hands for this purpose"; but with it, professed Page of Virginia, "I know not what the States will have left" (1499; cf. 1507, 1535–36).

As the session wore on the balance-of-power aspect of assumption was emphasized on both sides. Its advocates moved from expressions of the desirability of a stronger central government (1317) to grim warnings that the rejection of assumption would lead to the dissolution of the Union (1494, 1513, 1526, 1700). Its adversaries went from objections to reduced influence of the states (1344) to visions of their utter destruction. Page feared that assumption would "revive the ancient jealousies of the States" and "confirm the predictions" of the Antifederalists that the new government "would eventually swallow up the State Governments" (1418). Three weeks later he proclaimed that assumption tended to consolidation and hence to "monarchy" (1493). By July, Jackson of Georgia claimed that

> [t]he object certainly was the absorbing the whole of the State powers within the vortex of the all-devouring General Government. . . . The State powers are a most effectual and necessary check against encroachments from the Government of the Union. The assumption, by annihilating the powers of the State Governments, will prove a decisive and fatal stroke at that check. . . . The States will be deprived of every thing but the shadow of power; they will be reduced to the state of mere colonies, with not even the power they possessed previous to the Revolution. (1691–92)

There were, of course, a very large number of arguments regarding both the justice and the policy of assumption that were, in part, based on the great variety of circumstances surrounding the debts of the different states. It is not necessary to examine these; nor is it possible to estimate the relative influence of these pragmatic considerations, as against the constitutional questions, upon the votes cast. The issues of constitutionality and constitutional balance were more tenaciously argued than the removal power had been. Debate began on February 23, 1790, and consumed twenty days before the first rejection on April 12, 31 to 29. Attempts to reopen the question were made immediately and continued on the 15th, 16th, 21st, and 26th of April and on May 24 and 26. It was brought to a vote on April 16 and 26, and again on May 26, and decisively defeated each time.

The assumptionists, however, had more than one string to their bow. The funding bill being passed, without the state debts, on June 2, it was the Senate's turn to deal with the thorny matter.

Senator Maclay, who strongly opposed both funding and assumption, was told by speaker Muhlenburg early in April that "consolidation and uniting in one Government" was the reason for assumption (225).[30] On the 27th Senator Langdon of New Hampshire "avowed in the most unequivocal manner" to Maclay that "consolidation of the different governments was his object in the matter" (243). In May, Maclay exulted in the rejection of assumption by the House, saying, "The assumption would have completed the pretext for seizing every resource of government and subject of taxation in the Union, so that even the civil list of the respective governments would have to depend on the Federal Treasury. This was the common talk of the Secretary's tools" (246). By July 12, however, he feared that "Hamilton has got his number made up" to reinstate assumption (313), and by the 15th he saw clearly that the location of the national capital on the Potomac was "intimately connected" with the "abominations" of funding and the assumption (319).

The Senate reinserted assumption into the funding bill on July 16 by a vote of 15 to 11 (*Annals*, 1:1050). Two days later Maclay recorded that Fitzsimons of Pennsylvania had "averred, in the most unequivocal manner, the grand object of the assumption, to be the collecting all the resources of the United States into one treasury" (323). Thus, it would seem, this motive was not a figment of the agrarian imagination.

When the bill came back to the House of Representatives the constitutional objections were again presented by Jackson of Georgia. "Seven years were we fighting to establish props for liberty, and in less than two years since the adoption of the Constitution are we trying to kick them all away. . . . A friend, sir, to the state Governments, or the liberties of the people," he said sadly, "is as much lost at the present day, as if he had belonged to the last century, and had a resurrection in the present age" (*Annals*, 2:1691–92). His motion to reject the Senate amendment was also lost, 29 to 32 (1710). Four northern states cast all their votes for assumption and two southern ones all theirs against. Regional lines were more sharply drawn than they had been on the removal power, but still six states cast divided votes in the House and five in the Senate.

As has long been believed, this may have been achieved only by a bargain: the northern assumptionists agreed to a southern location of the national

---

30. Page citations in this and following paragraphs are to Maclay's *Journal*.

capital in exchange for enough votes to carry assumption in each house. But in addition, the sums to be assumed were specified, and the rules for the final settlement of accounts between the Union and the separate states were relaxed and the deadline for claims extended.[31]

The Bank

The Senate initiated the incorporation of the Bank of the United States, and in doing so, even more than with regard to assumption, showed itself a willing tool of the Hamiltonian financial policies. When the bill was introduced Maclay recorded: "It is totally in vain to oppose this bill" (353). A change of three votes would have given a majority against assumption, but on the Bank the conclusion was so foregone that several members apparently did not vote. Thus both actively and passively the Senate abdicated its role as the guardian of the states against the exercise by the central government of powers not delegated by the Constitution.

The opponents of the Bank bill in the House seem to have been asleep when it was read in committee of the whole, so the debate was conducted in the House on the third reading after a motion to recommit failed. The rules precluded the proposal of amendments; the House therefore lost its chance to modify the Senate's bill, which would not have happened if a majority had not been satisfied.

The minority took the view that Congress not only lacked power to enact the bill, but that the exercise of such an utterly unfounded power would signal the abandonment of the constitutional distribution of powers and would subvert the Constitution entirely. Admitting that no expressed power to create a corporation could be found in the Constitution, the spokesmen for the majority used the elastic clause and tried to show that a bank was necessary to the exercise of the powers to tax, to borrow, to regulate commerce, to defend against sudden attack, and to provide for the general welfare. In addition, Laurence of New York suggested that this government surely had more power than Congress under the Articles of Confederation, which had incorporated the Bank of North America (*Annals*, 2:1892).

---

31. See Jacob E. Cooke, "The Compromise of 1790," *William and Mary Quarterly* 27 (October 1970): 523–45, and Kenneth R. Bowling, "Dinner at Jefferson's: A Note on Jacob E. Cooke's 'The Compromise of 1790,'" with reply by Cooke, *William and Mary Quarterly* 28 (October 1971): 629–40. On the generous treatment of southern claims in the final settlement, see E. James Ferguson, *The Power of the Purse*, pp. 323–25.

In his first speech against the bill Madison remarked that he "well recollected that a power to grant charters of incorporation had been proposed in the General Convention and rejected."[32] He went on to say that the linking of the "necessary and proper" clause with "common defence and general welfare" would "give to Congress an unlimited power; would render nugatory the enumeration of particular powers; would supersede all the powers reserved to the State Governments" (1896–97). These objections were, of course, a neat summary of the objectives of his opponents.

Ames of Massachusetts replied: "Congress may do what is necessary to the end for which the Constitution was adopted, provided it is not repugnant to the natural rights of man, or to those which they have expressly reserved to themselves, or to the powers which are assigned to the States" (1906). By such arguments he and others hoped to shift the basis of constitutional interpretation away from the idea used during ratification and stated in the Tenth Amendment, that the powers not delegated are reserved, to the new idea that "it would be endless, useless, and dangerous" to declare what government may do; "exceptions of what it may not do are shorter and safer" (1905). Laurence of New York soon extended this idea, saying, "there is nothing in the Constitution that is expressly against it [the Bank], and therefore we ought not to deduce a prohibition by construction" (1914). And Sedgwick of Massachusetts supported them with the additional thought that the words "necessary and proper" do not mean "indispensable": "It is universally agreed that wherever a power is delegated for express purposes, all the known and usual means for the attainment of the objects expressed are conceded also" (1911). The broadest expression of purposes is in the Preamble, and Boudinot of New Jersey proceeded to quote it and to deduce the Bank from it by "necessary implication" (1921–22).

In opposition, Stone of Maryland prefaced a heated speech with the general observation that "[w]e differ in our ideas of Government, and in our sense of the sacredness of the written compact. We varied widely in our opinions of the direction of this Government" (1930). During the ratification struggle, he said, it had not been thus. "Never did any country more completely unite in any sentiment than America in this, 'that Congress ought not to exercise, by implication, powers not granted by the Constitution.' " But a strange and wondrous change had occurred. For the doctrine of implication "destroys the principle of our Government at a blow; it at once breaks down every barrier which the Federal Constitution had raised

32. See Farrand, *Records*, 2:325, 615–16.

against unlimited legislation." Attacking the ends/means argument, he too read the Preamble and then asked, Is there "any power under Heaven which cannot be exercised within the extensive limits of this preamble?" (1931–32). Noting "how eagerly men grasped at the slightest pretexts for exercise of power," Stone held that the "necessary and proper" clause itself supported his position: "This clause was intended to defeat those loose and proud principles of legislation which had been contended for. It was meant to reduce legislation to some rule. In fine, it confined the Legislature to those means that were necessary and proper" (1934).

Giles of Virginia also thought the bank bill to be subversive of the Constitution. "I have been taught to consider this as a Federal, not as a consolidated Government. . . . I presume the great object of the Constitution was to distribute all governmental rights between the several State governments and the Government of the United States; the expediency, therefore," of this distribution is properly "decided by the constitution, and not by the governments among which the distribution is made." All arguments for the Bank, however, tend to subvert this distribution, to threaten the very existence of the states, and "to end themselves in the unlimited ocean of despotism" (1942–43). According to Giles, the "peculiar relation" between the state and the national governments will "naturally produce a contest for governmental rights." The Bank bill he saw as "an unprovoked advance in this scramble for authority, and a mere experiment how far we may proceed without involving the opposition of the State governments" (1943–44). He described two "modes of administering this Government," the one "with mildness and moderation" within the known bounds of the Constitution, the other "by the creation and operation of fiscal mechanism." The latter, he predicted, "must be ultimately discarded, or [it will] bring about a radical change in the nature of our Government" (1944–45).

Giles was followed by Gerry of Massachusetts, who treated the House to an elaborate exposition of Blackstone's rules for interpreting a law. These included "considering the reason and spirit of it, or the cause which moved the Legislature to enact it." Gerry then used the Preamble to find "the causes which produced the Constitution" and immediately found in the elastic clause the power to carry out all the purposes mentioned in the Preamble (1950).

Following Gerry, Vining of Delaware made a speech remarkable for two features. Harking back to Madison's statement that the Convention had rejected a proposed power to issue charters of incorporation, Vining argued that, even if Madison's recollection was "the full sense of the members of the Convention, their opinion at that day, is not a sufficient authority by which for Congress at the present time to construe the Constitution" (1955). This amounted to a declaration of the independence of Congress from the influence of any opinions or decisions of the Convention, even if adequately established, beyond the words of the Constitution itself.

In a second move with even broader implications Vining advanced, for the first time in the new Congress, the doctrine of inherent powers. Citing the Declaration of Independence, he argued that by becoming an independent nation the United States "derive all the powers appertaining to a nation thus circumstanced, and consequently the power under consideration" (1955). The Declaration was thus called upon as a source of power preceding and superseding the distribution of powers made by the Constitution itself. In 1785 James Wilson had developed this doctrine in support of the Bank of North America, but it had obviously been repudiated in the ratification struggle, even by Wilson himself.[33] Vining did not succeed in resurrecting it, but his use of it showed clearly the cavalier attitude of the nationalists toward the Constitution.

In the last speech of the debate Madison remarked that this was "the first instance he had heard of" when the Preamble "has produced a new mine of power" (1957). He also reiterated the view that "[t]he constructions of the Constitution which have been maintained on this occasion, go to the subversion of every power whatever in the several States" (1958).

The vote was then taken and the Bank was incorporated, 39 to 20. Only one of the minority votes came from the North. The South also had improved its cohesion, particularly in Virginia, but still three of its five states were divided.

In each of these three cases the centralizers chose to exercise a power not mentioned in the Constitution in the face of determined opposition marshaling a variety of constitutional arguments against their proposals. The powers were clearly more important to them than the preservation of unity among the divergent interests that had united to secure ratification of the Constitution. It was not a matter of the unity being broken by a small minority: on the assumption issue, clearly, the opposition composed a majority of the House.

33. Wilson's view in 1785 is described above (p. 48). Interpreting the proposed Constitution on October 6, 1787, he argued instead that "the congressional power is to be collected, not from tacit implication, but from the positive grant expressed in the instrument of the union." *Pennsylvania and the Federal Constitution, 1787–1788*, ed. John Bach McMaster and Frederick D. Stone (Philadelphia, 1888), p. 143.

The Implications

In the First Session the exercise of the power to allocate the removal power was prevented by a maneuver that attained the end without the actual use of the power. In the Second Session the power to assume the state debts was effectively blocked until the logrolling of the Senate won for it a scant majority. Disheartened by that experience, the opposition was unable to muster similar strength against the Bank.

On removal, only four state delegations in the House cast undivided votes; on assumption the number increased to six; and on the Bank there were nine undivided states. In each case every solid southern state voted against every solid northern state. Yet the cohesion of the South lagged behind, and was a response to, the growing solidarity and aggressiveness of the North. The trend was similar in the Senate, where the Rice Index of Cohesion for the northern states improved from 33 to 100 while that for the southern states declined slightly from 50 to 43.[34]

As the centralizers grasped for power they presented ever-broader bases for their claims. The removal debate turned largely on logical deductions from the words of Article II, Section 2. Assumption brought in also data from the Philadelphia Convention and from the ratifying conventions. But it was not until the debate on the Bank that the full orchestration of sources of power was heard: the elastic clause, the Preamble, the Articles of Confederation, and the doctrine of inherent powers from the Declaration of Independence.

Table 1. Rice Index of Cohesion, by Region
             First Congress, House of Representatives

	Session 1	Session 2	Session 3
	Removal Power	Assumption of State Debts	Bank of the United States
Southern States	4.8	48.2	58.4
Northern States	26.6	47.0	94.2
New England	28.6	75.0	88.2
Middle States	75.0	22.2	100.0

34. The Rice index varies from 0 to 100 and is obtained by subtracting the percentage voting "yes" from the percentage voting "no," or vice versa if the "no" votes are less numerous.

In this process some definite theories of constitutional interpretation were advanced. The later generalizations of "broad" and "strict" interpretation were already given specific content in the First Congress:

1. Congress could supply laws to fill "gaps" in the Constitution; the silence of the Constitution need not be taken as a Convention decision against such laws (505).
2. The limits on the powers of Congress must be explicit in the Constitution, but the powers need not be; no implied limits could be erected by construction but implied powers could be.
3. Congress was not bound or limited by the views of the Convention, even when these views were known, unless the Convention had written them into the Constitution (753).
4. The elastic clause could supply the means for the achievement of purposes expressed anywhere in the Constitution, including the Preamble (1915).
5. The meaning of the words "necessary" and "proper" must be left to Congress to determine; there was no other basis to distinguish the convenient from the necessary (1926).
6. If a power was not expressly granted, nor prohibited, it could be exercised according to the "reason and spirit" of the Constitution, the intentions and purposes as found in the Preamble.[35]
7. Congress should more boldly exercise its discretion, since the Constitution is protected against legislative errors by the process of judicial review (1927).

Even the general proposition that the Constitution had established a balance of power between the Union and the states that should be preserved—

---

35. This interpretation by equity rules had been anticipated by the Antifederalist "Brutus," who may have been Robert Yates: "The inference is natural that the legislature will have an authority to make all laws which they shall judge necessary for the common safety, and to promote the general welfare. This amounts to a power to make laws at discretion." *New York Journal*, December 13, 1787, reprinted in Storing, *The Complete Anti-Federalist*, 2:389. See Ann Stuart Diamond, "The Anti-Federalist 'Brutus,'" *Political Science Reviewer* 6 (Fall 1976): 249–81.

Hadley Arkes credits "Brutus" with understanding that, with equity jurisdiction, the territory outside the text of the Constitution is not one without guideposts, given over to subjective whims and emotions, as Judge Robert Bork believes, but rather a land inhabited by principles and canons of moral reasoning. See Arkes's *Beyond the Constitution*, pp. 21–23. However, he ignores the fact that, for "Brutus," this was an argument against ratification. See also Arkes, *First Things* (Princeton, 1986), chapters 2 and 4.

eloquently defended by congressmen so divergent as Gerry of Massachusetts (2:1325), Stone of Maryland (586, 2:1328), and Madison of Virginia (1956)— was under attack. On the one side the powers of the states were seen as "a most effectual and necessary check against encroachments from the Government of the Union," as Jackson of Georgia phrased it (1692). On the other, "the separate sovereignties of the several States," Scott of Pennsylvania said, "are the most effectual bar to prevent the operations of the present system" (554). They were obstacles to be overcome, not contributing parts of the whole as the Convention had intended. Most members did not thus openly express their antagonism, but their actions spoke loudly. "A distrust of the States," Stone remarked toward the end of the Third Session, "is shown in every movement of Congress—will not this implant distrust also in the states?" (1936). Similarly in the Senate, a few days later, Maclay wrote that "[a]nnihilation of State government is undoubtedly the object of these people." He went on to describe their position and views as follows: "The general power to carry the Constitution into effect by a constructive interpretation would extend to every case that Congress may deem necessary or expedient. . . . The supreme power is with the General Government to decide in this, as in everything else, for the States have neglected to secure any umpire or mode of decision in case of differences between them. . . . This open point, this unguarded pass, has rendered the General Government completely uncontrollable." Thus, he said, "did these heroes vapor and boast of their address in having cheated the people and [in] establishing a form of government over them which none of them expected."[36]

That the central government was rendered completely uncontrollable is also the judgment of a modern analyst. Rudolph M. Bell found that, in the 1770s and 1780s, "Americans had overthrown governments or established them quite regularly—British rule by force, colonial governments by de facto action, a confederation by a delegate assembly. . . . The 'rights' extolled in the Declaration of Independence were freely exercised." From the First Congress, however, "A consistent majority fought successfully against any attempt to restrain national authority by establishing outside limits on its power," in the debates over amendments to the Constitution and reapportionment after the census of 1790, for example. Washington's response to the Whiskey Rebellion—his condemnation of the Democratic-Republican societies[37] and his massive military expedition to western Penn-

---

36. *The Journal of William Maclay*, pp. 378, 381–82.

37. Washington disparaged them as "self-created societies," a phrase equally applicable to many of the committees that had made the Revolution. See his State of the Union Message,

sylvania—was, in Bell's view, "an attack on all forms of meaningful opposition to an existing government. . . . The Sedition Act, passed only four years later, was not the aberration of men excessively driven by fear of foreign invasion; rather, it was an expression of Washington's vision of an effective government, that is, one unrestrained by externally determined limits." In 1794 the president and the Congress were not only "unusually willing to cast aside individual rights," but Bell made the further point that "the time had arrived when such an action was widely accepted."[38] The military expedition was made with militia from four states; and little public support could be found in other states for the Virginia and Kentucky Resolutions against the Alien and Sedition Laws.[39]

These events make it clear that the reign of law established under the Constitution had broad public support. They also make it clear that a rule of law without a spirit of consensus and respect for differences becomes distorted into tyranny. As the southerners had feared in the Convention (above, p. 91), they found that the northern Federalists were willing to use their majority to override determined opposition whenever they could. When they lacked a majority, as on assumption, they well knew how to roll logs; but, unwilling to back off from extremes as the Convention had learned to do, the Federalists rejected the delays and compromises needed to build consensus in favor of the coercion of majority rule—a subversion of the spirit and hope of the Convention. Both the Federalists and their opponents were willing to go that route, the former because they had the majority and believed they could continue to manipulate the voters, the latter because they thought the people would soon see the errors of Federalism.

This was the era when the idea of legitimate opposition to the holders of

---

November 19, 1794; see also Richard H. Kohn, "The Washington Administration's Decision to Crush the Whiskey Rebellion," *Journal of American History* 59 (December 1972): 567–84, and Thomas P. Slaughter, *The Whiskey Rebellion: Frontier Epilogue to the American Revolution* (New York, 1986).

38. Bell, *Party and Faction*, pp. 46–48. He believes, wrongly I think, that "factions" found solutions to policy issues, leading to an "ideological vacuum" in which "parties," from 1794, aimed to capture control of the unlimited regime (p. 53). I see the factional debates on policy as efforts by each side to convince the other, and the later pursuit of power as the abandonment of efforts at conviction in favor of the coercion of majority rule, a result of the radical polarization inherent in Hamilton's policies. There was no ideological vacuum.

39. See James Morton Smith, *Freedom's Fetters: The Alien and Sedition Laws and American Civil Liberties* (Ithaca, 1956), especially the 1966 Preface to the Cornell Paperbacks edition; William T. Mayton, "Seditious Libel and the Lost Guarantee of a Freedom of Expression," *Columbia Law Review* 84 (January 1984): 91–142; and Norman L. Rosenberg, *Protecting the Best Men: An Interpretive History of the Law of Libel* (Chapel Hill, 1986), chapters 3–5.

office was just beginning to be distinguished from subversion and rebellion. In England, Court party adherents still saw all opposition as subversion. The temperaments of Washington and Adams were such that they too could not accept this new conception of politics.

The Federalists in power thus embraced the Court Whig doctrine that the central government was the ultimate judge of its own powers—a doctrine against which the Revolution had been fought. Their program, so clearly patterned on England, predictably stimulated a resurgence of the Country, or Opposition, Whig ideology in the First Congress—as the attempts to gain consideration for limiting amendments, Madison's effort to discriminate in tonnage duties between countries in alliance with the United States (France) and those refusing to enter into an alliance (Britain), and the vigorous opposition to the excise tax, make clear. Although a minority in the First Congress, the Jeffersonian Republicans had an advantage not available to the English Opposition: they had a written Constitution that spoke against unlimited power.

The Federalists, overreacting to the X Y Z affair with their Sedition Act and divided by the conflict between Adams and Hamilton, lost some credibility and the election of 1800. The electorate was found to have a real power of choice, a crucial role in the governmental process. This election, in spite of the growing vituperation since 1798 and the acrimonious campaign, brought the maturity of a peaceful if not graceful transition of power. The forms of the Constitution held, in spite of the emotions aroused. For the first time the three branches of the government were not in the hands of the same party. The stage was also set for the discovery of a new dimension of the Constitution.

John Marshall's *Marbury* opinion presented, as was noted in chapter 5 (p. 150), a new claim to a power of final interpretation of the Constitution unlike any previous understanding of judicial power. After a dozen years of successful Federalist efforts to emancipate the central government from all external restraints, the dialectics of politics dictated that a Federalist judge could establish a strong restraint external to the other branches of the government. This form of judicial review makes judges political, however, and is of limited effectiveness in some issue areas. Yet precarious as this restraint is, being institutional it may be more predictable and reliable than external (and possibly violent) controls.

The Convention, starting from the extremes of state sovereignty on the one hand and a unitary project on the other, had learned that majority decision is not adequate for some political conflicts and had moved toward the achievement of consensus through debate. The First Congress generated equally vigorous debate; but, being established institutionally, it was not under equal constraints to achieve consensus. The delicate integration of divergent values and views that had been achieved at Philadelphia, by methods and debates then kept secret, was distorted in New York in favor of partial, even sectional values. The northern Federalists chose to use their majority to carry through the extreme provisions of Hamilton's program, and thus gradually alienated their supporters, especially in the South, and committed the country to a politics and a psychology of conflict.

Yet the "unguarded pass" that so troubled Maclay has at least two guardians, so that the central government is partially controllable, part of the time. The potential and actual judicial veto has kept the Constitution a living and enforceable body of law. And the voters can occasionally, rightly or wrongly, reverse establishment policy.

Perhaps as plans go among mice and men, and in spite of the Convention's great failure regarding slavery, that *is* a modest success.

Appendixes

Appendix A

State-Federalist Voting in the Philadelphia Convention

If the orientation of the state federalists was significantly different from those of other groups in the Convention, it should be possible to find a distinctive pattern in their voting. Aside from the remarks they made, which may be subject to interpretation, such a pattern of voting would be objective evidence of a special orientation.

A basic obstacle to the search for such a pattern lies in the fact that votes were recorded for states, rarely for individuals. Only from Connecticut were all the delegates state federalists, but the group also had control of the delegations of South Carolina and, usually, North Carolina. Many more votes, however, were taken on issues relating to the southern economy and southern apprehensions about a northern majority than on state-federalist issues, which strongly differentiated the group into northern and southern wings. So the search is unavoidably simplified to the question of whether Connecticut voted in a distinctive way.

Previous researchers using quantitative methods have found the state to be something of a maverick. Forrest McDonald, employing a percentage-of-agreement method, said that "Maryland and Connecticut acted as two lone wolves," and S. Sidney Ulmer, using Elementary Factor Analysis, suggested that those two states "might be classified as standing alone." They did not, however, suggest reasons for their findings.[1]

Of the several statistical methods by which voting blocs can be discovered, all of which tend to give similar results, perhaps the most sensitive is factor analysis. Proceeding from a matrix of correlation coefficients, it seeks to identify clusters of similar variables, thus facilitating a grasp of complex relationships.[2]

Treating each state as a dichotomous variable, by eliminating absences and divided votes, allows each cell of the matrix to show the degree of association between two states in yes and no voting. Since the data are nominal, an appropriate statistic would be *phi*; but since they are also dichotomous, it can be shown that, in such cases, *phi* is exactly equal to the product-moment correlation coefficient, Karl Pearson's *r*. The matrix, accordingly, can be regarded as either.

By retaining unity in the diagonal, the principle-component method factors common and specific variance. Each successive factor explains a smaller portion of the variance and tends to become more difficult to interpret.[3] Several of the optional techniques were tried, both orthogonal and oblique methods of rotation were employed, and different numbers of factors were rotated. While the several techniques give generally the same cluster, the clearest picture of the situation emerges from the factor-pattern matrix obtained by direct Oblimin (oblique) rotation.

It seemed that a distinctive pattern of voting by Connecticut should appear in the early part of the Convention, when the differences over representation were most acute, if it was to appear at all. Up to the Connecticut compromise 156 votes were taken, as numbered in Farrand's *Records*, the source of the basic data. These first 156 votes were examined, therefore, and the results are shown in table 2.

The "loading" of each state on a factor indicates the proximity of that state to the center of that cluster. It is clear that the three largest states form one

1. McDonald, *We the People*, p. 97; Ulmer, "Sub-Group Formation in the Constitutional Convention," *Midwest Journal of Political Science* 10 (August 1966): 295.

2. For invaluable assistance with this analysis I am particularly indebted to two former students referred to in footnote 25 on p. 64.

3. A painless introduction to this technique is R. J. Rummel, "Understanding Factor Analysis," *Journal of Conflict Resolution* 11 (December 1967): 444–78. There is no sampling-error variance in this study, since no sampling is involved. The question of the principal diagonal remains one of the most vexing in factor analysis. For a discussion of the merits see Rummel's *Applied Factor Analysis* (Evanston, 1970), pp. 112–13, 116–67, 310–20.

Table 2. Four-Factor Analysis of the First 156 Roll Call Votes

Factor Pattern After Direct Oblimin ($\Delta = 0$) Rotation with Kaiser Normalization

Factor	I	II	III	IV
Massachusetts	−.65	.08	−.33	.24
Connecticut	.14	−.01	−.06	.94
New York	.04	−.89	−.24	−.20
New Jersey	.17	−.76	.04	.21
Pennsylvania	−.86	.04	.10	−.16
Delaware	−.29	−.47	.43	.22
Maryland	−.44	−.44	.28	.30
Virginia	−.81	.02	−.10	−.08
North Carolina	−.49	.05	−.47	.33
South Carolina	.04	−.03	−.84	.12
Georgia	−.25	−.22	−.76	−.10

New Hampshire delegates arrived in time for vote no. 203; Rhode Island never sent delegates.

cluster, that the three deep South states form another, that the four small central states form a third, and that Connecticut stands alone.

The other loadings on factor IV are too low to indicate membership in a cluster, but they are interesting as indicators of attitudes toward the Connecticut position. Disregarding New York, which had departed before the vote was taken, the four states with the lowest loadings on this factor are precisely those that voted against the Connecticut compromise.

These four factors account for 71.5% of the total variance. If a fifth factor is added, New York and New Jersey appear on it as a group separate from Delaware and Maryland, which remain on factor II, but the alignment on factor IV is little changed.

If the hypothesis that Connecticut did vote in a distinctive way while the subject of representation was still unsettled is thus confirmed, a question may remain as to whether its pattern continued to be distinctive during the whole Convention. If so, it would appear that the state-federalist orientation affected the voting on many issues.

The same methodology, applied to the full 569 votes numbered by Farrand, should answer that question.[4]

The alignments thus revealed are less easily interpreted. The unity of the three large states was clearly temporary, while the small central states and the deep South bloc retain their cohesion. Massachusetts has pulled away

4. Professor Jillson is critical of attempts to find alignments for the whole Convention, since his methodology reveals three realignments. See his *Constitution Making*, especially chapter 2.

Table 3.   Five-Factor Analysis of All 569 Roll Call Votes

Factor Pattern After Direct Oblimin ($\Delta = 0$) Rotation with Kaiser Normalization

Factor	I	II	III	IV	V
New Hampshire	−.48	.18	.53	.11	.28
Massachusetts	−.52	.14	.51	−.07	−.01
Connecticut	−.05	.10	−.08	−.03	.96
New York	−.20	−.89	−.00	−.01	−.13
New Jersey	−.03	−.52	.28	.21	.39
Pennsylvania	.02	.16	.57	−.52	.04
Delaware	.13	−.36	.73	−.03	.01
Maryland	.15	−.48	.03	−.46	.28
Virginia	−.19	.01	.02	−.82	−.01
North Carolina	−.63	−.05	−.07	.30	.00
South Carolina	−.83	−.03	.05	.11	−.01
Georgia	−.75	−.18	−.13	−.09	.14

from Virginia; it and New Hampshire are almost equally divided in support of the deep South bloc and of Pennsylvania and Delaware. Comparing the two tables, other realignments are apparent, so it is obvious that the voting blocs did not remain stable throughout the Convention. Yet Connecticut continued to load heavily on a separate factor. New Jersey's .39 loading on that factor, coupled with .28 by both New Hampshire and Maryland, shows substantial support by those small states.

The very low loadings by North Carolina and South Carolina on factor V result from the overriding influence of North-South issues. When the Rice cohesion indexes for these two states with Connecticut are calculated, North Carolina reads 24 and South Carolina 12 before the Connecticut compromise; for the full 569 roll calls, they read 14 and 25, respectively.

These five factors account for 71.4% of the total variance. When an alternative procedure was tried, using only the 413 votes taken after the compromise, New Jersey loaded quite heavily (.73) with Connecticut. This indicates that most of the disagreement between these two delegations occurred in the early period when the state-sovereignty men and the state federalists were divided on the bases of representation.

It would also be interesting to know whether delegates from states other than Connecticut who expressed state-federalist views in debate voted with Connecticut. The official *Journal* does not record individual votes, but Forrest McDonald presented a table of sixteen roll calls on which he had deduced the positions of nearly all delegates. These included six that pertained to the "issue whether sovereignty . . . should be transferred to a new general government" and five that related to restrictions on state governments.[5]

Robert A. McGuire, using McDonald's table, found votes 30 and 74 (both on the sovereignty issue) irreconcilable with data in Farrand's *Records* and that vote 228 was really vote 230, but otherwise accepted McDonald's attributions.[6]

The data in McDonald's table, thus corrected by McGuire, make possible a comparison of the individuals who expressed state-federalist leanings (as listed above on p. 62) with the position of Connecticut on fourteen roll calls—an admittedly small sample. The data can also be used to detect delegates who voted with Connecticut without clearly expressing such leanings. Carroll and Jenifer of Maryland, for example, agreed with Connecticut on 11 and 10 of the fourteen roll calls, illustrating the wider support that enabled the state federalists to achieve what they did.

Only vote 34 occurred before the Connecticut compromise, and most of the tabulated roll calls came in late August. Clearly the support for Connecticut varied greatly from issue to issue; other considerations could override the general state-federalist orientation. On these roll calls, the three delegates who refused to sign the Constitution (Gerry, Mason, and Randolph) were about as supportive of the Connecticut position as anyone— until August 29, when the final vote (no. 399) was taken rejecting the two-thirds requirement for navigation laws. This divisive issue suggests that the cohesion of the state federalists was weaker than the primary division between North and South.

The North-South differences are evident also in the degree of support the state federalists received from other delegates on the two categories of votes, those on sovereignty and on state restrictions. Of the fourteen votes, five (387, 391, 392, 393, 394) pertained to restrictions on the states. Excluding the Pennsylvanians, whom McDonald did not tabulate, only Madison and Washington voted against Connecticut's position on all five. They were joined by twelve northerners on three or four of these votes, but by only

5. *We the People*, pp. 100–103. He assumed that on these issues (Farrand's vote numbers 30, 34, 74, 203, 228, 268, 336, 345, 387, 391, 392, 393, 394, 399, 415, and 559) the Pennsylvania delegates, all representing personal-property interests, voted together. Other delegates were divided into real- and personal-property groups and were listed on each roll call as supporting or opposing Pennsylvania's personalty orientation—as a test of Beard's hypothesis.

6. "Constitution Making: A Rational-Choice Model of the Federal Convention of 1787," *American Journal of Political Science* 32 (May 1988): 483–522, at 496.

Table 4. Votes of Connecticut and of State Federalist Delegates of Other States on Fourteen Roll Calls as Tabulated by McDonald, *We the People*, pp. 102–3

+ = yes   − = no   0 = not voting

McDonald vote number	2	4	5	6	7	8	9	10	11	12	13	14	15	16	Votes cast	With Connecticut Number	Percentage
Farrand vote number	34	203	230	268	336	345	387	391	392	393	394	399	415	559			
Connecticut	−	+	−	−	+	−	+	−	−	−	−	−	+	+	14		
Mass. Gerry	−	+	+	+	+	−	+	0	+	−	−	−	+	−	13	8	62
Dela. Dickinson	+	0	−	0	−	−	+	+	+	+	−	−	+	0	11	5	45
Va. Mason	−	−	+	+	+	−	+	−	−	−	+	+	−	−	14	8	57
Randolph	−	−	−	+	+	+	+	−	−	−	+	+	−	−	14	8	57
N.C. Davie	−	−	+	−	0	0	0	0	0	0	0	0	0	0	4	2	50
Spaight	−	−	+	−	+	+	+	+	+	+	−	−	+	−	14	7	50
Williamson	−	−	+	−	+	+	+	−	+	+	+	+	+	−	14	6	43
S.C. Butler	−	−	−	−	+	+	+	+	−	−	−	−	+	−	14	9	64
C. C. Pinckney	−	−	−	−	+	+	+	+	−	−	−	−	+	−	14	9	64
Rutledge	−	−	−	−	+	+	+	+	−	−	−	−	+	−	14	9	64
Ga. Pierce	−	0	0	0	0	0	0	0	0	0	0	0	0	0	1	1	100
Baldwin	−	−	+	−	+	+	+	+	−	−	+	+	+	−	14	8	57
Percentage voting with Connecticut	92	10	45	70	90	30	100	22	50	70	70	60	70	0	0		

Table 5. Rice Index of Cohesion of Individual Voting on Roll Calls as Tabulated by McDonald, *We the People*, pp. 102–3

	Vote	34	(N)	Vote	203	(N)	Vote	345	(N)	Vote	399	(N)	Average of 14 Votes
All State Federalists		73	15		38	13		8	13		38	13	48
Northern State Federalists	yes	20	5	yes	100	4	yes	100	5	yes	100	5	62
Southern State Federalists	yes	100	10	no	100	9	no	75	8	no	0	8	59
All Other Northern Delegates (except Pennsylvanians)	yes	17	12	no	20	10	no	100	11	yes	100	11	61
All Other Southern Delegates		0	8	no	60	10	no	20	10	no	60	10	35

Vote 34: Madison's congressional negative on state laws.
Vote 203: Ratification of the Constitution by state legislatures.
Vote 345: National power over state militias.
Vote 399: Require two thirds of each house to pass navigation acts.
"Yes" and "no" indicate agreement or disagreement with the Connecticut position on each issue.

three southerners on three of the five votes. On the other side, Connecticut was joined by one northerner (Gerry) on three votes, and by thirteen southerners—four of them on all five votes and five on four votes.

Four of the fourteen votes (34, 268, 345, 415) dealt with issues of state versus national sovereignty. Jenifer of Maryland alone supported Connecticut on all four votes, joined on three by eight other southerners but by only two northerners (Brearley and Livingston of New Jersey). Four Delaware delegates, plus King and Randolph, were the only ones who opposed Connecticut's position on as many as three of the four votes, indicating less cohesion in the North on this issue than in the South, and less than on restricting the states.

The Rice cohesion index (p. 201, note 34) can be used on these fourteen votes to examine the relations between the northern and southern wings of the state-federalist group.

The North-South division was a significant influence in reducing the cohesion of the state federalists as a voting bloc. They displayed more cohesion in each geographical area than other delegates from the same area. Yet the two wings of the group could stand solidly on the two sides of an issue, as vote 203 illustrates, or on the same side, as in vote 387. The southern wing, although it included twice as many delegates, was only slightly less cohesive than the northern wing. As an analysis of table 3 shows, however, the Carolina delegates were cohesive as parts of the deep South bloc rather than as state federalists.

Perhaps a cautionary reminder is warranted: McDonald's 14 votes are only 2.46% of the 569 roll calls of the Convention.

Appendix B

The First Senate

There being no records of debates in the First Senate (other than Maclay's journal), the roll call votes displayed in the Senate *Journals* provide our best glimpses into the minds of the individual senators. Many votes were taken, of course, without the roll call, but we have an even hundred recorded votes from the three sessions. Of these, thirty-two concerned the location and other aspects of the choice of a national capital. This large number of votes on a single subject, on which geography had a special influence, makes it desirable to separate the seat-of-government votes from the others.

Many members of the Convention had seen the Senate as a body representing the states (or even the state governments) rather than the people, and as the part of the new government expected to uphold the interests of the separate states. Thus, it would be desirable to know whether the senators, as individuals, thought of themselves primarily as state agents or, on the contrary, as wheels in the new national machinery of government.

In the old Congress and in the Convention it had been necessary for the members of state delegations to cast a single state vote. The new rule of per capita voting, however, permitted each member to cast an individual vote. If a state's two senators disagreed, and voted their disagreement, they would effectively cancel out their state's influence on the outcome. Each might, of course, be conscientiously pursuing his state's interests as he saw them, but, in the absence of coordinated votes, the state's influence would necessarily be reduced.

One measure, therefore, of the degree to which senators saw themselves as state agents is the degree of their coordination in voting. This is a rough measure, perhaps better stated in this way: when the two senators failed to vote together they were sacrificing state influence to their disagreement; they either read their state's interests differently or one or both senators were not trying to pursue the state's interests—perhaps being nationally oriented.

In seat-of-government voting, where state orientations might be expected to predominate, levels of agreement were quite high, although three states were more divided on this than on non-seat voting. The extreme case of Pennsylvania, where Maclay and Robert Morris generally agreed on seat votes but on little else, clearly displays the need to segregate those votes in examining levels of agreement on other subjects. There is almost no correlation between the last two columns of table 6—the rank-order coefficient (Spearman's *rho*) is $-.05$.

In non-seat voting, complete agreement was achieved by four states in the first session, by three in the third, but by only one in the divisive second session. Only two states achieved it in two sessions and none in all three, so six different states did so at least once. On the other hand, completely random voting should result in 50 percent agreement, and there are eight instances of that figure or less on seat and non-seat votes in the three sessions. It may be concluded that the senators did not generally feel a need to coordinate their votes in defense of state interests.

Table 6. Percentage Agreement in State Delegations, First Senate, 1789–1791

| | Non-Seat-of-Government Votes | | | | Seat Votes |
	Session 1	Session 2	Session 3	Total	Total
New Hampshire	100	34	67	50	70
Massachusetts	100	80	100	87	96
Rhode Island	absent	81	67	77	77
Connecticut	73	79	100	84	77
New York	58	100	100	92	94
New Jersey	80	67	92	75	48
Pennsylvania	11	15	33	19	81
Delaware	82	79	83	80	87
Maryland	69	49	80	59	97
Virginia	100	56	88	69	97
North Carolina	absent	86	82	85	60
South Carolina	91	71	77	76	78
Georgia	100	50	44	59	65
Average	79	65	78	70	79
Number of votes	16	38	14	68	32

Another dimension of senatorial decision making is the exploration of the clusters by which majorities were reached. (Frequently they were not reached: John Adams was able to decide sixteen questions after tie votes.) To uncover such clusters, several types of factor analysis were tried, with different parameters.[7]

A two-factor analysis of the seat-of-government votes (table 7) reveals four clusters, with heavy positive and negative loadings on each factor and a correlation of only −.25 between factors. A northern bloc of four states confronted a middle-state bloc from Pennsylvania to Virginia (joined by New Hampshire because of its long-standing conflict with New York over Vermont), with New Jersey divided between them.

The negative loadings of the deep South show three things: southern senators' dissatisfaction with the alternatives available, their divided votes, and their power, even though divided, to pull the capital to the Potomac— since neither of the blocs could win without deep South votes. The first factor explains more than half of the variance, and the middle-state bloc had greater cohesion. Three-, four-, and five-factor analyses were run but are not presented as tables since they did not yield much additional under-

7. In the tables the factor-structure loadings are correlations with the oblique factor axes. To reduce the size and complexity, loadings that account for less than 25% of the variance (.50) are usually omitted.

Table 7. Two-Factor Analysis of Seat-of-Government Votes in the First Senate, 1789–1791

Factor Structure After Direct Oblimin ($\Delta = 0$) Rotation with Kaiser Normalization

	Factor I, Positive				*Factor II, Positive*	
N.H.	Langdon	.94		Mass.	Dalton	.79
	Wingate	.75			Strong	.72
N.J.	Elmer	.87		R.I.	Foster	.86
Pa.	Maclay	.79			Stanton	.65
	Morris	.90		Conn.	Ellsworth	.74
Dela.	Bassett	.89			Johnson	.74
	Read	.90		N.Y.	King	.85
Md.	Carroll	.69			Schuyler	.87
	Henry	.75		N.J.	Paterson	.84
Va.	Lee	.79				
	Walker	1.00				

	Factor I, Negative				*Factor II, Negative*	
R.I.	Stanton	−.70		Pa.	Maclay	−.54
Conn.	Johnson	−.63		Ga.	Gunn	−.74
N.Y.	King	−.52		Md.	Carroll	−.63
	Schuyler	−.50			Henry	−.63
N.C.	Johnston	−.59		N.C.	Hawkins	−.70
S.C.	Butler	−.46		Va.	Lee	−.59
	Izard	−.77			Walker	−.61
Ga.	Few	−.66				

standing. On July 1 the factor I cluster (without Wingate), joined by Butler, Gunn, Hawkins, and Johnston, carried the final decision (*Annals,* 1:1040).

In non-seat voting (table 8) the clusters account for less of the variance, and the positive cluster on factor I is not a winning coalition. As with the seat voting, a two-factor analysis gives four clusters; but they are smaller, and two states, Maryland and South Carolina, do not appear in any cluster. Only five states have both their senators in the same cluster, whereas in seat voting ten states did.

When the Senate reinserted the assumption of state debts into the funding bill (July 16, *Annals,* 1:1050) only one senator, Few of Georgia, deviated from the alignments of the two-factor solution. It was carried by

Table 8.   Two-Factor Analysis of Non-Seat Votes in the First Senate,
1789–1791

Factor Structure After Direct Oblimin (Δ = 0) Rotation with Kaiser Normalization

	Factor I, Positive			*Factor II, Positive*	
N.H.	Wingate	.64	Mass.	Dalton	.63
R.I.	Foster	.52		Strong	.85
	Stanton	.77	Conn.	Ellsworth	.88
N.C.	Hawkins	.78		Johnson	.61
	Johnston	.70	N.J.	Elmer	.61
Pa.	Maclay	.66	Dela.	Read	.60
Dela.	Bassett	.52			
Va.	Lee	.69			
Ga.	Few	.67			

	Factor I, Negative			*Factor II, Negative*	
N.H.	Langdon	−.48	Va.	Walker	−.79
N.Y.	King	−.76	Ga.	Gunn	−.67
	Schuyler	−.77	(correlation between		
N.J.	Paterson	−.71	factors is −.018)		
Pa.	Morris	−.79			

the joint votes of the factor II group and the factor I opposition, plus the South Carolina senators and Carroll of Maryland (who were not in any cluster) and Few. On the Bank bill, the only close vote recorded came on a motion to extend the incorporation to 1815 (Jan. 13, 1791, *Annals,* 2:1745). Again, in a thin Senate, only one vote, this time Bassett of Delaware, deviated from the clusters of the two-factor solution, the South Carolina senators and Henry of Maryland voting "no."

The usually dominant coalition, the factor I negative and factor II positive groups, included eight former members of the Constitutional Convention (some of them state federalists), while the other two groups counted only two. More significant, this coalition contained not a single southerner. The factor I positive group was very evenly balanced, North and South, bringing together against northern dominance all the senators from the two "rejecting" states, the Antifederalist Lee and two Signers, Bassett and Few, plus the two northern mavericks, Maclay and Wingate. Such a disparate group, although large, lacked the cohesion for effective resistance to the Hamiltonian program for central power.

Appendix C

The First House

An unusual feature of voting in the First House of Representatives was the large number of votes taken on a single issue. In each of the first two sessions, almost exactly two fifths of all roll calls related to the location of the national capital. As a geographical issue, these votes might produce a sectional distortion in the analysis of roll calls that might not be accurate for other issues.

The data summarized in tables 9 and 10 give some rough indication of the directions and extent of the effects of the seat-of-government votes. Since there were some sixty-odd members of the First House and over a hundred roll calls, several decisions designed to simplify the presentation of the evidence were made. Each session was treated separately. First, only members who voted on 40% or more of the roll calls were included in the analysis. Second, only those representatives who participated in a factor group to the extent of 16% of their variance (a loading of .40) were counted as members of that cluster. Finally, to make clear the roles of the separate states and regions, the members of each cluster were grouped by states, and the states were then listed from north to south in order to group regions.

Some similarities appear when the clusters with and without seat votes are compared in the First Session. A middle bloc of members from New Jersey to Virginia shows up on factor 2 positive each way, but on the seat votes Pennsylvania goes with the North. Also, each way, a strong southern cluster of nine or more shows up on factor 1 negative. Without the seat votes it has the support of six northerners; with the seat votes, however, that support evaporates. Including the seat votes sharpens the regional differentiations; the northern clusters have no southern adherents, and vice versa (except for New Jersey), whereas without seat votes the factor 1 clusters stretch from New England to Georgia. These clusters also have ten more members and account for 41.5% of the variance, as against 36.2% with the seat votes. With seat votes, members voted more cohesively with their clusters, so that nearly all loadings are higher; and no state is found in three different clusters, whereas without the seat votes New Hampshire, Massachusetts, and Virginia are so divided.

In the Second Session (tables 11 and 12) such differences between the clusters, with and without seat votes, are less apparent. Three clusters show up each way, with members from the same states. The factor 1 positive

Table 9. Two-Factor Analysis of Non-Seat Votes, First House, First Session ($N = 21$) Representatives with Loadings $\geq .40$; Orthogonal (Verimax) Rotation

	Factor 1 +		Factor 1 –		Factor 2 +		Factor 2 –	
N.H.	Foster	.70	Livermore	–.49			Foster	–.45
	Gilman	.61						
Mass.	Ames	.75	Gerry	–.53			Leonard	–.41
	Goodhue	.57	Grout	–.92			Partridge	–.60
							Thatcher	–.55
Conn.	Sherman	.54						
	Trumbull	.88						
	Wadsworth	.87						
N.Y.	Benson	.89	Floyd	–.90			Hathorn	–.44
	Laurence	.91	Hathorn	–.83				
	Silvester	.48	Van Rensselaer	–.82				
N.J.	Cadwallader	.71			Boudinot	.55		
	Schureman	.56						
	Sinnickson	.54						
Pa.	Clymer	.82			Hartley	.66		
	Fitzsimmons	.82			Heister	.64		

State						P. Muhlenberg	.91
	Hartley	.61				Scott	.56
	Scott	.60					
	Wynkoop	.96					
Dela.	Vining	.77				Vining	.46
Md.	Carroll	.50				Carroll	.43
	Gale	.96				Contee	.66
	Smith	.45				Seney	.57
Va.	Brown	.44	Coles	−.86		Brown	.87
	Lee	.67	Page	−.61		Griffin	.73
			Parker	−.70		Lee	.47
			White	−.61		Madison	.81
						Moore	.64
S.C.			Burke	−.56			
			Sumter	−.94			
			Tucker	−.68			
Ga.	Baldwin	.56	Jackson	−.64			
			Matthews	−.53			
Variance		41.5%					15.1%

Rhode Island and North Carolina had not yet ratified the Constitution.

Table 10. Two-Factor Analysis of All Votes, First House, First Session ($N = 35$)
Representatives with Loadings $\geq .40$; Orthogonal (Verimax) Rotation

	Factor 1 +		Factor 1 –	Factor 2 +		Factor 2 –	
N.H.	Foster	.79				Livermore	–.71
	Gilman	.74					
Mass.	Ames	.85				Gerry	–.52
	Goodhue	.76				Grout	–.88
	Leonard	.56				Partridge	–.60
	Partridge	.43				Thatcher	–.48
	Thatcher	.54					
Conn.	Sherman	.69					
	Trumbull	.92					
	Wadsworth	.91					
N.Y.	Benson	.93				Floyd	–.86
	Laurence	.92				Hathorn	–.89
	Silvester	.70				Van Rensselaer	–.83
N.J.				Boudinot	.58		
				Cadwallader	.56		
Pa.	Clymer	.89					
	Fitzsimmons	.85					

State		Factor 1 (36.2%)		Factor 2 (19.3%)
	Hartley	.78		
	P. Muhlenberg	.60		
	Scott	.77		
	Wynkoop	.95		
Dela.			Vining	.73
Md.	Contee	−.57	Carroll	.72
			Gale	.53
Va.	Bland	−.86	Brown	.86
	Coles	−.89	Griffin	.47
	Griffin	−.41	Lee	.85
	Page	−.74	Madison	.83
	Parker	−.77	Moore	.61
	White	−.65		
S.C.	Burke	−.67		
	Sumter	−.94		
	Tucker	−.61		
Ga.	Jackson	−.71	Baldwin	.67
	Matthews	−.75		
Variance		36.2%		19.3%

Table 11. Two-Factor Analysis of Non-Seat Votes, First House, Second Session ($N = 30$) Representatives with Loadings $\geq .40$; Orthogonal (Verimax) Rotation

	Factor 1 +		Factor 1 –		Factor 2 +		Factor 2 –	
N.H.							Foster	–.41
Mass.	Ames	.67						
	Gerry	.59						
	Goodhue	.56						
	Leonard	.58						
	Partridge	.41						
	Sedgwick	.77						
	Thatcher	.59						
Conn.	Huntington	.64			Huntington	.41		
	Trumbull	.57						
N.Y.	Benson	.65					Hathorn	–.49
	Laurence	.40						
N.J.	Boudinot	.64			Cadwallader	.75		
	Cadwallader	.43			Sinnickson	.53		
Pa.			P. Muhlenberg	–.43	Clymer	.92		
					Fitzsimmons	.86		
					Hartley	.83		
					Heister	.78		
					P. Muhlenberg	.65		

State	Representative	Loading		Representative	Loading
				Scott	.56
				Wynkoop	.81
				Vining	.68
				Carroll	.86
				Contee	.40
				Gale	.81
				Griffin	.58
				Lee	.93
				Madison	.58
				Page	.49
				Parker	.42
				White	.53
Dela.	Vining	.41			
Md.	Contee	−.62			
	Seney	−.73			
Va.	Brown	−.65			
	Coles	−.61			
	Madison	−.56			
	Moore	−.56			
N.C.	Ashe	−.65			
	Bloodworth	−.66			
	Sevier	−.45			
	Steele	−.65			
	Williamson	−.78			
S.C.	Smith	.61			
Ga.	Baldwin	−.65			
	Jackson	−.70			
	Matthews	−.87			
Variance		23.3%			18.4%

Rhode Island had ratified but was not yet represented.

Table 12. Two-Factor Analysis of All Votes, First House, Second Session ($N = 51$) Representatives with Loadings $\geq .40$; Orthogonal (Verimax) Rotation

	Factor 1 +	Factor 1 –	Factor 2 +	Factor 2 –
N.H.	Foster .52			Foster –.44
Mass.	Ames .76			
	Gerry .64			Gerry –.46
	Goodhue .40			Grout –.41
	Grout .53			
	Leonard .67			
	Partridge .55			
	Sedgwick .81			
	Thatcher .57			
Conn.	Huntington .82			
	Sherman .60			
	Sturges .58			Sturges –.44
	Trumbull .71			
	Wadsworth .95			
N.Y.	Benson .77			Hathorn –.58
	Laurence .61			Silvester –.41
	Silvester .57			Van Rensselaer –.58
N.J.	Boudinot .84		Cadwallader .91	
	Schureman .61		Sinnickson .71	
Pa.		P. Muhlenberg –.45	Clymer .98	
		Scott –.42	Fitzsimmons .88	
			Hartley .82	
			Heister .84	
			P. Muhlenberg .75	

State	Member	Factor I	Factor II
	Scott		.68
	Wynkoop		.90
Dela.	Vining		.87
Md.	Carroll		.90
	Contee	−.56	.58
	Gale		.91
	Stone		.42
Va.	Brown	−.62	.55
	Coles	−.62	
	Griffin		.70
	Lee		.96
	Madison	−.49	.64
	Moore	−.55	.52
	Page	−.44	.60
	Parker	−.43	.64
	White		.68
N.C.	Ashe	−.64	.47
	Sevier	−.66	
	Steele	−.64	
	Williamson	−.72	.41
S.C.	Burke	.51	
	Huger	.41	
	Smith	.62	
	Sumter	−.52	
Ga.	Baldwin	−.64	
	Jackson	−.67	
	Matthews	−.77	
Variance		41.6%	12.0%

Table 13. Two-Factor Analysis of All Votes, First House, First Session, Representatives with Loadings $\geq$ .40, and Their Vote on Removal Power[a]

	Factor Structure After Oblique (Direct Oblimin, $\Delta = 0$) Rotation with Kaiser Normalization ($N = 35$)			
	Factor 1 +	Factor 1 −	Factor 2 +	Factor 2 −
N.H.	○ Foster .80			− Livermore − .72
	+ Gilman .75			
Mass.	+ Ames .84			− Gerry − .51
	+ Goodhue .77			− Grout − .87
	− Leonard .58			− Partridge − .61
	− Partridge .46			− Thatcher − .50
	− Thatcher .57			
Conn.	− Sherman .70			
	+ Trumbull .91			
	○ Wadsworth .91			
N.Y.	+ Benson .90			○ Floyd − .86
	+ Laurence .91			− Hathorn − .89
	+ Silvester .71			− Van Rensselaer − .83
N.J.			+ Boudinot .59	
			+ Cadwallader .56	
Pa.	+ Clymer .88			
	+ Fitzsimmons .84			

State	Factor 1 name	Factor 1	Factor 2 name	Factor 2
	+ Hartley	.77		
	+ P. Muhlenberg	.59		
	+ Scott	.77		
	○ Wynkoop	.95		
Dela.			+ Vining	.73
Md.	+ Contee	−.59	+ Carroll	.72
			+ Contee	.42
			○ Gale	.52
Va.	○ Bland	−.88	+ Brown	.86
	− Coles	−.89	+ Griffin	.49
	+ Griffin	−.44	+ Lee	.85
	− Page	−.75	+ Madison	.83
	− Parker	−.77	+ Moore	.62
	− White	−.64		
S.C.	+ Burke	−.68		
	− Sumter	−.94		
	− Tucker	−.60		
Ga.	− Jackson	−.71	○ Baldwin	.68
	− Matthews	−.77		

Variance: Factor 1 (+ and −) = 36.2%   Variance: Factor 2 (+ and −) = 19.3%

aFinal vote on the Foreign Affairs Department, June 24, 1789, as printed in the *Annals of Congress*, 1:614. Before a name, + = a "yes" vote, − = a "no" vote, and ○ = not voting in that roll call.

Table 14. Two-Factor Analysis of All Votes, First House, Second Session, Representatives with Loadings ≥ .40, and Their Vote on Assumption[a]

	Factor Structure after Oblique (Direct Oblimin, Δ = 0) Rotation with Kaiser Normalization (N = 51)			
	Factor 1 +	Factor 1 −	Factor 2 +	Factor 2 −
N.H.		+ Foster −.61		+ Foster −.50
		− Livermore −.45		
Mass.		+ Ames −.76		+ Gerry −.53
		+ Gerry −.74		+ Grout −.47
		+ Grout −.61		+ Thatcher −.41
		+ Leonard −.69		
		+ Partridge −.61		
		+ Sedgwick −.85		
		+ Thatcher −.64		
Conn.		+ Huntington −.78		+ Sturges −.50
		+ Sherman −.59		
		+ Sturges −.67		
		+ Trumbull −.72		
		+ Wadsworth −.94		
N.Y.		+ Benson −.79		− Hathorn −.60
		+ Laurence −.64		+ Silvester −.48
		+ Silvester −.65		− Van Rensselaer −.60
N.J.		+ Boudinot −.83	+ Cadwallader .89	
		+ Schureman −.65	+ Sinnickson .72	
Pa.	+ Clymer .41		+ Clymer .99	
	− Hartley .45		+ Fitzsimmons .88	
	− Heister .53		− Hartley .85	
	− P. Muhlenberg .62		− Heister .87	
	− Scott .58		− P. Muhlenberg .80	

State	Member	Factor 1	Factor 2
	−Scott		.73
	+Wynkoop		.89
Dela.	+Vining		.87
Md.	+Carroll		.91
	−Contee	.69	.64
	+Gale		.90
	−Stone	.45	.46
Va.	−Brown	.74	.62
	−Coles	.70	.45
	−Griffin		.72
	+Lee		.95
	−Madison	.63	.69
	−Moore	.66	.58
	−Page	.58	.65
	−Parker	.58	.69
	+White	.48	.71
N.C.	−Ashe	.74	.54
	−Sevier	.69	
	−Steele	.70	.40
	−Williamson	.80	.49
S.C.	+Burke	−.52	
	o Huger	−.48	
	+Smith	−.65	
	−Sumter	.59	.40
Ga.	−Baldwin	.72	.47
	−Jackson	.66	
	−Matthews	.84	.47

Variance: Factor 1 (+ and −) = 41.5%   Variance: Factor 2 (+ and −) = 12.0%

aVote on Senate amendment, July 24, 1790. *Annals of Congress*, 2:1710. Before a name, + = a vote for assumption, − = a vote against, and o = not voting.

Table 15. Two-Factor Analysis of All Votes, First House, Third Session, Representatives with Loadings ≥ .40, and Their Vote on the Bank[a]

	Factor Structure After Oblique (Direct Oblimin, Δ = 0) Rotation with Kaiser Normalization (N = 22)			
	Factor 1+	Factor 1−	Factor 2+	Factor 2−
N.H	+ Foster .80			
	+ Gilman .63			
Mass.	+ Ames .91			
	+ Gerry .78		− Grout .43	
	+ Goodhue 1.02			
	+ Leonard .77			
	+ Partridge .72			
	+ Sedgwick .91			
	+ Thatcher .64			
R.I.	+ Bourne .51		+ Bourne .43	
Conn.	+ Huntington .85			
	+ Sherman .77			
	+ Sturges .97			
	+ Trumbull .88			
	+ Wadsworth .92			
N.Y.	+ Benson .93			
	+ Laurence .87			+ Van Rensselaer −.47
N.J.	+ Boudinot .40			
	+ Cadwallader .87			
	+ Schureman .71			
	+ Sinnickson .66			

State	Factor 1 (+)		Factor 1 (−)		Factor 2	
Pa.	+ Clymer	.90			+ Hartley	−.61
	+ Fitzsimmons	.87			+ Heister	−.57
	+ Wynkoop	.87			+ P. Muhlenberg	−.44
Dela.	+ Vining	.62				
Md.			− Contee	−.55	− Carroll	.75
			− Stone	−.50	− Contee	.72
					− Gale	.63
					+ Smith	.53
Va.			− Brown	−.84	o Griffin	.44
			− Giles	−.43	− Lee	.83
			− Moore	−.91	− Madison	1.00
			− Parker	−.84	− White	.67
N.C.			− Ashe	−.91		
			− Bloodworth	−.97		
			+ Steele	−.52		
			− Williamson	−.77		
S.C.	+ Smith	.51	− Burke	−.76	+ Smith	.47
			o Sumter	−.57	o Sumter	.65
			− Tucker	−.94		
Ga.			− Baldwin	−.77	− Baldwin	.399
			− Jackson	−.93		
			− Matthews	−.91		

Variance: Factor 1 (+ and −) = 44.5%   Variance: Factor 2 (+ and −) = 12.8%

aFinal vote, February 8, 1791. *Annals of Congress*, 2:1960. Before a name, + = a "yes" vote, − = a "no" vote, and o = not voting.

cluster still stretches from New England to South Carolina with or without
seat votes, but the negative cluster is almost purely southern, each way. In
further contrast to the First Session, the factor 1 clusters have eight more
members with the seat votes than without, and account for 41.6% of the
variance, as against 23.3% without seat votes. No state is represented in all
three clusters, with or without seat votes. Pennsylvania now votes almost
solidly with the middle-state cluster each way. Its transition effectively made
this coalition, running from New Jersey to Virginia, the largest and potentially the dominant group.

In view of the seeming differences in the ways in which the seat votes
may have influenced the clusters based on all votes in each of the two
sessions, a question may be raised regarding the continuity of clusters from
one session to another. Such scholars as Bell and Hoadley, who apply
quantitative methods to the votes of all three sessions as one group, may
detect changes from one Congress to another, but they may also obscure
the developments from one session to another.[8] A member's voting pattern
may evolve even within a single session, but no attempt is made here to
measure these intra-session changes.

Tables 13, 14, and 15 apply the oblique-factoring technique (which
permits correlations among factors, if any exist) to the sessions so that the
clusters displayed are comparable. Comparisons of tables 10 with 13 and of
12 with 14 clearly indicate that both orthogonal and oblique techniques of
factoring reveal the same clusters, although marginal differences in loading
may include or exclude individuals. The tables also give the actual votes cast
on the three issues treated as examples in chapter 6. In assessing these
actual votes, one needs to remember that cluster members may have been
absent and also that some representatives who voted were not cluster
members. Moreover, the same representative may participate for a quarter
or more of his variance in more than one cluster; but, more frequently, he
may not be found in any cluster.

It will be noticed that the northern cluster on factor 1 appears with
negative loadings in the Second Session, even though it is the same cluster
that loaded positively in the First and Third Sessions—with some changes
in membership. Massachusetts, almost evenly divided in the First Session,
is only marginally divided in the Second; by the Third, the only northern
maverick on the Bank bill, Grout, loads at $-.36$ on factor 1. New York,

8. Bell, *Party and Faction*; John F. Hoadley, *Origins of American Political Parties, 1789–
1803* (Lexington, Ky., 1986).

similarly divided in the First Session, is less so in the Second, and fully united on the Bank in the Third, even though three of its six representatives failed to cluster.[9] Pennsylvania, with six of its eight members in the northern cluster during the First Session (F. A. Muhlenberg had been elected Speaker and did not vote), shifted decisively in the Second Session, all seven of its representatives loading heavily with the middle-state cluster. Three of them also supported the southern cluster and, along with Hartley, voted against the assumption of state debts.

The southern states display very divergent voting patterns. Maryland and Virginia, both divided, adhere in part to the factor 1 southern cluster through all three sessions, but Maryland especially and Virginia also support the middle-state group including New Jersey and Delaware. This group gained great strength in the Second Session with the adhesion of Pennsylvania, and then lost it in the Third as the three northern states joined the cohesive northern coalition. Even less cohesion was displayed by South Carolina, which divided on each of the three specific votes. Loading fairly cohesively on a single factor in the First Session, it joined two clusters in the Second and three in the Third, being the only southern state to be represented in the factor 1 northern cluster. Georgia, on the contrary, after participating in two clusters in the First Session, achieved the most consistent loading of any state in the southern cluster in both the following sessions. North Carolina also found a different path: its Antifederalist representative, Bloodworth, did not join any cluster until the Third Session, yet voted with his colleagues solidly against assumption, and with two of them against the Bank—while their western colleagues, Sevier and Steele, supported it. One may conclude that, by the Third Session, the northern states had achieved a degree of unity, individually and collectively, that still eluded the South.

When the specific roll calls are compared with the factor groups, it is apparent that each conformed to the pattern prevalent in that session.

Of the complicated removal-power votes in the First Session, Benson's crucial first motion was carried by 30 to 18 (*Annals*, 1:603, June 22). Of these 48 votes, only 3 deviated from the clusters revealed by the two-factor-structure solution for all 35 votes taken during the session, as shown in table 13: the two positive clusters joined to defeat the two negative clusters. Only

9. The three Antifederalists from Long Island and west of the Hudson still voted differently from the three Federalists from New York City and eastern counties, but less consistently. See Alfred F. Young, *The Democratic Republicans of New York: The Origins, 1763–1797* (Chapel Hill, 1967), pp. 156–59.

Sherman of Connecticut and Cadwallader of New Jersey deserted their respective clusters to vote "no," and Burke of South Carolina left the factor 1 negative group to vote "yes." Thatcher of Massachusetts, who loaded on factor 2 negative, also loaded on factor 1 positive and voted "yes," and Contee of Maryland and Griffin of Virginia, who loaded on both factor 1 negative and factor 2 positive, voted "yes." Of the 30 supporters of Benson's motion, 24 were from the positive clusters; of the 18 opponents, 13 were from the negative clusters. Thus, 77.1% of the vote followed the clusters, 6.2% deviated, and the remaining 16.7% came from congressmen who loaded less than 16% of their variance on any cluster.

The final vote to establish a Department of Foreign Affairs, on which the negative votes reflected dissatisfaction with the removal provision, was carried 29 to 22 (*Annals*, 1:614; see table 13). Of these 51 votes cast, only 3 deviated from the two-factor-structure solution: the two positive clusters again joined to defeat the two negative ones. The same persons again deviated, except that Cadwallader returned to his cluster and Leonard and Thatcher of Massachusetts, from the factor 1 positive cluster, voted "no." With these changes, and the absentees, the result again showed 37 members voting with their clusters.

When the final assumption vote of July 24, 1790, is compared with the two-factor structure of the 51 roll calls of the Second Session (see table 14), it will be found that every member of the factor 1 positive cluster (22), save two, voted to reject, and that every member of the factor 1 negative cluster who voted (21), save one, voted to assume. The exceptions, Clymer, White, and Livermore, loaded less than a quarter of their variance on factor 1, and Clymer and White were more closely aligned with factor 2 positive. But factor 2, both positive and negative, was divided on this roll call, the northern members voting to assume (except for the New York Antifederalists and the Pennsylvanians outside Philadelphia) and the southern members voting to reject (except 2 each from Maryland and Virginia). Of the 61 votes cast, 40, or 65.6%, conform to the clusters on factor 1. This is substantially more than factor 1 alone accounted for on the removal power (20 of 51 votes, or 39.2%), when there were also deviations.

If the assumption roll call is compared with the two-factor structure of the 30 non-seat votes (which is not given in the tables), the results are different, yet much the same. Again, every member of the factor 1 positive cluster (22), save White, voted to reject, and every factor 1 negative member (11) voted to assume. Every member of factor 2 positive (19) voted to assume (with the exceptions of Hartley and Heister of Pennsylvania and Griffin of

Virginia), and the 2 members loading on factor 2 negative voted to reject. Thus, eliminating duplication, 23 of 29 negative votes and 26 of 32 positive votes conform exactly to these clusters: 80.3%.[10]

Coming to the Third Session, of the 39 votes for the Bank bill on February 8, 1791, 30 came from two clusters of the two-factor structure (*Annals*, 2:1960; see table 15). All members of the factor 1 positive and factor 2 negative groups voted for the Bank. Of the 20 opposing votes, all were cast by members of the other two clusters. All members of the factor 1 negative and the factor 2 positive clusters (who voted) opposed the Bank, with four exceptions: Smith of Maryland and Steele of North Carolina, who had low loadings, and Bourne of Rhode Island and Smith of South Carolina, who loaded more on and voted with factor 1 positive. Thus, 50 of the 59 votes cast, or 84.7%, came from the two-factor clusters. Of this total, 40, or 67.8%, were from the factor 1 groups, an increase over the figure for the assumption vote.

From all this it seems clear that, although levels of cohesion may have increased in later Congresses, voting in the First Congress, even in the First Session, was not without like-minded groups. With the political implications of Hamilton's economic program as the primary line of cleavage, individual members gradually found their positions in an increasingly polarized environment—both inside and outside Congress.[11] The summary in table 16 brings together some of the evidence for this.

While the two factors together "explain" approximately the same 55% of the variance in each session, the amount explained by the primary polarization, factor 1, clearly increases. So, too, does the number of members in the northern cluster (factor 1 positive). Paradoxically, so also does the

10. Lee and White, the two Virginians who supposedly voted reluctantly for assumption as part of the deal to bring the capital to the Potomac, were not strangers to the factor 2 positive cluster. Lee, in fact, loaded more of his variance on that cluster than anyone else, and White loaded marginally (from .39 to .52) on that factor more consistently, with varying numbers of factors used, than on any other. Was the "dinner at Jefferson's" really necessary?

11. Mary P. Ryan's view is thus supported, her "fundamental discovery" of "the emergence in the first session of the United States Congress of two voting blocs" that "reached maturity by the Third [Congress], well before the Jay Treaty controversy," and "remained remarkably stable" through the four Congresses she had studied. Ryan, "Party Formation in the United States Congress, 1789 to 1796: A Quantitative Analysis," *William and Mary Quarterly* 28 (October 1971): 523–42, at pp. 531, 541. Hoadley agrees with Bell that these groups should be termed factions rather than parties, because the alignments differed on different issues. Yet he recognizes that the factions aroused by Hamilton's program were "substantially different" from the others and that "this opposition group became the core of the Republican party." Hoadley, *Origins of American Political Parties*, pp. 106, 107.

Table 16. Summary of Two-Factor Structures, First House of Representatives

	Session 1	Session 2	Session 3
Variance Explained			
Factor 1	36.2%	41.5%	44.5%
Factor 2	19.3%	12.0%	12.8%
Total	55.5%	53.5%	57.3%
Members Factored and in Clusters			
Factor 1 positive	19	22	26
Factor 1 negative	12	22	16
Factor 2 positive	12	29	13
Factor 2 negative	8	8	4
Total, without duplications	47	55	54
Members Factored but not in Clusters	6	7	7
Percentage not in clusters	11%	11%	11%
Northerners not in clusters	3	3	5
Southerners not in clusters	3	4	2
Correlation between Factors	−.102	.367	−.028

number of northern members not adhering to any group, or displaying marginal loadings. The southerners, on the other hand, did not display similar advances in cohesion. By the third session, only one northern state was divided by delegates loading above 25% of their variance on different factors, while three of the southern states continued more than marginally divided, South Carolina having delegates in three clusters.

Works Cited

Books

Ackerman, Bruce. *We the People*. Vol. 1, *Foundations*. Cambridge, Mass., 1991.
Adams, John. *Defence of the Constitutions of Government of the United States of America* (1787–88). In his *Works*, edited by Charles F. Adams, vols. 4 and 6.
———. *Works of John Adams*. Edited by Charles F. Adams. Boston, 1850–56.
Adams, John Quincy. *Journal, Acts and Proceedings of the Convention, . . . Which Formed the Constitution of the United States*. Boston, 1819.
Adams, Randolph G., ed. *Selected Political Essays of James Wilson*. New York, 1930.
Ahlstrom, Sydney E. *A Religious History of the American People*. New Haven, 1972.
Allen, J. W. *English Political Thought, 1603–1660*. London, 1938.
Annals of Congress, 1st Congress and 18th Congress, 1 Session.
Anonymous. *Fleta* (late 13th century). Edited and translated by H. G. Richardson and G. O. Sayles. London, 1955.
Arendt, Hannah. *On Revolution*. New York, 1965.
Arkes, Hadley. *Beyond the Constitution*. Princeton, 1990.
———. *First Things*. Princeton, 1986.
Ashcraft, Richard. *Revolutionary Politics and Locke's "Two Treatises of Government."* Princeton, 1986.
Atkyns, Sir Robert. *The Power, Jurisdiction and Priviledge of Parliament: And the Antiquity of the House of Commons Asserted*. London, 1689.
Bailyn, Bernard. *The Ideological Origins of the American Revolution*. Cambridge, Mass., 1967.
———. *The Origins of American Politics*. New York, 1968.
Ball, Terence, and J.G.A. Pocock, eds. *Conceptual Change and the Constitution*. Lawrence, Kans., 1988.
Bancroft, George. *History of the Formation of the Constitution*. New York, 1882.
Baxter, Stephen B. *The Development of the Treasury, 1660–1702*. London, 1957.
Beard, Charles A. *An Economic Interpretation of the Constitution of the United States*. New York, 1913.

————. *The Supreme Court and the Constitution*. New York, 1912.

Beauté, Jean. *Un grand juriste anglais, Sir Edward Coke, 1552–1634: Ses idées politiques et constitutionnelles*. Paris, 1975.

Beeman, Richard, Stephen Botein, and Edward C. Carter, III, eds. *Beyond Confederation: Origins of the Constitution and American National Identity*. Chapel Hill, 1987.

Bell, Rudolph M. *Party and Faction in American Politics: The House of Representatives, 1789–1801*. Westport, Conn., 1973.

Belz, Herman, Ronald Hoffman, and Peter J. Albert, eds. *To Form a More Perfect Union: The Critical Ideas of the Constitution*. Charlottesville, 1992.

Bennett, G. V. *The Tory Crisis in Church and State, 1688–1730: The Career of Francis Atterbury, Bishop of Rochester*. Oxford, 1975.

Benson, Lee. *Turner and Beard, American Historical Writing Reconsidered*. Glencoe, Ill., 1960.

Bickford, Charlene B., and Helen E. Veit, eds. *Legislative Histories*. Baltimore, 1986.

Bickford, Charlene B., Kenneth R. Bowling, and Helen E. Veit, eds. *Documentary History of the First Federal Congress*. Baltimore, 1972–.

Black, Jeremy. *Robert Walpole and the Nature of Politics in Early Eighteenth-Century Britain*. New York, 1990.

Black, Jeremy, ed. *Britain in the Age of Walpole*. London, 1984.

Blackstone, William. *Commentaries on the Laws of England*. London, 1811.

Bodin, Jean. *De la République* (1576) and *De Republica* (1586). Translated by Richard Knolles. London, 1606; Cambridge, Mass., 1962.

Boyd, Julian P., ed. *The Papers of Thomas Jefferson*. Princeton, 1950–.

Bracton, Hugh de. *De Legibus et Consuetudinibus Angliae*. Edited by George E. Woodbine. New Haven, 1922.

Brady, Robert. *Complete History of England*, vol. 1. London, 1685.

Brennan, Ellen E. *Plural Office-Holding in Massachusetts, 1760–1780*. Chapel Hill, 1945.

Brewer, John. *The Sinews of Power: War, Money, and the English State, 1688–1783*. Cambridge, Mass., 1990.

Brown, Robert E. *Charles Beard and the Constitution*. Princeton, 1956.

Browning, Reed. *Political and Constitutional Ideas of the Court Whigs*. Baton Rouge, 1982.

Burnett, Edmund C., ed. *Letters of Members of the Continental Congress*. Washington, 1921–36.

Butzner, Jane, ed. *Constitutional Chaff: Rejected Suggestions of the Constitutional Convention of 1787*. New York, 1941.

Calamy, Edmund. *An Abridgement of Mr. Baxter's History of His Life and Times*. 2d ed., vol. 2. London, 1713.

Calhoun, Craig, ed. *Habermas and the Public Sphere*. Cambridge, Mass., 1992.

Calhoun, John C. *The Works of John C. Calhoun*. Edited by Richard K. Crallé. Vol. 6. New York, 1879.

Cannon, John, ed. *The Whig Ascendancy*. New York, 1981.

Carlyle, R. W. and A. J. *A History of Medieval Political Theory in the West*. Edinburgh, 1915, 1950.

Charles I. *His Majesty's Answer to the Nineteen Propositions of Both Houses of Parliament* (1642). Reprinted in Kenyon, *The Stuart Constitution*.

Chastellux, François Jean, Marquis de. *De la Félicité Publique*. Amsterdam, 1772; English translation, two vols., London, 1774.

Chrimes, S. B. *English Constitutional Ideas in the Fifteenth Century*. Cambridge, 1936.

Christie, Ian R. *Stress and Stability in Late Eighteenth-Century Britain*. Oxford, 1984.

Clark, J.C.D. *English Society, 1688–1832: Ideology, Social Structure, and Political Practice during the Ancien Regime*. Cambridge, 1985.

Clinton, Robert L. *"Marbury v. Madison" and Judicial Review*. Lawrence, Kans., 1989.

Cobbett, William, ed. *Parliamentary History of England*. London, 1806–.

Coke, Edward. *Institutes of the Laws of England; or, A Commentary Upon Littleton*. London, 1644.

————. *Reports*. Vol. 8 Dr. Bonham's Case (1609); vol. 12 *Case of Prohibitions* (1607). London, 1658.

Coker, Francis W. *Readings in Political Philosophy*. New York, 1938.

Colbourn, Trevor. *The Lamp of Experience: Whig History and the Intellectual Origins of the American Revolution*. Chapel Hill, 1965.

Continental Congress, Journals of the. Edited by W. C. Ford. Washington, 1904–37.

Continental Congress, Papers of the. No. 41, X, folios 79–86.

Cooke, Jacob E., ed. *The Federalist*. Middletown, Conn., 1961.

Crallé, Richard K., ed. *The Works of John C. Calhoun*, vol. 6. New York, 1879.

Crosskey, William W., and William Jeffrey, Jr. *Politics and the Constitution*, vol. 3. Chicago, 1980.

Davis, David Brion. *Revolutions: Reflections on American Equality and Foreign Liberations*. Cambridge, Mass., 1990.

Davis, Joseph L. *Sectionalism in American Politics, 1774–1787*. Madison, 1977.

DePauw, Linda G. *The Eleventh Pillar*. Ithaca, 1966.

DePauw, Linda Grant, ed. *Documentary History of the First Federal Congress*. Baltimore, 1972.

Dickinson, H. T. *Liberty and Property*. New York, 1977.

Dickson, P.G.M. *The Financial Revolution in England: A Study in the Development of Public Credit, 1688–1756*. London, 1967.

Documentary History of the Constitution of the United States of America. Washington: Department of State, 1894.

Documentary History of the First Federal Congress. Edited by Charlene B. Bickford, Kenneth R. Bowling, and Helen E. Veit. Baltimore, 1972–.

The Documentary History of the Ratification of the Constitution. Edited by Merrill Jensen, John P. Kaminski, Gaspare J. Saladino, Richard Leffler, and Charles H. Schoenleber. Madison, 1976–.

Dumbauld, Edward. *The Bill of Rights and What It Means Today*. Norman, Okla., 1957.

Dunbar, Louise B. *A Study of "Monarchical" Tendencies in the United States from 1776 to 1801*. Urbana, 1922.

Eidelberg, Paul. *The Philosophy of the American Constitution*. New York, 1968.

Elliot, Jonathan, ed. *The Debates in the Several State Conventions on the Adoption of the Federal Constitution*. 2d ed. Philadelphia, 1888.

Farrand, Max, ed. *The Records of the Federal Convention of 1787*. New Haven, 1911, 1937.

The Federalist. Edited by Jacob E. Cooke. Middletown, Conn., 1961.

Ferguson, E. James. *The Power of the Purse*. Chapel Hill, 1961.

Ferguson, Robert. *A Brief Justification of the Prince of Orange's Descent into England* (40-page anonymous edition). London, 1689.

Fink, Zera S. *The Classical Republicans: An Essay in the Recovery of a Pattern of Thought in Seventeenth-Century England*. Evanston, 1945.

Fitzpatrick, John C., ed. *The Writings of George Washington*. Washington, 1937.

Force, Peter, ed. *American Archives*. Fourth series, vol. 1. Washington, 1837.

Ford, Paul L., ed. *The Works of Thomas Jefferson*. New York, 1905.

Ford, Worthington C., then Gaillard Hunt, eds., *Journals of the Continental Congress, 1774–1789*. Washington, 1904–37.

Fortesque, John. *De Laudibus Legum Angliae* (1468–1471). Edited by S. B. Chrimes. Cambridge, 1942.

Franklin, Julian. *Jean Bodin and the Rise of Absolutist Theory*. Cambridge, 1973.

Gillespie, Michael A., and Michael Lienesch, eds. *Ratifying the Constitution*. Lawrence, Kans., 1989.

Glanvil, Ranulf de. *Tractatus de Legibus et Consuetudinibus Regni Angliae*. Edited by John Rayner. London, 1780. Translated by John Beames. Washington, 1900.

Grey, Anchitel. *Debates of the House of Commons, 1667–1694*. London, 1763.

Haines, Charles G. *The American Doctrine of Judicial Supremacy*. 2d ed. New York, 1959.

Hall, David D., John M. Murrin, and Thad W. Tate, eds. *Saints and Revolutionaries*. New York, 1984.

Haller, William, ed. *Tracts on Liberty*. New York, 1933.

Hamilton, Alexander. *The Papers of Alexander Hamilton*. Edited by Harold C. Syrett. New York, 1961–87.

Hamilton, John C., ed. *The Works of Alexander Hamilton*. New York, 1851.

Hanson, Russell L. *The Democratic Imagination in America*. Princeton, 1985.

Hart, James. *The American Presidency in Action, 1789*. New York, 1948.

Henderson, H. James. *Party Politics in the Continental Congress*. New York, 1974.

Herle, Charles. *A Fuller Answer to a Treatise Written by Doctor Ferne*. London, 1642.

Hildreth, Richard. *The History of the United States of America*. New York, 1851.

———. *The Theory of Politics*. New York, 1853.

Hoadley, John F. *Origins of American Political Parties, 1789–1803*. Lexington, Ky., 1986.

Hofstadter, Richard. *The Paranoid Style in American Politics*. New York, 1965.

Holdsworth, William. *A History of English Law*. London, 1938.

Howe, John R., Jr. *The Changing Political Thought of John Adams*. Princeton, 1966.

Hunton, Philip. *A Treatise of Monarchie*. London, 1643.

Hutson, James H., ed. *Supplement to Max Farrand's Records*. New Haven, 1987.

Jefferson, Thomas. *The Papers of Thomas Jefferson*. Edited by Julian P. Boyd. Princeton, 1950–.

Jensen, Merrill. *The Articles of Confederation: An Interpretation of the Social-Constitutional History of the American Revolution, 1774–1781*. Madison, 1940.

———. *The Making of the American Constitution*. New York, 1964.

———. *The New Nation*. New York, 1950.

Jensen, Merrill, and Robert A. Becker, eds. *Documentary History of the First Federal Elections, 1788–1790*. Madison, 1976–.

Jensen, Merrill, John P. Kaminski, Gaspare J. Saladino, Richard Leffler, and Charles H. Schoenleber, eds. *The Documentary History of the Ratification of the Constitution*. Madison, 1976–.

Jillson, Calvin C. *Constitution Making: Conflict and Consensus in the Federal Convention of 1787*. New York, 1988.

Jones, Clyve, ed. *Party and Management in Parliament, 1660–1784*. Leicester, 1984.
Jones, J. R. *The Revolution of 1688 in England*. New York, 1972.
Judson, Margaret A. *The Crisis of the Constitution: An Essay in Constitutional and Political Thought in England, 1603–1645*. New Brunswick, N.J., 1949.
Justinian. *Digest, or Pandects* (533; *Digesta Seu Pandectae*). Edited by Theodore Mommsen. Vol. 1. Berlin, 1962.
———. *Institutes* (533; *Institutiones*). Translated by J. R. Moyle. Oxford, 1896.
Kenyon, J. P. *Revolution Principles: The Politics of Party, 1698–1720*. Cambridge, 1977.
Kenyon, J. P., ed. *The Stuart Constitution, 1603–1688*. 2d ed. Cambridge, 1986.
King, C. R., ed. *Life and Correspondence of Rufus King*. New York, 1900.
Kramnick, Isaac. *Bolingbroke and His Circle: The Politics of Nostalgia in the Age of Walpole*. Cambridge, Mass., 1968.
———. *Republicanism and Bourgeois Radicalism: Political Ideology in Late Eighteenth-Century England and America*. Ithaca, 1990.
Langford, Paul. *The Excise Crisis: Society and Politics in the Age of Walpole*. Oxford, 1975.
Leder, Lawrence H. *Liberty and Authority: Early American Political Ideology, 1689–1763*. Chicago, 1968.
Levy, Leonard W., and Dennis J. Mahoney, eds. *The Framing and Ratification of the Constitution*. New York, 1987.
Lewis, Ewart. *Medieval Political Ideas*. London, 1954.
Lienesch, Michael. *New Order of the Ages: Time, the Constitution, and the Making of Modern American Political Thought*. Princeton, 1988.
Lovejoy, David S. *The Glorious Revolution in America*. New York, 1972.
Lutz, Donald S. *The Origins of American Constitutionalism*. Baton Rouge, 1988.
———. *Popular Consent and Popular Control: Whig Political Theory in the Early State Constitutions*. Baton Rouge, 1980.
Lynd, Staughton. *Class Conflict, Slavery, and the United States Constitution*. Indianapolis, 1967.
Maclay, William. *The Journal of William Maclay*. New York, 1927.
Main, Jackson T. *The Antifederalists: Critics of the Constitution, 1781–1788*. Chapel Hill, 1961.
Marston, Jerrilyn Green. *King and Congress: The Transfer of Political Legitimacy, 1774–1776*. Princeton, 1987.
Martin, Luther. *The Genuine Information, Delivered to the Legislature of the State of Maryland*. Baltimore, 1788.
Matson, Cathy D., and Peter S. Onuf. *A Union of Interests*. Lawrence, Kans., 1990.
McCloskey, Robert G., ed. *The Works of James Wilson*. Cambridge, Mass., 1967.
McCormick, Richard P. *The Presidential Game: The Origins of American Presidential Politics*. New York, 1982.
McDonald, Forrest. *Novus Ordo Seclorum*. Lawrence, Kans., 1985.
———. *We the People*. Chicago, 1958.
McIlwain, Charles H. *Constitutionalism: Ancient and Modern*. Rev. ed. Ithaca, 1947.
McKendrick, Neil, ed. *Historical Perspectives*. London, 1974.
McMaster, John Bach, and Frederick D. Stone, eds. *Pennsylvania and the Federal Constitution, 1787–1788*. Philadelphia, 1888.
Melone, Albert P., and George Mace. *Judicial Review and American Democracy*. Ames, Iowa, 1988.
Mendle, Michael. *Dangerous Positions: Mixed Government, the Estates of the Realm,*

and the Making of the "Answer to the xix Propositions." University, Ala., 1985.

Michaelsen, William B. *Creating the American Presidency, 1775–1789* Lanham, Md., 1987.

Morgan, Edmund S. *Inventing the People: The Rise of Popular Sovereignty in England and America.* New York, 1988.

Muratori, Ludivico. *Della pubblica felicità.* Lucca, 1749; French translation, two vols., Lyons, 1772.

Narrett, David E., and Joyce S. Goldberg, eds. *Essays in Liberty and Federalism: The Shaping of the United States Constitution.* College Station, Tex., 1988.

Nedelsky, Jennifer. *Private Property and the Limits of American Constitutionalism: The Madisonian Framework and Its Legacy.* Chicago, 1991.

Neville, Henry. *Plato Redivivus* (1681). Reprinted in Robbins, *Two English Republican Tracts.*

Onuf, Peter S. *Maryland and the Empire, 1773.* Baltimore, 1974.

———. *The Origins of the Federal Republic: Jurisdictional Controversies in the United States, 1775–1787.* Philadelphia, 1983.

Otis, James. *Rights of the British Colonies Asserted and Proved.* Boston, 1764.

Pangle, Thomas L. *The Spirit of Modern Republicanism: The Moral Vision of the American Founders and the Philosophy of Locke.* Chicago, 1988.

Parker, Henry. *Observations upon Some of His Majesties Late Answers and Expresses* (1642). Reprinted in Haller, *Tracts on Liberty.*

Plumb, J. H. *The Growth of Political Stability in England, 1675–1725.* London, 1967.

Pocock, J.G.A. *The Ancient Constitution and the Feudal Law.* 2d ed. New York, 1987.

———. *The Machiavellian Moment: Florentine Political Thought and the Atlantic Republican Tradition.* Princeton, 1975.

———. *Virtue, Commerce, and History.* Cambridge, 1985.

Pocock, J.G.A., ed. *The Political Works of James Harrington.* Cambridge, 1977.

———. *Three British Revolutions: 1641, 1688, 1776.* Princeton, 1980.

Pole, J. R. *The Gift of Government.* Athens, Ga., 1983.

Polybius. *The Histories.* Translated by W. R. Paton. Cambridge, Mass., 1927. Book 6.

Rakove, Jack N., ed. *Interpreting the Constitution: The Debate over Original Intent.* Boston, 1990.

Robbins, Caroline. *The Eighteenth-Century Commonwealthman: Studies in the Transmission, Development, and Circumstances of English Liberal Thought from the Restoration of Charles II until the War with the Thirteen Colonies.* Cambridge, Mass., 1959.

Robbins, Caroline, ed. *Two English Republican Tracts.* Cambridge, 1969.

Rodgers, Daniel T. *Contested Truths: Keywords in American Politics since Independence.* New York, 1987.

Rohr, John A. *The President and the Public Administration.* Washington, 1989.

Rosenberg, Norman L. *Protecting the Best Men: An Interpretive History of the Law of Libel.* Chapel Hill, 1986.

Roseveare, Henry. *The Treasury, 1600–1870: The Foundations of Control.* London, 1973.

Rummel, R. J. *Applied Factor Analysis.* Evanston, 1970.

Rushworth, John. *Historical Collections.* London, 1659, 1682.

Sandoz, Ellis. *A Government of Laws: Political Theory, Religion, and the American Founding*. Baton Rouge, 1990.

Schechter, Stephen L., ed. *The Reluctant Pillar*. Troy, N.Y., 1985.

Schmidhauser, John R. *The Supreme Court as Final Arbiter in Federal-State Relations, 1789–1957*. Chapel Hill, 1958.

Schwoerer, Lois G. *The Declaration of Rights, 1689*. Baltimore, 1981.

———. *"No Standing Armies!" The Anti-Army Ideology in Seventeenth-Century England*. Baltimore, 1974.

Scott, Walter, ed. *A Collection of Scarce and Valuable Tracts . . . of the Late Lord Somers*. 2d ed., vol. 10. London, 1813.

Slaughter, Thomas P. *The Whiskey Rebellion: Frontier Epilogue to the American Revolution*. New York, 1986.

Smith, J. Allen. *The Spirit of American Government*. New York, 1907.

Smith, James Morton. *Freedom's Fetters: The Alien and Sedition Laws and American Civil Liberties*. Ithaca, 1956.

Smith, Thomas. *De Republica Anglorum* (1562). Edited by Mary Dewar. Amsterdam, 1970.

Snowiss, Sylvia. *Judicial Review and the Law of the Constitution*. New Haven, 1990.

Sparks, Jared. *The Life of Gouverneur Morris*. Vol. 1. Boston, 1832.

Speck, W. A. *Stability and Strife: England, 1714–1760*. Cambridge, Mass., 1977.

Spelman, John. *The Case of our Affairs, in Law, Religion, and other Circumstances briefly examined, and Presented to the Conscience*. Oxford, 1644.

———. *A View of a Printed Book, Intituled Observations . . .* Oxford, 1643.

Stimson, Shannon C. *The American Revolution in the Law*. Princeton, 1990.

Storing, Herbert J., ed. *The Complete Anti-Federalist*. Chicago, 1981.

Stoudinger, Susan M. "An Analysis of Voting Behavior in the Constitutional Convention of 1787." M.A. thesis, University of Maryland, 1968.

Taft, Barbara, ed. *Absolute Liberty: A Selection from the Articles and Papers of Caroline Robbins*. Hamden, Conn., 1982.

Taylor, John. *Construction Construed, and Constitutions Vindicated*. Richmond, 1820.

Trenchard, John, and Thomas Gordon. *Cato's Letters: or, Essays on Liberty, Civil and Religious, and Other Important Subjects*. 6th ed. London, 1755. Reprint. New York, 1971.

Tushnet, Mark. *Red, White, and Blue: A Critical Analysis of Constitutional Law*. Cambridge, Mass., 1988.

Ulpian. *Book of Rules* (3d century; Domitius Ulpianus, *Liber Singularis Regularum*). Edited and translated by James Muirhead. Edinburgh, 1895.

Van Buren, Martin. *Inquiry into the Origin and Course of Political Parties in the United States*. New York, 1867.

Veit, Helen E., Kenneth R. Bowling, and Charlene B. Bickford, eds. *Creating the Bill of Rights: The Documentary Record from the First Congress*. Baltimore, 1991.

Vile, John R. *The Constitutional Amending Process in American Political Thought*. New York, 1992.

Vile, M.J.C. *Constitutionalism and the Separation of Powers*. Oxford, 1967.

Warren, Charles. *The Making of the Constitution*. Cambridge, Mass., 1928.

Weston, Corinne C., and Janelle R. Greenberg. *Subjects and Sovereigns: The Grand Controversy over Legal Sovereignty in Stuart England*. Cambridge, 1981.

White, Stephen D. *Sir Edward Coke and "The Grievances of the Commonwealth," 1621–1628*. Chapel Hill, 1979.

Wilson, James. *Selected Political Essays of James Wilson.* Edited by Randolph G. Adams. New York, 1930.
————. *The Works of James Wilson.* Edited by Robert G. McCloskey. Cambridge, Mass., 1967.
Wood, Gordon S. *The Creation of the American Republic, 1776–1787.* Chapel Hill, 1969.
Yates, Robert. Notes of the Convention. Edited by E.C.É. Genêt as *A Letter to the Electors of President and Vice-President of the United States.* New York, 1808.
Yolton, John W., ed. *John Locke: Problems and Perspectives.* Cambridge, 1969.
York, Niel L., ed. *Toward a More Perfect Union: Six Essays on the Constitution.* Provo, Utah, 1988.
Young, Alfred. *The Democratic Republicans of New York: The Origins, 1763–1797.* Chapel Hill, 1967.

Articles and Other Sources

Adams, John. "Thoughts on Government" (1776). In his *Works,* edited by Charles F. Adams, vol. 4.
Aldrich, John H., and Ruth W. Grant. "The Antifederalists, the First Congress, and the First Parties." *Journal of Politics,* 55 (May 1993): 295–326.
Bayard v. Singleton (North Carolina Superior Court, May 1787).
Benhabib, Seyla. "Models of Public Space: Hannah Arendt, the Liberal Tradition, and Jürgen Habermas." In Craig Calhoun, ed., *Habermas and the Public Sphere.* Cambridge, Mass., 1992.
Bogin, Ruth. " 'Measures So Glareingly Unjust': A Response to Hamilton's Funding Plan by William Manning." *William and Mary Quarterly* 46 (April 1989): 315–31.
Bowling, Kenneth R. "Dinner at Jefferson's: A Note on Jacob E. Cooke's 'The Compromise of 1790,' " with reply by Cooke. *William and Mary Quarterly* 28 (October 1971): 629–40.
Bruchey, Stuart, and E. James Ferguson. "Forces behind the Constitution." *William and Mary Quarterly* 19 (July 1962): 429–38.
Calder v. Bull, 3 Dallas 386 (1798).
Cooke, Jacob E. "The Compromise of 1790." *William and Mary Quarterly* 27 (October 1970): 523–45.
Corwin, Edwin S. Review of Charles A. Beard's *Supreme Court and the Constitution. American Political Science Review* (May 1913).
Cruickshanks, Evaline. "The Political Management of Sir Robert Walpole, 1720–42." In Black, *Britain in the Age of Walpole.*
Curtenius, Peter. Letter to George Clinton, March 2, 1788. George Clinton Papers, New York Public Library.
DePauw, Linda G. "The Anti-Climax of Antifederalism: The Abortive Second Convention Movement, 1788–1789." *Prologue* 2 (Fall 1970): 98–114.
Diamond, Ann Stuart. "The Anti-Federalist 'Brutus,' " *Political Science Reviewer* 6 (Fall 1976): 249–81.
Diamond, Martin. "The American Idea of Equality: The View from the Founding." *Review of Politics* 38 (July 1976): 313–31.

————. "Democracy and *The Federalist*: A Reconsideration of the Framers' Intent." *American Political Science Review* 53 (March 1959): 52–68.

Diggins, John P. "Power and Authority in American History: The Case of Charles A. Beard and His Critics." *American Historical Review* 86 (October 1981): 701–30.

Dunn, John. "The Politics of Locke in England and America in the Eighteenth Century." In Yolton, *John Locke*, 45–80.

Ferguson, E. James, and Elizabeth M. Nuxoll. "Investigation of Governmental Corruption during the American Revolution." *Congressional Studies* 8, no. 2 (1981): 13–35.

Finkelman, Paul. "James Madison and the Bill of Rights: A Reluctant Paternity." *Supreme Court Review, 1990* (Chicago, 1991): 301–47.

Fletcher v. Peck, 6 Cranch 87 (1810) at 138–39.

Frankle, Robert J. "The Formulation of the Declaration of Rights." *Historical Journal* 17 (June 1974): 265–79.

Goldie, Mark. "The Roots of True Whiggism, 1688–94." *History of Political Thought* 1 (June 1980): 195–236.

Goldstein, Leslie F. "Popular Sovereignty, the Origins of Judicial Review, and the Revival of Unwritten Law." *Journal of Politics* 48 (February 1986): 51–71.

"A Hartford Convention in 1780, Proceedings" [November 8–14]. *Magazine of American History* 8 (October 1882): 688–98.

Hayton, David. "The 'Country' Interest and the Party System, 1689–c.1720." In Clyve Jones, *Party and Management in Parliament, 1660–1784*, 37–85.

Hobson, Charles F. "The Negative on State Laws: James Madison, the Constitution, and the Crisis of Republican Government." *William and Mary Quarterly* 36 (April 1979): 215–35.

Holmes, Geoffrey S. "The Attack on 'the Influence of the Crown,' 1702–1716." *Bulletin of the Institute of Historical Research* 39 (May 1966): 47–68.

Holmes, Geoffrey. "The Achievement of Stability: The Social Context of Politics from the 1680s to the Age of Walpole." In Cannon, *The Whig Ascendancy*.

Honig, Bonnie. "Declarations of Independence: Arendt and Derrida on the Problem of Founding a Republic." *American Political Science Review* 85 (March 1991): 97–113.

Horwitz, Henry. "Parliament and the Glorious Revolution." *Bulletin of the Institute of Historical Research* (University of London) 47 (May 1974): 36–52.

Hume, David. "Of the Independency of Parliament." In his *Essays, Literary, Moral and Political*. London, 1870.

Humfrey, John. "Advice Before It Be Too Late" (1688). In Scott, *Collection of Scarce and Valuable*, 198–202.

Hutson, James H. "The Creation of the Constitution: The Integrity of the Documentary Record." *Texas Law Review* 65 (November 1986): 1–38.

————. "The Paranoid Style in American Politics." In David D. Hall, John M. Murrin, and Thad W. Tate, eds., *Saints and Revolutionaries*.

Innes, Joanna. "Jonathan Clark, Social History, and England's 'Ancien Regime.' " *Past and Present*, no. 115 (May 1987): 165–200.

Jensen, Merrill. "The Idea of a National Government during the American Revolution." *Political Science Quarterly* 58 (1943): 356–79.

Jillson, Calvin C. "The Executive in Republican Government: The Case of the American Founding." *Presidential Studies Quarterly* 9 (Fall 1979): 386–402.

————. "Political Culture and the Pattern of Congressional Politics under the Articles of Confederation." *Publius* 18 (Winter 1988): 1–26.

Kenyon, J. P. "The Revolution of 1688: Resistance and Contract." In McKendrick, *Historical Perspectives*, 43–69.

Kohn, Richard H. "The Inside History of the Newburgh Conspiracy: America and the Coup d'Etat." *William and Mary Quarterly* 27 (April 1970): 187–220.

———. "The Washington Administration's Decision to Crush the Whiskey Rebellion." *Journal of American History* 59 (December 1972): 567–84.

Langdon, John. Letter to George Washington, February 28, 1788. Washington Papers, Library of Congress.

Laslett, Peter. "The English Revolution and Locke's 'Two Treatises of Government.' " *Cambridge Historical Journal* 12 (no. 1, 1956): 40–55.

Lewis, John Underwood. "Sir Edward Coke (1552–1633): His Theory of 'Artificial Reason' as a Context for Modern Basic Legal Theory." *Law Quarterly Review* 84 (July 1968): 330–42.

Lienesch, Michael. "The Constitutional Tradition: History, Political Action, and Progress in American Political Thought, 1787–1793." *Journal of Politics* 42 (February 1980): 2–30.

London Journal (a Walpole paper, 1730, 1733, 1734).

Lutz, Donald S. "Bernard Bailyn, Gordon S. Wood, and Whig Political Theory." *Political Science Reviewer* 7 (Fall 1977): 111–44.

———. "Connecticut: Achieving Consent and Assuring Control." In Gillespie and Lienesch, *Ratifying the Constitution*.

———. "The Relative Influence of European Writers on Late Eighteenth-Century American Political Thought." *American Political Science Review* 78 (March 1984): 189–97.

Main, Jackson T. "Charles A. Beard and the Constitution." *William and Mary Quarterly* 17 (January 1960): 86–110.

———. "Government by the People: The American Revolution and the Democratization of the Legislatures." *William and Mary Quarterly* 23 (July 1966): 391–407.

Maryland Gazette (Annapolis), February 10 to June 4, 1748.

Matthews, Richard K. "Liberalism, Civic Humanism, and the American Revolution: Understanding Genesis." *Journal of Politics* 49 (November 1987): 1127–53.

Mayton, William T. "Seditious Libel and the Lost Guarantee of a Freedom of Expression." *Columbia Law Review* 84 (January 1984): 91–142.

McCorkle, Pope. "The Historian as Intellectual: Charles Beard and the Constitution Reconsidered." *American Journal of Legal History* 28 (October 1984): 314–63.

McCulloch v. Maryland 4 Wheat. 316 (1819).

McGuire, Robert A. "Constitution Making: A Rational-Choice Model of the Federal Convention of 1787." *American Journal of Political Science* 32 (May 1988): 483–522.

McGuire, Robert A., and Robert L. Ohsfeldt. "Economic Interests and the American Constitution: A Quantitative Rehabilitation of Charles A. Beard." *Journal of Economic History* 44 (June 1984): 509–19.

McIlwain, Charles H. "A Forgotten Worthy, Philip Hunton, and the Sovereignty of King in Parliament." In his *Constitutionalism and the Changing World*. Cambridge, 1939.

Nelson, Jeffrey M. "Ideology in Search of a Context: Eighteenth-Century British Political Thought and the Loyalists of the American Revolution." *Historical Journal* 20 (September 1977): 741–49.

Nelson, Paul D. "Horatio Gates at Newburgh, 1783: A Misunderstood Role." *William and Mary Quarterly* 29 (January 1972): 143–58.

Nelson, William E. "The Eighteenth-Century Background of John Marshall's Constitutional Jurisprudence." *Michigan Law Review* 76 (May 1978): 893–960.

———. "Reason and Compromise in the Establishment of the Federal Constitution, 1787–1801." *William and Mary Quarterly* 44 (July 1987): 458–84.

Onuf, Peter S. "Reflections on the Founding: Constitutional Historiography in Bicentennial Perspective." *William and Mary Quarterly* 46 (April 1989): 341–75.

———. "Toward Federalism: Virginia, Congress, and the Western Lands." *William and Mary Quarterly* 34 (July 1977): 353–74.

Radding, Charles M. "The Origins of Bracton's *Addicio de Cartis*." *Speculum* (April 1969): 239–46.

Rakove, Jack N. "The Great Compromise: Ideas, Interests, and the Politics of Constitution Making." *William and Mary Quarterly* 44 (July 1987): 424–57.

Riker, William H. "The Senate and American Federalism." *American Political Science Review* 49 (June 1955): 452–69.

Roane, Spencer. Articles from the *Richmond Enquirer*. Reprinted in *John P. Branch Historical Papers of Randolph-Macon College* 2 (June 1905): 51–121.

Robbins, Caroline. "The Pursuit of Happiness" (1974). In Taft, *Absolute Liberty*.

Roberts, Clayton. "The Constitutional Significance of the Financial Settlement of 1690." *Historical Journal* 20 (March 1977): 59–76.

Rummel, R. J. "Understanding Factor Analysis." *Journal of Conflict Resolution* 11 (December 1967): 444–78.

Ryan, Mary P. "Party Formation in the United States Congress, 1789 to 1796: A Quantitative Analysis." *William and Mary Quarterly* 28 (October 1971): 523–42.

Schmitt, Gary J., and Robert H. Webking. "Revolutionaries, Antifederalists, and Federalists: Comments on Gordon Wood's Understanding of the American Founding." *Political Science Reviewer* 9 (Fall 1979): 195–229.

Schultz, Fritz. "Bracton on Kingship." *English Historical Review* 60 (May 1945): 136–76.

Seed, John. "Gentlemen Dissenters: The Social and Political Meanings of Rational Dissent in the 1770s and 1780s." *Historical Journal* 28 (June 1985): 299–325.

Skeen, C. Edward. "The Newburgh Conspiracy Reconsidered." *William and Mary Quarterly* 31 (April 1974): 273–98.

Snowiss, Sylvia. "From Fundamental Law to the Supreme Law of the Land: A Reinterpretation of the Origin of Judicial Review." In Karen Orren and Stephen Skowronek, eds., *Studies in American Political Development*, vol. 2, 1–67. New Haven, 1987.

Tenney, Samuel. Letter to Nicholas Gilman, March 12, 1788. Gratz Collection, Pennsylvania Historical Society, Philadelphia.

Thompson, M. P. "The Reception of John Locke's *Two Treatises of Government*, 1690–1705." *Political Studies* 24 (June 1976): 184–91.

Trevett v. Weeden (Rhode Island Superior Court of Judicature, September 1786).

Ulmer, S. Sidney. "Sub-Group Formation in the Constitutional Convention." *Midwest Journal of Political Science* 10 (August 1966): 288–303.

Villa, Dana R. "Postmodernism and the Public Sphere." *American Political Science Review* 86 (September 1992): 712–21.

Waterman, Julius S. "Thomas Jefferson and Blackstone's *Commentaries*." In David

H. Flaherty, ed., *Essays in the History of Early American Law*, 467–72. Chapel Hill, 1969.

Wood, Gordon S. "Conspiracy and the Paranoid Style: Causality and Deceit in the Eighteenth Century." *William and Mary Quarterly* 39 (July 1982): 401–41.

Yarbrough, Jean. "Republicanism Reconsidered: Some Thoughts on the Foundation and Preservation of the American Republic." *Review of Politics* 41 (January 1979): 61–95.

Zaller, Robert. "The Continuity of British Radicalism in the Seventeenth and Eighteenth Centuries." *Eighteenth-Century Life* 6 (January 1981): 17–38.

Zuckert, Michael P. "Federalism and the Founding: Toward a Reinterpretation of the Constitutional Convention." *Review of Politics* 48 (Spring 1986): 166–210.

Index